Marxism and Beyond

Marxism and Beyond

SIDNEY HOOK

ROWMAN AND LITTLEFIELD
Totowa, New Jersey

HX
73
.H66
1983

First published in the United States 1983 by
Rowman and Littlefield
81 Adams Drive, Totowa, New Jersey 07512.

Library of Congress Cataloging in Publication Data

Hook, Sidney, 1902-
  Marxism and beyond.

  Includes bibliographical references and index.
  1. Communism—Addresses, essays, lectures.
  2. Marx, Karl, 1818-1883—Addresses, essays,
lectures. I. Title.
HX73.H66 1983   335.43   82-20542
ISBN 0-8476-7159-3

83 84 85/10 9 8 7 6 5 4 3 2 1

Printed in the United States of America

Contents

Preface   vii
Acknowledgments   xi

PART ONE   STUDIES IN MARXISM
1   Karl Marx versus the Communist Movement   3
2   Marxism: A Synoptic Exposition   23
3   Spectral Marxism   54
4   Lenin and the Communist International   72
5   Communism and the American Intellectuals
       from the Thirties to the Eighties   84
6   The Twilight of Capitalism: A Marxian Epitaph   96
7   Marx for All Seasons   103
8   Disremembering the Thirties   108
9   Home Truths about Marx   114
10   Reflections on the Frankfurt School   120
11   John Reed, Romantic   130
12   Out of the Depths   135
13   Some Fables of American "Fear & Terror"   141
14   The Worldly Views of John Kenneth Galbraith   159

PART TWO   BEYOND MARXISM
15   What Means This Freedom?   175
16   In Defense of the Cold War,
       Neither Red nor Dead   187
17   On Western Freedom   197
18   A Critique of Conservatism   208

Index   219

Preface

All of the studies in this book, with the exception of most of the first chapter and Chapters 10 and 16, have been published before. They are here reproduced substantially unaltered because they deal with similar, loosely interrelated themes, the central one of which is the intellectual legacy of Karl Marx. Fifty years ago on the fiftieth anniversary of Karl Marx's death when I published my *Towards the Understanding of Karl Marx*, I believed there was an empirical justification for his analysis of the capitalist system and the predictions that flowed from it. On the hundredth anniversary of his death, although the largest and most populous nations of the world call themselves "Marxist," their existence as economies are far from what Marx envisaged as a successor to capitalism, while their cultures—the regulating principles that govern their political, social, and intellectual experience—are in crass opposition to Marx's own ideals of freedom and human dignity.

On the other hand, Western Europe, the North American states, and Japan, although far from being socialist economies in Marx's sense, have by political democratic means modified the operation of their free enterprise systems (never completely free to begin with), and developed a Welfare State not anticipated by either Marx or his predecessors and their critics. History itself, as has often been observed, has been guilty of lese-Marxism.

As an historical movement Marxism has spread faster and further in the last five decades than Christianity as a movement in the first five centuries of its emergence. It does not seem to me to be too much of an exaggeration to say that the ideals and practices of Christianity, after it became the state religion of the Roman Empire, are as far removed from the ideals and practices of primitive Christianity as the ideals and practices of the self-characterized Marxism of the Russian and Chinese Empires today are from the animating ideals of Marx and his early followers.

In evaluating Marx and his thought it seems to me that only an historical approach can do justice to his intent and contributions. It is sometimes forgotten that Marx came to maturity during the period of the Metternichean reaction, when democratic political

vii

institutions had not yet developed except in a very truncated form in England. Marx is not the only thinker whose central predictions have been falsified by historical events. Nevertheless, unless we arbitrarily disregard Marx's words and actions we must acknowledge the authenticity and intensity of his identification with the politically and economically oppressed. His remarks on the Polish insurrections against czarist authority have a contemporary ring as well as other observations he made on the brooding threat of Russian despotism to the emergence of democratic forces in Western Europe. Nor can one question both the existence and moral justification of his high hopes for a better social order in which those who are able and willing to work do not lack the goods and services necessary for a decent human existence while others who make no social contribution wallow in needless luxuries.

By natural impulse strengthened by reflective thought, Marx was a fighter for human freedom who sought to enrich and expand the legacy of the Renaissance, the Reformation, and the American and French Revolutions. This can hardly be called into question even if we note the full measure of the blemishes on his character and his cantankerous personality. He was not free from the Victorian and class prejudices of the society he was trying to revolutionize, and it is not too fanciful to believe that he would have been a dissenter, if not a rebel, in the utopia of the classless and stateless community of the future he claimed to foresee. The utopian elements in Marx's thought are additional evidence of what he hoped for and thought history would provide. That he was not less mistaken in his expectations than the other great utopians who were his predecessors does not gainsay the nobility of his aspirations.

No one who takes an historical approach to Marx and examines his contributions in the scientific spirit that Marx believed he himself was following can reasonably consider himself a Marxist today. To go beyond Marx is not a form of apostasy but of development required by the recognition of the pluralistic factors at work in history.

One of the unmistakable signs that the Marxist movement is not as scientific as Marx himself hoped it would be is the reaction by "orthodox Marxists" to any erstwhile adherent of his ideas who believes that the evidence justifies conclusions that are incompatible with some of Marx's major beliefs. They are all too often judged in the same way as individuals who have surrendered one religious confession for another. Religious converts are abhorred by those whose religion they have renounced and not seldom regarded with condescension if not contempt by the birthright members of the new religious faith they have embraced. This was the fate of the first and greatest of all Marxist revisionists, Eduard Bernstein, whose stature as man and thinker has grown with the years.

Since the chapters that follow were written at different times and independently of each other, in the nature of the case a certain amount of repetition in phrase and thought was unavoidable. I must beg the readers' indulgence for any passages that may sound repetitive. Even the truth may become boring but unless I am very much mistaken, in view of the forthcoming multiple rediscoveries of Marx in these commemorative years, whatever be the truths this book contains, they will not appear obvious to those who refuse to go beyond Marx.

Sidney Hook
South Wardsboro, VT
1982

Acknowledgments

"Karl Marx versus the Communist Movement" was first published under the title "Myth and Fact in the Marxist Theory of Revolution and Violence" in the *Journal of the History of Ideas* 34, no. 2 (April 1973): 271–80. It is reprinted with permission.

"Marxism—A Synoptic Exposition" was first published under the title "Marxism" in *Dictionary of the History of Ideas*, under the general editorship of Philip P. Weiner, copyright © 1973 Charles Scribner's Sons, and is reprinted with permission.

"Spectral Marxism" was first published in *The American Scholar* (Spring 1980) and is reprinted with permission.

"Lenin and the Communist International" was first published in *Russian Review* 32, no. 1 (January 1973) and is reprinted with permission.

"Communism and the American Intellectuals from the Thirties to the Eighties" was first published in *Free Inquiry* (Fall 1981) and is reprinted with permission.

"The Twilight of Capitalism: A Marxian Epitaph" was first published in *The New Republic* (August 1976) and is reprinted with permission.

"Marx for All Seasons" was first published in *Commentary* (July 1980) and is reprinted with permission.

"Disremembering the Thirties" was first published in *The American Scholar* (Autumn 1980) and is reprinted with permission.

"Home Truths about Marx" was first published in *Commentary* (September 1978) and is reprinted with permission.

"John Reed, Romantic" was first published in *The New Republic* (September 1973) copyright © 1973 The New Republic, Inc., and is reprinted with permission.

"Out of the Depths" was first published in *The American Scholar* (Spring 1982) and is reprinted with permission.

"Some Fables of American 'Fear & Terror'" was first published under the title "David Caute's Fable of 'Fear & Terror'" in *Encounter* (January 1980) and is reprinted with permission.

"The Worldly Views of John Kenneth Galbraith" was first published in *The American Spectator* (October 1981), copyright © 1981 *The American Spectator*, and is reprinted with permission.

"What Means This Freedom?" was first delivered as a Feinstone Lecture at the United States Military Academy, West Point, 1976.

"On Western Freedom" was first published under the title "Solzhenitsyn and Western Freedom" in *World Literature Today* (Autumn 1979) and is reprinted with permission.

"A Critique of Conservatism" was first delivered as an address to the National Convention of Social Democrats U.S.A. 1978.

PART ONE

Studies
in
Marxism

CHAPTER ONE

Karl Marx versus the Communist Movement

There is a double paradox in the expression "Karl Marx versus the Communist Movement." It results from the natural but unfortunate identification of Marx with the multitudinous varieties of Marxism offering their ideological wares today in his name. Currently there are almost as many types and kinds of Marxists in Europe, Asia, the Americas, and even Africa claiming the legacy of Marx as Christian cults professing fidelity to the authentic teachings of Christ. Logically, with respect to both historical figures, although their self-characterized disciples cannot all be right in their doctrinal interpretations, they may very well all be wrong or at least partial and inadequate.

The other kernel of the paradox is that although Marx described the ideal society that was coming on the wings of history as "communist," Communist societies as they exist everywhere today are in marked variance to the ideals that inspired his social vision and heroic personal commitment. The man who concluded the preface to his *magnum opus* with a defiant line from Dante, "Follow your own course and let people talk," would have come to a violent and inglorious end in any Communist country of the world whether it be China, Cuba, or the Soviet Union.

One may protest that freedom as the right and power of the individual to determine his own life may have been Marx's *personal* ideal, but that the kind of society he envisaged for the future was one in which such freedom did not exist. His favorite slogan may have been "Doubt everything," but his classless society of the future was one in which the coordinated activities of its members would make effective doubt and its public expression irrelevant if not dangerous. There are many scholars who are convinced that Marx's projected ideal of a Communist society was one in which

3

there would be no room for genuine individuality at all. Far from there being a variety of projects among which individuals would be able to choose, society would be ordered in such a way that there would be no more variation among its citizens than among the leaves of a multibranching tree or the bees in a hive. Society would function without dissension or conflict because its members would have been shaped by its institutions to coexist in functional harmony. In other words, the end of history would be a benign totalitarianism in which every person would know his place and no person would be out of place.

If one could imagine modern Communist societies ever solving their problems of legitimacy and productivity and the myriad of other endemic problems that breed hostility within and between them, this might be the upshot of their development. But there is overwhelming evidence that this was not Marx's ideal. Although he was reluctant to describe in any detail what the classless society of the future would be like, he says enough to indicate that it would be quite different from the benign totalitarianism some critics attribute to him or from any of the current varieties of malignant totalitarianism in Communist countries today. This can be established without reference to his early manuscripts, in which Marx was not yet a Marxist. It is implicit in the writings of his mature years.

These writings show how Marx conceives of the individual whom he regards as free. He is contrasted with the typical wage worker under capitalism who, although legally and politically free, is constrained by the necessity of earning his living from enjoying what Marx calls true freedom. In a striking passage Marx suggests that the worker's real life begins only when his working life is over.

The worker who for twelve hours works, spins, drills, turns, builds, shovels, breaks stones, carries loads, etc.—does he consider this twelve hours' weaving, spinning, drilling, turning, building, shovelling, stone-hauling as a manifestation of his life, as life? On the contrary, life begins for him where this activity ceases, at the table, in the public house, in bed. The twelve hours labor has no meaning for him as weaving, spinning, drilling, etc., but as earnings which bring him to the table, to the public house, into bed. If the silkworm were to spin in order to continue its existence as a caterpillar, it would be a complete wage-worker. ("Wage, Labor and Capital," *Collected Works,* Vol. IX, p. 203.)

The true realm of freedom for human beings is one in which the exertion of energy is directed by goals autonomously chosen by themselves, and not dictated by any other person's will or the necessities of the market. The first prerequisites for this state of affairs are an economy of abundance and superabundance and, for most people, the shortening of the working day. But these are not sufficient, for what Marx is saying is that with respect to the most important values of life, a man's work must be meaningful to him, not as a means to leisure or to the wherewithal on which his other pursuits depend, but as a way of fulfilling himself. For the free man work is not a curse but a vocation or calling in which he realizes his desirable potentials. There have always been a few fortunate human beings for whom earning a living is a satisfactory way of living one's life, but until now that has not been the human estate. Marx sought to generalize this ideal of work as a personal need as well as fulfillment in the unrealistic expectation that the development of science and technology would not only abolish material want but all other scarcities as well. In such a situation every human being is viewed as a potential source of some creative thought or action.

Marx goes even further and lapses into a utopianism more extreme than any of the projections of his great predecessors. Influenced by the Greek ideal of the harmonious all-round developed personality and repelled by the extremes of specialization imposed by industrial society, he decries the division of labor. He suggests that any kind of professionalization is a deplorable one-sidedness that limits the powers of growth in other areas of human interest that are equally legitimate and worthy of cultivation.

The starting point of Marx's criticism of the effects of excessive specialization of labor under capitalism is legitimate enough, and from *The Communist Manifesto* to *Capital* he inveighs fiercely against it. The development of productive forces

mutilate the laborer into a fragment of a man, degrade him to the level of an appendage to a machine, destroy every remnant of charm in his work and turn it into hated toil; they estrange him from the intellectual potentialities of the labor process . . . they transform his lifetime into working-time, and drag his wife and child beneath the wheels of the Juggernaut of capital. (*Capital*, Vol. 1, p. 645.)

Whatever may have been true for the early days of capitalism, as a description today of the actual conditions of work for the overwhelming majority of wage earners this would be far from the mark. The excessive specialization of labor is a consequence of industrial society rather than of capitalism. Under nationalized industries, whether in capitalist or socialist economies, the assembly line still operates. The legitimate disapproval of excesses in the division of labor leads Marx into an unqualified denunciation of the principle of division of labor that takes him beyond the confines of common sense. But—and this is the relevant point—his very exaggeration indicates how he conceives of the individual.

The following passage is from *die deutsche Ideologie*, but the attack upon the division of labor, albeit recognized as a necessary evil in the development of capitalism, runs through all of Marx's writings:

For as soon as the division of labor comes into being, each man has a particular, exclusive sphere of activity, which is forced upon him and from which he cannot escape. He is a hunter, a fisherman, a shepherd, or a critical critic [the reference here is to Bruno Bauer and his circle], and must remain so if he does not want to lose his means of livelihood; whereas in communist society, where no one has one exclusive sphere of activity but each can become accomplished in any branch he wishes, society regulates the general production and thus makes it possible for me to do one thing today and another tomorrow, to hunt in the morning, fish in the afternoon, rear cattle in the evening, criticize after dinner, just as I have a mind, without ever becoming hunter, fisherman, shepherd, or critic. (*Collected Works*, Vol. V, p. 275.)

We are trying to establish what Marx means by human freedom and individuality, not whether his conceptions are valid. I submit that this passage is sufficient to destroy completely the views of those who attribute to him the notion that he conceives of man in his ideal society as a creature in a beehive or as a leaf almost indistinguishable from other leaves on a tree. Marx's man had the individuality of a Leonardo da Vinci, capable of becoming accomplished in any branch of knowledge or skill he wishes, and free to turn from one accomplishment to another day by day. Such a man would be unfit for any totalitarian society and would certainly be barred from the enlightened totalitarianism of the Platonic Republic.

Taken literally such a man would be as rare as a Leonardo, and the notion that he could be *everyman* is an absurdity. It runs counter to the well-attested insight of Goethe and Charles Peirce that the secret of great achievement lies in limitation, and that when an ordinary man tries his hand at everything he is not likely to do anything of great significance. All we need to do to show its bizarre character is to recast Marx's schedule of activities in terms of modern vocations and avocations "to perform brain surgery in the morning, engage in nuclear research in the afternoon, do some gene splicing in the evening, and conduct a symphony after dinner, just as I have a mind to, without ever becoming a brain surgeon, or nuclear physicist, or geneticist, or conductor." Not even the Greek freeman, whose physical needs were supplied by slaves, had that degree of versatility. Marx's citizen of the future was certainly an individual, but his mode of life suggests the hopeless amateurism of a British squire. Capitalism did not create the brutalized "man with a hoe." Marx may have been justified in writing of "the idiocy of rural life" in 1847, but no one familiar with the mode of existence of the small farmer today—even in Tuscany—despite his precarious economic future, can properly characterize it in the same way.

When we inquire what kind of society would nurture and sustain an association of such individuals, all of whom are as different as they choose to be, it becomes clear that it is a society of anarchism wishfully imputed by Marx to the objective processes of history. By anarchism Marx meant more than a social organization characterized by the absence of state power of any kind. In more positive terms, anarchism, which is interchangeable with the highest phase of Communism as described in his *Critique of the Gotha Program*, is a community of harmonious self-determined individuals whose association gives rise naturally to forms of accepted authority and legitimacy without the presence of any coercive institutions whatsoever. That Marx could believe in the viability of such a society testifies to his faith not only in the perfectability of man but in a secular millenarianism as extreme as any of his great utopian predecessors. Marx was amused by the fantasies of a Fourier, who expected the applied science of the future to transform the seas into potable lemonade, but he was serious about the possibility of transforming human beings into creatures of an angelic nature by modifying their social institutions, despite the empirical evidence that geniuses from Leonardo to Marx himself were conspicuously lacking in those traits that made for harmonious relations with others. It was not the ideals of man professed by the utopians of the past or their vision of a harmonious community of persons with which Marx took issue, but only with the methods they advocated to achieve them.

Another feature of Marx's thought that should dispel the myth that he had no conception of genuine individuality is his impatience with egalitarianism. To him the belief in the moral and political equality of all members of society no more entailed that they would receive the same treatment, goods, offices, and rewards than the belief that everyone is morally entitled to medical care implied that everyone is to receive the same treatment regardless of his or her ailment. Parents know that it is possible to love their children equally without treating them identically. It is more legitimate to criticize Marx's ideal for its unrealistic assumption that an entire community can be organized by the same loving relationship that exists in a family, bound together by ties of affection, than to conflate his ideal with the organizing principle or discipline that binds an army. Marx's impatience with egalitarianism expresses itself in his rejection of the view that even the introduction of a uniform principle of distribution or reward for services or labor under socialism will result in equality. That is to say, even when private ownership in the instruments of social production has been abolished and the socialist state that has replaced the employers undertakes to treat everyone by the same principle or standard, equality will not result. Different individuals will end up with more or less than others by virtue of their natural inequalities. As Marx puts it, "they would not be different individuals if they were not unequal." The same holds true in the golden future in which individuals are rewarded, not according to their labor time or what they produce, but according to their needs. Needs, once we go beyond the basic needs of food, clothing, and shelter, are so variable and elastic that they could hardly be used to define self-identity. Not only is Marx's ideal community one of a vast plurality of different persons, it is also one in which the personalities of its denizens are not fixed.

That Marx apparently sees no problem in conceiving of this multitude of individuals voluntarily coordinating their activities as "associated producers rationally regulating their intercourse with nature" and each other, a complex planned society in which interlocking schedules for the movement of vast numbers of men and materials must mesh, is a mystery. In the absence of any coercive power, what will make things happen and guarantee the cornucopia of universal abundance once the rational will of men and women does not manifest itself? These are troublesome questions not only for Marx; they face any anarchist view that imagines that the administration of things can ever replace the administration of human beings who, unlike bees in a hive or leaves on a tree, have purposes that are often at cross purposes with each other.

Only a naive person would believe that modern transportation in our crowded cities and express highways can flow safely and expeditiously without traffic rules. It is hardly less naive to believe that all that is required, once traffic rules are established, is the presence of someone to direct the flow of traffic. To be sure, such persons do not require the badge of authority to exercise their task. But unless they have at their call the power of a coercive authority to arrest drunken drivers and other alleged lawbreakers, and courts to determine their guilt or innocence, before long the transportation system would be in chaos.

What is distinctive about Marx is not the ideal of a cooperative commonwealth of freedom-loving individuals for whom private property in the instruments of social production does not exist. This was the common coin of many socialist and anarchist groups of his day. He differentiated himself from them, first, by his theory of social change that tried to spell out the objective historical conditions that had to be fulfilled before such a society could become a realistic possibility; and second, by his views about the means and methods to be followed in the struggle to actualize it. Although Marx's writings are neither clear nor consistent, the general drift of his meaning can be discovered when considered in their historical context.

Failure to take into account the historical context of Marx's thought and a too literal reading of his text sometimes makes nonsense of his meaning. It has led to the strange view that because for Marx ethical judgments are not completely autonomous of social and economic facts and tendencies, that therefore Marx had no moral theory. This accounts for his repudiation of any attempt to justify socialism on the basis of principles of justice or humanity. It is granted—indeed, it is sometimes insisted upon—that the overwhelming motivation for the support of Marx's proposals in the West is rooted in feelings and judgments that the inequalities of distribution under capitalism are unjust. But this is taken to be evidence of Marx's confusion and incoherence on the subject of morality and the relation between the factual and the normative.

For Marx morality is natural, social, and, at its best, rational. He differs from both Kant and Hegel. For Kant morality is ultimately independent of any empirical consequences. It expresses imperatives that transcend the facts of nature and human nature. "Let justice prevail though the heavens fall" is a Kantian dictum that Marx's position rejects as fanatical. There is something wrong with a conception of justice that results not only in the destruction of human life but in all the other moral values associated with the possibility of intelligent social life. On the other hand, partly as a response to the formalistic and nonnatural elements in Kant's stark opposition between the empirical and the ideal, Hegel elaborated a doctrine that, despite its obscurities and ambiguities, identified the actual or real with the ideal or what ought to be. The brutal upshot of this view is that whatever is, is right, or with respect to history, "Die Weltgeschichte ist das Weltgericht."

When Marx abandoned Hegelian idealism he unfortunately retained some of the Hegelian terminology. Although his writings are pervaded by passionate ethical judgments, he never developed a systematic ethical theory. His impatience with do-gooders and those preaching either the doctrine of love or salvation by violence as solutions to the social problem led him to deny that his condemnation of the evils of capitalism was based on any judgment of its injustice. Sometimes it resulted in his writing sentences that seem downright silly if the historic context of moral judgment is disregarded. For example, in trying to explain the differences in the schemes of distribution between the lower and higher stages of Communism, he declares: "Right can never be higher than the economic structure of and the cultural development of society conditioned by it." Taken literally, this means that there can be no rational justification for urging support of a social system like that of socialism or even of the welfare state with a more equitable system of distribution while the capitalist economy is functioning—which would cut the nerve of agitation for a better society. This position would make unintelligible the meaning of the term "higher" when Marx speaks of "right" as higher or lower. If the concept of right can never be differentiated from a specific economic structure, what independent meaning can be given it? The higher right would simply reflect the higher economic structure. But unless "the higher economic" structure already involved an implicit value or moral judgment, all Marx would be saying is that every economic structure has a different concept of right, whether it be a primitive cannibalistic society that lives by war and in which all captives are owned and eaten in common, an Asiatic despotism, a slave society, or a feudal, or capitalist, or socialist society. We could not morally order such societies. Under such circumstances what sense would it make for those living in a slave society morally to condemn it? On what grounds could we morally approve the revolt of Spartacus, or the leaders of the Peasant Wars, or of the Paris Commune who sought to overthrow the economic structure under which they lived, in the light of moral ideals different from those that prevailed at the time?

Yet, despite Marx's unfortunate formulation, what he is saying makes sense—even common sense. This may be conveyed in the form of a parable. Suppose two castaways find themselves the only survivors on an island. After making a survey of its resources, A proposes that they dig a well for water. B refuses in the expectation that their luck will turn and rain or rescue will come in time. The digging is difficult and toilsome for A, aggravated by B's mockery of his efforts. Neither rain nor succor arrives, but at the point of utter exhaustion after several days, A opens up a seam of gushing water. B by this time is parched and requests some of the water. Would it be right for A to deny it to him? Since there is no alternative supply and B cannot survive without water, A's refusal to share some of the water would be tantamount to a sentence of death, a punishment whose severity seems disproportionate to B's thoughtlessness and irresponsibility. Since the water is so plentiful, most of it beyond any possible use by A, running out into the sand, it would be unjust to deprive B of any share of it.

Change the material condition of the problem. Suppose as a consequence of his labor, A finds an amount of water sufficient to keep only one person alive. Would it be wrong for him to deny B a share of it? Certainly not. We might praise him for his generosity or saintliness if he does share the water with B. But we could not justifiably condemn him if he refused to assume these roles.

What is the difference in the applicability of these two principles of distribution? Obviously the difference in supply. If any good or service is as plentiful and costless as air, we do not need any principle of distribution. Marx assumed that would be the case with respect to all human needs in a world of unlimited energy. We have seen how utopian such an assumption is. There will always be relative scarcities, if only with respect to temporal priority in the consumption of what is ultimately universally distributed. And with respect to the awards of honor, prizes, recognition— the very situation is defined in terms of scarcity. Not everyone can come in first.

We cannot do without some ethical principles. The fact that they are applied differently in different historical situations where material conditions are varied does not gainsay their validity. It is clear that Marx recognizes several ethical principles—not only the absence of needless suffering, but dignity, self-respect, intellectual independence, and the right to individual self-fulfillment— i.e., the development of one's desirable potential abilities. He does not seek to reduce them to each other, but assumes that in a rational, cooperative, socialized society mankind has the best possibility of realizing them. Although democracy was for him a political concept that was to be introduced wherever it was absent in any modern society and extended to other areas in societies in which it was present, when we bear in mind his concept of individual freedom, it is not reading a foreign element into his thought to say that for him the functioning of an authentic socialist society could be characterized as democracy as a way of life.

But how can such a faith be reconciled with advocacy of "the dictatorship of the proletariat?" This phrase, employed by Marx three or four times in the course of millions of words, fell into desuetude in the international socialist movement after his death and was revived by Lenin and his followers shortly before they seized power in Russia in October 1917. The meaning of the phrase is hotly contested for it combines political and economic connotations. A clue to Marx's meaning is that he contrasts "the dictatorship of the proletariat," not with "the democratic rule of the proletariat," but with "the dictatorship of the bourgeoisie." The latter exists whenever the conflict of economic interests between the working class and its employers—which follows from the economic structure of class society—is systematically resolved in favor of the employers. According to Marx and Engels, this is the case regardless of whether the political system of capitalist society is autocratic or democratic, monarchical or republican. Whether it was England and the United States, imperial Germany or czarist Russia, the dictatorship of the bourgeoisie operated.

The socialist revolution that exemplifies "the dictatorship of the proletariat" is transitional until it abolishes all classes. Marx's conception of class is narrowly defined in terms of the role men play in the mode of economic production. Once production is socialized, then by definition, since ownership is vested in the entire community, economic classes no longer exist. Marx apparently assumed that any other conception of class would not carry with it the possibility of exploitation, great disparities in standards of living, and conflicts over the distribution of social wealth—assumptions shattered in every country today whose economy is collectivized. Presumably an orthodox Marxist would argue in Marx's defense that this outcome, the emergence of "a new class" or a "privileged bureaucracy," was to be expected because the objective conditions of genuine social equality were lacking in the countries in which collectivism had been introduced and that they were therefore unripe and unready for Socialism. This is precisely what Karl Kautsky and the leading Social Democratic followers of Marx maintained in contradistinction to the Bolshevik-Leninist-Stalinist view. However, even if in the light of historical development one grants that Marx's vision of socialism as a cooperative commonwealth of free and socially equal individuals was transformed into a totalitarian despotism by the Bolshevik-Leninist disregard of Marx's principle of historical materialism, this would not be a confirmation of that principle. For although it would explain why Socialism or Communism, even in its first phase, failed in Russia and the other underdeveloped countries in which it had been introduced, it would not explain the attempt to introduce it, and the peculiar economy—neither capitalist nor socialist—and totalitarian culture that resulted from it.

But how was it possible for the Bolshevik-Leninists who began their political careers convinced that they were the executors of the Marxist legacy to end up as the chief executioner of its theories and ideals? How was it that, intent upon liberating the working class from the yoke of capitalist society, they fastened an even more oppressive yoke on the workers and, in the judgment of some erstwhile sympathizers, discredited the entire idea of socialism in our time? Perhaps the single most important explanation lay in the transformation of that unfortunate phrase of Marx, "the dictatorship of the proletariat"—unfortunate in that Marx's meaning could have been expressed without the use of the term "dictatorship"—into the dictatorship of the Communist Party *over* the proletariat and all other classes.

According to Marx and Engels, revolution can be violent or peaceful depending upon the presence of democratic political possibilities, but whether peaceful or not, the socialist revolution must be democratic. At the time of the *Communist Manifesto* there were no realistic possibilities in view of the severe restrictions on suffrage that profound social change could be introduced through parliamentary means. Indeed the *Manifesto* indicates that among the first things that would be done after the revolution would be to introduce democratic institutions. Nonetheless both Marx and Engels assumed that revolutionary action even under oppressive or narrowly restrictive political institutions would have the support of the majority of the population behind it, and that it could justifiably be considered democratic. (The empirical evidence, however, that the working class actually constituted a majority of the population was lacking. It was based on an extrapolation of certain economic tendencies of capitalist development.) Subsequently, Marx and Engels, as is well known, anticipated the possibility that socialism could be introduced peacefully by parliamentary means in countries like England, the United States, and Holland. Toward the end of his life Engels explicitly declared that "the dictatorship of the proletariat" could express itself under the political form of the bourgeois parliamentary republic.

Marx and Engels and their followers disassociated themselves strongly from men like Blanqui and Bakunin on two grounds. The first was the latter's failure to recognize the controlling importance of the objective economic-social situation as providing a necessary condition for a successful political revolution. The second was their undisguised elitism. For Marx "the emancipation of the working class can be achieved only by the working class." This is of central significance in distinguishing between Marx's conception of revolution and the Leninist-Stalinist (Bolshevik) view. *There is not a line in Marx's writings that states or implies that "the dictatorship of the proletariat" must be exercised through "the dictatorship of the Communist Party."*

For Marx the concept of dictatorship, as we have seen, is primarily social and economic. The "dictatorship of the bourgeoisie" refers to the fact that the rule of the bourgeoisie is to its own economic advantage and to the economic disadvantage of the working class. But the dictatorship of the bourgeoisie could be exercised either through democratic or nondemocratic political forms. For Lenin, on the other hand, "dictatorship" is primarily a political concept. "Dictatorship," he tells us, "is rule based directly upon force and unrestricted by any laws." It is really unmitigated *Faustrecht*. Whereas for Marx and Engels "the dictatorship of the proletariat" could be established through peaceful parliamentary victory, for Lenin "the revolutionary dictatorship of the proletariat is rule won and maintained by the use of violence by the proletariat against the bourgeoisie, rule that is unrestricted by any laws." (*Selected Works* [Moscow, 1951], Vol. 2, Part II, p. 41 ff.)

In contradistinction to Marx and Engels, Lenin proceeds to interpret the "dictatorship of the proletariat" as viable only through the dictatorship of the Communist Party, which constitutes a small minority of the population many of whose members are not even proletarians. Although Marx and Engels' interpretation of the Paris Commune of 1871 as a socialist revolution is extremely dubious, nonetheless they both refer to it as an exemplification of "the dictatorship of the proletariat" in which there was no dictatorship of any political party whatsoever. The followers of Blanqui seemed to be most numerous, then the followers of Proudhon, while the partisans of Marx and Engels, whose chief spokesman was Leo Frankel, were minisucular. Actually there was no basic socialist content whatsoever to the reforms of the Paris Commune. No industries were socialized. The abolition of night work for bakers was no more socialist than the abolition of child labor and other "bourgeois" reforms. The real achievements of the Paris Commune, whose launching Marx disapproved, was the extension of democratic processes and principles, most of which could be implemented in a nonsocialist economy. The Leninist view that the Russian socialist revolution of October 1917 is a continuation or fulfillment of the heritage of the Paris Commune is sheer myth.

Lenin makes no bones about the fact that "the dictatorship of the proletariat" is exercised through "the dictatorship of the Communist Party." In his pamphlet on *The Infantile Sickness of Left-Communism*, he states: "Not a single important political or organizational question is decided by any state institution in our republic without the guiding instructions of the Central Committee of the Party." And Stalin, here as elsewhere when he touches on doctrinal matters, echoes his teacher:

Here in the Soviet Union, in the land of the dictatorship of the proletariat, the fact that not a single important political or organizational question is decided by our Soviet and other mass organizations without directions from the Party must be regarded as the highest expression of the leading role of the Party. *In this sense* it could be said that the dictatorship of the proletariat is *in essence* the "dictatorship of its vanguard," "the dictatorship" of its Party, as the main guiding force of the proletariat. (*Foundations of Leninism* [Moscow, 1934], Ch. VIII.)

If, as Lenin declares, "dictatorship is rule based directly upon force and unrestricted by any laws," the dictatorship of the Party entails that it may very well be a dictatorship, not *of* the proletariat, but *over* the proletariat as well as over others.

Aware of the enormity of this transformation of the concept of the "dictatorship of the proletariat" into the "the dictatorship of the Communist Party," Lenin and other Bolshevik leaders adopted several semantic devices to conceal their abandonment of the democratic component of the Marxist theory. In the early years the exigencies of the struggle for power led them to a forthrightness of utterance that becomes qualified in subsequent apologetic rationalizations when faced by critics invoking Marx's democratic principles.

Nothing signifies the non-Marxist undemocratic stance of Bolshevik-Leninism more clearly than Lenin's writings on the Constituent Assembly. Referring to his thesis on the Constituent Assembly, Lenin observes:

My thesis says clearly and repeatedly that the interests of the revolution are higher than the formal rights of the Constituent Assembly. The formal democratic point of view is precisely the point of view of the bourgeois democrat who refuses to admit that the interests of the proletariat and of the proletarian class struggle are supreme. (*Selected Works, op. cit.,* p. 78.)

The plain meaning of this declaration exposes as a hypocritical rationalization the pretexts Lenin offers for forcibly dispersing the Constituent Assembly after the Bolsheviks' miserable showing in the elections (19 percent) and after the Social Revolutionary and

Menshevik majority refused to accept Lenin's ultimatum to yield power to the Bolsheviks. Justifying his refusal to accept the legitimacy of the Constituent Assembly, Lenin claims that although elections to the Constituent Assembly had been held *after* the Bolsheviks seized power in October, the mood or sentiment of the masses had changed by early January and that in reality they favored the Bolsheviks (*op. cit.*, p. 81). Rosa Luxemburg, in sharply criticizing Lenin's view, retorted that if this were so, the Bolsheviks could have called for new elections without disputing the legitimacy of the Constituent Assembly, particularly since in their propaganda against Kerensky they had agitated so fiercely for the convocation of the Constituent Assembly.

In the light, however, of Lenin's thesis on the Constituent Assembly cited above, his *ex post facto* talk about improper lists and unrepresentative elections is revealed as a feeble and irrelevant cover-up. Assume that the election on the basis of new lists had been as democratic as Lenin had desired. If, as he unwaveringly claims, "the interests of the proletariat and the proletarian class struggle are supreme," what difference would it have made to Lenin if the new electoral results showed that the Russian masses had even more completely repudiated the Bolsheviks than they did on the basis of the old lists? Would Lenin have recognized the sovereignty of the Constituent Assembly? Certainly not! For if, as he insists, "the interests of the proletariat," as interpreted by the Bolsheviks, of course, are "supreme," Lenin would have felt justified by his political philosophy to take power against the Constituent Assembly even if it had an overwhelming mandate from the masses—provided he could get away with it.

If there is any doubt about this, an analysis of Lenin's article "On Slogans" will confirm it (*Selected Works, op. cit.*, p. 87ff). When Lenin seeks excuses to ban the Constituent Assembly, he bases himself on the authority of the Soviets. But in July 1917 when his article "On Slogans" was published he repudiates the slogan "All Power to the Soviets" because the Soviets "are dominated by the Social Revolutionary and Menshevik parties" (p. 95). In January, having seized power and already begun the terror, and after having acquired a majority in the Soviets of Petrograd and Moscow, the slogan "All Power to the Soviets" is restored and used as a foil and excuse to prorogue the Constituent Assembly. In every case what is decisive for Lenin is the question of *power*, not the question of democracy, formal or concrete, or representation, authentic or not, viz., whether the Bolshevik Party has a likely prospect of seizing and retaining power.

Lenin and Stalin explicitly disavow Marx's belief that socialism could be legally and peacefully achieved through the democratic political process in countries like England and the United States. Further, the conditions of affiliation to the Third International drawn up by Lenin imposed on *every* Communist Party of the world, the organization of illegal cadres and the resort to armed insurrection in the conquest of political power in all countries, including "the most free in the world." Even ambiguity on this point was not tolerated except as a linguistic maneuver to disarm the political enemy and to win suffrance to organize the seizure of power. The Russian road to power became the paradigm for all Communist Parties of the world under the discipline of the Third International. This may be illustrated in the programmatic declaration of William Z. Foster, head of the Communist Party of the United States, at a time when it enjoyed complete legality and freedom of propaganda:

Even before the seizure of power, the workers will organize the Red Guard. Later on this loosely constructed body becomes developed into a firmly-knit, well-disciplined Red Army. The leader of the revolution in all its stages is the Communist Party. . . . Under the dictatorship all the capitalist parties—Republican, Democratic, Progressive, Socialist, etc.,—will be liquidated, the Communist Party functioning alone as the party of the toiling masses. Likewise will be dissolved all other organizations that are political props of bourgeois rule, including Chambers of Commerce, employers' associations, rotary clubs, American Legion, Y.M.C.A. and such fraternal orders as the Masons, Odd Fellows, Elks, Knights of Columbus, etc. (*Towards Soviet America* [N.Y., 1932], p. 275.)

Under Khrushchev's rule the Leninist dogma of the inevitability of war between the Communist world and the Western world was abandoned, although the inevitability of world Communist victory was still proclaimed. But the insistence upon the view that the triumph and rule of the revolution could be achieved only through "the dictatorship of the party" was retained. It was asserted that the Communist Party in a "coalition" with other parties might come to power peacefully, but only if the Communist Party exercised leadership, which meant at least control of the Ministry of the Interior (police).

An analysis of the concept of "the dictatorship of the party" in official Communist literature (as well as the historical evidence) will show that even where Communist Parties, either alone or in formal coalition, come to power peacefully, their rule is based upon continuous exercise of force and violence. For, to repeat, the very meaning of "dictatorship," in the words of Lenin, "is rule based directly upon force and unrestricted by any laws." This dictatorship is directed not only against overt hostile elements seeking to restore the overthrown economic and social order, but against any dissenting thought in art, literature, science, and philosophy of which the Central Committee of the Communist Party disapproves.

With some variations, depending upon a number of historical and national factors, all Communist states that profess to be inspired by Leninist doctrine follow the Russian Soviet pattern, which is demonstrably incompatible with Marx's and Engels' commitment to socialist democracy and their criticism of elitist rule. These Communist views have remained unaffected by the Sino-Soviet split and by the emergence of "polycentrism."

Naturally, in democratic Western countries where there are large Communist Parties (and/or dissident Communist groups critical of the Leninist tradition) engaged in the parliamentary political process, attempts have been made to soften and tone down the harsh features of Leninist principles according to which "the dictatorship of the proletariat" results in the terror of a Communist Party dictatorship of varying degrees of intensity over the proletariat and all other groups of the population until the advent of the classless society. In these countries some theoretical spokesmen of Communism tend to blur the difference between the Marxist views on revolution, including the possibility of a peaceful transition to socialism through a multiparty democratic political process, and the Communist-Leninist position.

The lineaments of that position not long ago were authoritatively restated by the Institute of Marxism-Leninism of the Central Committee of the Communist Party of the Soviet Union, and reprinted in the Soviet official theoretical journal *Kommunist* (No. 3, 1972) under the title "Falsifiers of the Theory of Scientific Communism and their Bankruptcy." It is directed against Communist dissidents, characterized as "modern revisionists," who envisage the transition from capitalism to socialism as a process of "evolution" or "reform" or "renovation," and who believe that "the dictatorship of the proletariat" is possible without the dictatorship or leadership (a euphemism for dictatorship) of the Communist Party. The article declares:

We know the numerous statements in which V. I. Lenin developed the basic Marxist thesis that the dictatorship of the proletariat is inconceivable without the leadership of the Communist Party. Practical experience has shown that even the existence of a multiparty system does not refute the necessity of such leadership. The Communist Party is the vanguard of

the working class, its most conscious, organized and unified part. Only under the leadership of the Party can the working class implement its dictatorship over the defeated exploiting classes.

As if to leave no doubt that the Leninist line applies not only to the seizure of political power but to its exercise after the Communist Party has come to power, the article concludes:

The grave consequences of any attempt to depart from the Marxist-Leninist teaching on the leading role of the Party and to renounce Leninist organizational principles are well illustrated by the events of 1968 in Czechoslovakia.

Although Marx's views on revolution, violence, and democracy are quite different from those identified as Bolshevik-Leninist, they suffer from certain basic difficulties, some of which have already been adverted to and others developed in subsequent chapters. Most of them flow from the failure clearly to recognize the primacy of political freedom in relation to all other desirable social and cultural freedoms, and the consequent underestimation of the possibility of modifying the economic structure of society by political democratic means.

Whatever the inadequacies of Marx's theory of revolution are, his commitment to a *scientific* or rational method of achieving a nonexploitative society permits—actually it should encourage—a modification of his specific views on political strategy in the light of historical evidence and shifting social forces. Marx was not born a socialist and certainly not a Marxist. What was distinctive about his theories concerning how socialism—which *au fond* was an extension of democracy to a way of life—was to be achieved have largely been disproved by historical events. History, alas!, has been guilty of lese-Marxism. Marx underestimated the capacity of capitalist societies to raise the standard of living of its population, including even the longevity of the working class; he underestimated the growth and intensity of nationalism; he was mistaken in interpreting all forms of coercion and exploitation as flowing from private ownership of the social means of production; he ignored the prospect of bureaucratic forms of collectivism; and the very possibility of war between collectivist economies, illustrated in the nuclear threat of Communist Russia against Communist China, was inconceivable to him by definition. As we have seen, he shared the naïveté of anarchist thinkers in believing that the state would disappear with universal collectivism, and that "the administration of things" could ever completely replace administration by men and women and the possibility of its abuse. He underestimated the role of personality in history, and although he contributed profoundly to our understanding of the determining influence, direct and indirect, of the mode of economic production on many aspects of culture, he exaggerated the degree of its determination and its "inevitability" and "necessity." That is why those who have learned most from Marx, if faithful to his own commitment to the scientific, rational method, should no more consider themselves "Marxists" today than modern biologists should consider themselves "Darwinians" or modern physicists "Newtonians." "Marxism" today signifies an ideology in Marx's original sense of that term, suggestive more of a religious than of a strictly scientific or rational outlook on society.

In speaking of Marx's failure to do justice to personality in history, one may cite the life and work of Lenin, the greatest revisionist of Marx, as decisive evidence. The Russian Revolution of October 1917 has been regarded as among the most influential events, and some have even characterized it as *the* most influential event because of its consequences upon·world history. Yet it is incontestable that if Lenin had not lived there would in all likelihood have been no Russian October Revolution (Cf. my *The Hero in History: A Study in Limitation and Possibility* [New York, 1943]). Among the fateful consequences of the October Revolution under Lenin's guidance was the creation of the Communist International, which organized Communist Parties in most of the countries of Europe, Asia, and America. Its chief accomplishment was to split the European working class in the face of threats of social and political reaction.

It has been argued by some that the October Revolution was responsible for reforms introduced in non-Communist countries and that the development of the Welfare State was primarily motivated out of fear of domestic Communist revolution abetted by the armed intervention of the Red Army. It would be very hard to establish such a thesis. The history of political and social reform in Western Europe and America was impressive long before the Russian Revolution and was primarily the result of indigenous class struggles that resulted in the extension of the democratic ethos· to economic and social life. The New Deal in the United States, for example, as well as the emergence of the Welfare State in Great Britain, were in no way undertaken to meet any danger of a domestic Communist revolution.

It is far closer to the truth to assert that rather than inspiring democratic social reforms in the Western world, the Bolshevik Revolution and the operation of the Communist International were largely responsible for the rise of Fascism in Italy and Nazism in Germany. They not only weakened the democratic structure of pre-Mussolini Italy and Weimar Germany by splitting the working class, but by their activities, including abortive attempts at insurrection, they enlarged the mass base and support for the demagogic propaganda of the forces of social reaction. It is not unlikely that if there had been no October Revolution and attempts by the Communist International, serving as the instrument of the Kremlin, to organize revolutions in western Europe, there would have been no victory of Fascism in Italy and of Hitlerism in Germany. It may be difficult to predict in detail what the history of western Europe would have been if Lenin had not succeeded in overthrowing Kerensky's regime and destroying the democratic Constituent Assembly. In the light of what actually did occur as a consequence of the rule of Bolshevism—Fascism and Nazism—it is hard to see what could have been worse.

It remains to ask what light this analysis casts on identifying contemporary expressions of Marxism with respect to revolutionary thought and action. A position, of course, may be morally sound or justifiable regardless of whether it is Marxist or not. The question I pose here is this: what are the criteria for determining the truth of the claim of any party program or activity, independently of its own labels, to be Marxist? For example, on the above analysis, any movement based on the ideas of Herbert Marcuse is clearly non-Marxist. This follows not only from his repudiation of the working class as unfit for the role and honor of carrier of the socialist idea, but because of his undisguised elitism and unabashed justification of forcible repression of ideas, persons, or institutions that are not "progressive" according to his lights. Here Marcuse is a faithful Leninist. Other criteria are discussed in subsequent chapters.

Where socialist parties, alone or in alliance with others, come to power through the democratic political process, the crucial question is whether or not they permit freedom of political propaganda to parties that reject their program, and in the event of an electoral defeat, relinquish the reins of government to those who have won the support of the majority. Any political party, regardless of what it calls itself, that holds on to power by refusing to conduct free elections or to abide by their consequences is not Marxist.

The theory of Marxism makes no claim that the working masses are always right or even aware of what is to their best interests. At any definite time a Marxist party may know better than the masses what their best interests are. But this knowledge does not give it any right to impose upon the masses a program in opposition to their wishes and will. Indeed, this is integral to the very meaning of "democracy" in any political context.

In envisaging the democratic road to political power, Marx and Engels were realistic in considering the possibility of an antidemocratic revolt to defeat the will of the majority. This possibility has led some Leninists to justify the seizure of power without the support of the majority of the population, and when in power, to repress parties and individuals who dissent from the socialist program, and even from the Leninist version of that program, on the pretext that they *may* revolt. But such rationalizations are transparent evidence that they have no faith in the democratic process.

In dealing with children or mental incompetents, it is sometimes necessary, and therefore justifiable, to act in behalf of their genuine interests even when it runs against their wishes and will. What Marx would have thought of such procedure with respect to the proletariat or working class may be inferred from his declaration that this class "regards its courage, self-confidence, independence and sense of personal dignity as more necessary than its daily bread" (*Gesamtausgabe*, Abt. I, Bd. 6, p. 278). Marx may have been wrong in believing this, but it is not wrong that he believed it.

Mistaken as Marx's historical theories and economic predictions may have been or turn out to be, and regardless of the crimes and infamies committed in his name in the Soviet and Chinese Gulag Archipelagos, a critical but objective assessment of his ideas justifies including him in the calendar of fighters for human freedom. Hegel would not have recognized his progeny in Marx nor Marx in Lenin. The intellectual sins, like all sins of the fathers, should not be visited on the heads of their children. There is even less warrant for attributing the sins of the children to their fathers, especially when there is strong doubt of their legitimacy.

CHAPTER TWO

Marxism:
A Synoptic Exposition

Marxism, like Christianity, is a term that stands for a family of doctrines attributed to a founder who could not have plausibly subscribed to all of them, since some of these doctrines flatly contradict each other. Consequently any account that professes to do justice to Marxism must be more than an account of the ideas of Karl Marx even if it takes its point of departure from him.

As a set of ideas one of the remarkable things about Marxism is that it is continually being revived despite formidable and sometimes definitive criticisms of its claims and formulations. For this and other reasons, it cannot be conceived as a purely scientific set of ideas designed "to lay bare the economic law of motion of modern society" (Preface to first edition of *Capital*) and to explain all cultural and political developments in terms of it. There is little doubt that Karl Marx himself thought that his contributions were as scientific in the realm of social behavior as Newton's in the field of physics and Darwin's in biology. But there is no such thing as a recurring movement of Newtonianism or Darwinism in physics or biology. The mark of a genuine science is its cumulative development. The contributions of its practitioners are assimilated and there is no return to the original forms of theories or doctrines of the past.

The existence of Marxism as a social and political *movement* inspired by a set of ideas, sometimes in open opposition to other movements, is further evidence that we are dealing with a phenomenon that is not purely scientific. For such a movement obviously goes beyond mere description or the discovery of truth. That its normative goals may in some sense be based upon descriptive truths, i.e., not incompatible with them, may justify using the term "scientific" at best to differentiate these goals from those that are arbitary or impossible of achievement.

Marxism has often been compared with, and sometimes characterized as, a religion with its sacred books, prophets, authoritative spokesmen, etc. But this is not very illuminating until there is agreement about the nature of religion, a theme which is even more ambiguous and controversial than that of Marxism. Nonetheless there are some important features which Marxism shares with some traditional religions that explain at least in part its recurrent appeal despite its theoretical shortcomings.

Marxism is a monistic theory that offers an explanatory key to everything important that occurs in history and society. This key is the mode of economic production, its functioning, the class divisions and conflicts it generates, its limiting and, in the end, its determining effect upon the outcome of events. It provides a never failing answer to the hunger for explanation among those adversely affected by the social process. That the explanations are mostly ad hoc, that predictions are not fulfilled, like the increasing pauperization of the working class, that important events occur that were not predicted like the rise of Fascism, the emergence of a new service-industry oriented middle class, the discovery of nuclear technology—are not experienced as fatal, or even embarrassing, difficulties. Just as belief that everything happens by the will of God is compatible with whatever occurs, so belief in the explanatory primacy of the mode of economic production and its changes is compatible with any social or political occurrence if sufficient subsidiary hypotheses are introduced. That is why although Marxism as a social and political movement may be affected by the events and conditions it failed to explain (like the latter-day affluence of capitalist society), as a set of vague beliefs it is beyond refutation. In the course of its history, now more than a century old, few, if any, Marxists have been prepared to indicate under what empirical or evidential conditions they were prepared to abandon their doctrines as invalid.

A second reason for the recurrence of Marxism in various guises—there are today existentialist Marxisms and even Catholic Marxisms—is that its theories are an expression of hope. Marxisms of whatever kind all hold out the promise, if not the certainty, of social salvation, or at the very least, relief from the malaise and acute crises of the time. Whether the future is conceived in apocalyptic terms or less dramatically, it is one with a prospect of victory through struggle, a victory that will insure peace, freedom, prosperity, and surcease from whatever evils flow from an improperly organized and unplanned society, dominated by the commodity producing quest for ever renewed profit.

The third reason for the recurrence of Marxism is a whole series of semantic ambiguities that permit Marxists to appeal to individuals and groups of democratic sentiment despite the fact that Marxists often direct savage and unfair criticisms against nonsocialist democracies. The growth of democratic sentiment and the allegiance to the principle of self-determination in all areas of personal and social life are universal phenomena. They are marked by the fact that almost every totalitarian regime seeks to pass itself off as one or another form of democracy. Marxists, for reasons that will be made clearer below, are the most adept and successful in presenting Marxism as a philosophy of the democratic left, despite the existence of ruthless despotisms in the USSR and Red China, and other countries that profess to be both socialist and Marxist. Although the existence of these two dictatorial regimes and of other avowedly Marxist regimes in Eastern Europe creates some embarrassment for those who identify the Marxist movement with the movement toward democracy, the terrorist practices of these regimes are glossed over and explained away. They are represented either as excesses of regimes unfaithful to their own socialist ideals or as temporary measures of defense against enemies of democracy within or without.

Finally there are certain elements of truth in Marxism that, however vague, explain some events and some facets of the social scene that involve the growth of industrial society and its universal spread, the impact of scientific technology, the pressure of conflicting economic class interests and their resolution. Although not exclusively Marxist, these insights and outlooks have been embodied in the Marxist traditions. They function to sustain by association, so to speak, the more specific Marxist doctrines in the belief system of their advocates. Although they are generalized beyond the available evidence, they bestow a certain plausibility on Marxist thought when other conditions further their acceptance.

This brings us to the important and disputed question of what constitutes the nature of Marxism. What are the characteristic doctrines associated with the Marxist outlook upon the world? For present purposes we are distinguishing Marxism and its variants from the question of what Marx and Engels *really* meant. Historically, this question is by far not as significant as what they have been *taken* to mean. Marx like Christ might have disowned all of his disciples: it would not affect how their meaning has been historically interpreted and what was done in the light of that interpretation. It may be that in the future there will be other interpretations of what Marx really meant. Even today there are several esoteric views of his thought different from those to be considered but they obviously cannot be considered as part of intellectual history.

There are three main versions of Marxism identifiable in the history of ideas that have received wide support. The first, oldest, and closest to the lives of Karl Marx and Friedrich Engels in point of time is the Social-Democratic version. The second version which acquired widespread influence after the October 1917 Russian Revolution is the Communist version, sometimes called the Bol-shevik-Leninist view. The third version, which emerged after the Second World War, may be called "existentialist." Marxism is regarded from an existentialist view as primarily a theory of human alienation, and of how to overcome it. It is based primarily on Marx's unpublished Paris economic-philosophical manuscripts first made available in 1932. Although these three interpretations of Marxism are not compartmentalized in that they share some common attitudes, values, and beliefs, some of their basic theories are incompatible with each other. It would not be too much to say that if the basic theories of any one of these three interpretations are taken to be true they entail the falsity of the corresponding basic theories of the other two.

I

The first version of Marxism is represented mainly by the writings of the later Engels, the early Eduard Bernstein, Karl Kautsky, George Plekhanov, and in the United States by Daniel De Leon. It accepts as literally valid six interrelated complexes of propositions.

1. The fundamental and determining factor in all societies is the mode of economic production. All important changes in the culture of a period—its politics, ethics, religion, philosophy, and art—are ultimately to be explained in terms of changes in the economic substructure.

2. The capitalist mode of economic production is fundamentally unstable. It cannot guarantee, except for very limited periods, continued employment for the masses, a decent standard of living, and sufficient profit for the entrepreneurs to justify continued production. The consequence is growing mass misery culminating in the crisis and breakdown of the system of production. The deficiencies and fate of capitalism are not due to any specific persons or human actions, but flow from the law of value and

surplus value in a commodity-producing society. The collapse of capitalism and its replacement by a socialist classless society are inevitable.

3. Classes are defined by the role they play in production. Their conflicting economic interests give rise to economic class struggles that override on crucial occasions and, in the long run, all other kinds of struggle—religious, racial, national, etc. The variations in the intensity of these types of struggle, even their origin, are directly or indirectly a consequence of the "underlying" economic class struggle.

4. The state is an integral part of the political and legal order. It therefore has a class character which must be changed through class struggles, peaceful where possible, violent where not, before the forces of production can be liberated from the quest for ever-renewed profit and utilized for the benefit of the entire community, in which the economic exploitation of men by other men is no longer possible.

5. Capitalism prepares the way for the new socialist society by intensive development and centralization of industry, concentration of capital, and rationalization of the techniques of production. These are necessary presuppositions of a socialized, planning society in which the abolition of private ownership of the social means of production, and its vestment in the community as a whole, abolishes the economic class divisions of the past.

6. The movement towards socialism is a movement towards democracy. *Political* democracy must be defended against all its detractors and enemies but from the point of view of democracy as a way of life, it is necessary but not sufficient. Political democracy must be used to achieve a complete democracy by extending democratic values and principles into economic and social life. Where democracy does not exist the socialist movement must introduce it. (The *Communist Manifesto*, because of the absence of political democracy of the European Continent, advocated revolution by forcible overthrow.) Where democracy already exists, the working class can achieve power by peaceful parliamentary means (cf. Engels' critique of the Erfurt Program in 1891 and also his introduction to the first English translation of *Capital*).

There are many other doctrines that are part of the Marxist position (like equality between the sexes, self-determination for national minorities, the desirability of trade unions and cooperatives) that are easily derivable from the above propositions and some implicit value judgments about the desirability of human dignity, freedom, and creative self-fulfillment, even though they are obviously not uniquely entailed by them.

Marxism, in this its original version, was primarily a social philosophy. Its spokesmen as a rule adopted positions in philosophy and religion only in opposition to those metaphysical or theological doctrines whose suspected impact obstructed the growth of the working class movement and the development of its socialist consciousness. Philosophical and religious freedom of thought were extended to all thinkers who accepted the complex of social and economic propositions enumerated above which defined the theoretical Marxist orthodoxy of the German Social-Democratic Party and the majority of the members of the Second International. Dialectical materialism, for example, despite its espousal by Engels in his *Anti-Dühring* (1878) and *Ludwig Feuerbach* . . . (1888; trans, as *Ludwig Feuerbach and the Outcome of Classical German Philosophy*, 1934), was of peripheral importance in the Marxism that flourished up to 1917. The attack on Eduard Bernstein as a revisionist of Marxism was motivated primarily by his criticism of the first four of the complex of propositions identified above, and of the party programs of the political movement based on Marxism. It was only because he rejected the economic analysis of his party comrades and the political program presumably based on it (he approved its day-by-day activities) that attacks were made on his philosophical views.

The predominant characteristic of Social-Democratic Marxist thought is its determinism, its reliance upon the immanent processes of social development to create the conditions that would impel human beings to rationalize the whole of economic production in the same explicit and formal way in which an efficient industrial plant is organized. Formulated during an era in which the theory of evolution was being extrapolated from the field of biology to all other fields, especially the social and cultural areas of human activity, the laws of social development were considered universal, necessary, and progressive. The vocabulary was not very precise, partly because of the popular audience to which the teachings of Marxism were addressed. But even in *Capital*, as well as in his more popular writings, Marx used the term "inevitable" in describing the laws of economic change in heralding the collapse of capitalism. Engels was particularly addicted to the vocabulary of necessitarianism. Although aware of the differences in the subject matter of the natural and social sciences, and opposed to the reduction of the latter to the former, Marxists regarded the laws in both domains as working themselves out with an ineluctable "iron" necessity.

The concept of social necessity remained unexamined by the

Marxist theoreticians and could not be squared, when strictly interpreted, with the recognition of alternatives of development, alternatives of action, and objective possibilities presupposed in the *practical* programs of the Marxist movement of the time. Nonetheless it possessed a rational kernel of great importance. For it stressed the importance of social readiness, preparedness, and maturity as a test and check on proposals for reform and revolution. It served as a brake upon the adventurism and euphoria of action induced by revolutionary rhetoric, and also as a consolation in defeat when objective conditions were proved to be unripe.

On the other hand, belief in the concept of social necessity tended psychologically to inhibit risk-taking actions, especially as the Marxist movement and its political parties increased in influence and acquired a feeling of responsibility. Belief in determinism, and in the heartening conviction that the structure of the socialist society was being built within the shell of the old even by those opposed to socialism, could not obviate the necessity of making choices in economics and politics, whether it was a question of supporting a call for a general strike, or voting for welfare and/ or war budgets. But it naturally tended to reinforce in practice, if not in rhetoric, the choice of the moderate course, the one *less* likely to provoke opposition that might eventuate in violence and bloodshed. And why not, if the future, so to speak, was already in the bag?

This attitude of caution and restraint was reinforced by the implicitly teleological interpretation of evolutionary processes. What came later in time was assumed to be "higher" or "better"; setbacks were only temporary, the reverse stroke of an historical spiral that had only one direction—upward to a higher level. This led in practice to a commitment to the *inevitability of gradualism* so that the very pace of reforms tended to slow down as a sense of the urgent, the critical, and the catastrophic in history eased, and became replaced by a feeling of security in the overall development of history. Even the outbreak of the First World War in 1914, which destroyed the belief in the necessarily progressive character of change, failed to dispel the moderation of the Social-Democratic variant of Marxism. It was unprepared not only to take power but to exercise it vigorously when power was thrust upon it—at the close of the First World War in Germany. It moved towards the welfare state very slowly, partly in fear of provoking civil war.

Beginning with the last decade of the nineteenth century, as Social-Democratic movements gained strength in Europe, an enormous literature has been devoted to the exposition, criticism, and

evaluation of Marxism. At first neglected, then refuted, then reinterpreted, modified, and qualified, Marxism in all its varieties has
become at present perhaps the strongest single intellectual current
of modern social thought. It has left a permanent impress upon
economic historians like Max Weber and Charles Beard, even as
they disavowed belief in its basic ideas. Here we shall offer only
a brief review of the principal interpretations of the historical role
and validity of the central notions of Marxism.

1. The doctrine of historical materialism is accepted by many
historians as a heuristic aid in describing the ways a society
functions, its class power relations, and their influence on cultural
activities. But it is woefully deficient in clarity with respect to all
its basic terms. It is clear enough that it is not an economic
determinism of human motives of a Benthamite variety, nor a
technological determinism *à la* Veblen. But the connection between
"the social relations of production" and "the material forces of
production" is left obscure, so that there is some doubt whether
the basic motor forces of historical development are tools, techniques, and inventions, especially what Whitehead calls "the invention of the method of invention," all of which express the
productive drive of human beings—a drive which would open the
door to a psychological, idealistic interpretation—or whether the
immanent laws of the social relations of production are the ultimate
determinants. Actually although many historians express indebt-
edness to Marxism for its theory of historical materialism, they
mean no more by this doctrine than that "economics," in one of
its many different meanings, must always be taken into account
in an adequate understanding of history. But so must many other
things that are not economic.

There is a further difficulty in ascertaining whether Marxism
asserts that "social relations of production" or "the mode of
economic production" *determines* the cultural superstructure, and
if so to what degree, or merely *conditions* it. If it is taken to mean
that it determines culture in all important aspects—historical mo-
nism—it is obviously untenable. In the face of evidence to the
contrary, Marxists are wont to introduce reference to other factors
reserving the determination of these factors by the mode of economic
production—"in the last analysis"—despite the fact that scientifically speaking there is no such thing as "the last analysis."

The monistic determinism of Marxism is conspicuous in its
treatment of "great men" in history. From Engels to Kautsky to
Plekhanov to all lesser lights it is dogmatically assumed that no
event-making personality has existed such that in his absence

anything very important in history would have been different. With respect to any great event or phase of social development it is assumed that "no man is indispensable." Nonetheless, to cite only one difficulty, the overwhelming evidence seems to show that without Lenin there would in all likelihood have been in 1917 no October Russian Revolution.

Even if all problems of meaning are resolved and every trace of incoherence is removed from the theory of historical materialism, its claims that the mode of economic production determines politics, that "no social order ever perishes before all the productive forces for which there is room in it have developed," and that no new social order can develop except on the basis of the economic foundations that have been prepared for it—have all been decisively refuted by the origin, rise, and development of the USSR and Communist China. Marxism as a theory of social development has been proved false by the actions of adherents of the Marxism of Bolshevik-Leninism. Lenin and his party seized political power in an industrially backward country and proceeded to do what the theory of historical materialism declared it was impossible to do—build the economic foundations of a new society by the political means of a totalitarian state.

2. The economic theory of Marxism is clearer than the theory of historical materialism, and events have more clearly invalidated it by negating its specific predictions especially the pauperization of the working classes, and the continuous decline in the rate of profit. The theory failed to predict the rise of what has been called the "new middle class' of the service industries as well as the economics of the totalitarian state, on the one hand, and of the welfare state, on the other. Even before events invalidated the Marxist economic assumptions, the theoretical structure of Marxist economics never recovered from Eugen Böhm-Bawerk's searching critique in the 1890s of its inconsistencies. Much more successful were the Marxist predictions about the historical development of capitalism, even though they did not uniquely follow from its theory of value and surplus value. The Marxists foresaw the growth of monopolistic tendencies, the impact of science on industrial technology, the periodic business cycle (although mistaken about its increasing magnitude), and imperialistic expansion in quest for foreign markets. Although Marxists anticipated progressive and cumulative difficulties for the capitalist system, as Joseph Schumpeter and others in the twentieth century have pointed out, they failed to see that these difficulties resulted from the successes of the system rather than from its failures.

3. The Marxist theory of the class struggle differs from all other theories of the class struggle in that it weights the component of economic class membership more heavily than any other theory in relation to other social groupings and associations, and in its expectation that economic class struggles will cease when the social instruments of production are collectivized. Although economic class interests and struggles play a large and indisputable role in political, social, and cultural life, on crucial occasions nationalist and religious ties have exercised greater weight. Although the international Marxist movement was pledged to a general strike against war, when World War I broke out, French workmen, instead of making common cause with German workmen against their respective ruling classes, joined their "domestic exploiters," the French capitalists, in a common "national front" or "sacred union." The same was true in all major countries. National allegiance almost always proves stronger than class allegiance when national interest and class interest conflict. The union of capitalist Great Britain and United States supporting the socialist USSR against the invasion by capitalist Germany not only constitutes a difficulty for the theory of historical materialism—since the mode of economic production here was not decisive—but also for the theory of the class struggle, since the differences between the economic interests of the capitalist class as a whole and those of the USSR, especially in its opposition to capitalism declared from its very birth, are obviously far greater than the differences among the capitalists themselves. Even within the culture of a single capitalist country the Marxist theory of the class struggle fails to account for the degree and extent of class cooperation. The organized American labor movement seems just as hostile to collectivism as an economy and to communism as a political system as is the National Association of Manufacturers.

With the advent of collectivist economies in the Soviet Union and elsewhere, class struggles have not disappeared but have taken on a new form, sometimes expressed in strikes that are legally forbidden, in widespread pilfering, the use of a private sector to buy and sell, growth of bureaucratic privileges that some observers regard as indicia of a new class, and disparities in income and standards of living that are not too far removed from the upper and lower ranges of earned income in some capitalist countries. V. Pareto and Robert Michels, who agreed with Marxism that class struggles rage in society but disagreed with Marxism in holding that these struggles would continue even after Marxists came to power in what they call a socialist society, seem to have been justified by events.

Very little was done to solve some of the obvious difficulties in using the concept of class consistently with its definition, viz., the role played by individuals in the mode of production. In ordinary discourse, the various meanings of class take their meanings from the varied contexts in which they are used. One would have expected an attempt by Marxists to show that the chief uses of the term "class" that are different are derivative from the central Marxist one. Even more important was the failure to relate the concept of class interest to individual interest. Marxism is not a theory of human motivation, and especially not a theory of self-interest or egoism. The question remains: how does class interest get expressed? Classes are not individuals. They are abstractions. Only individuals act in history. On the Marxist theory of class, regardless of whether individual members of the class are selfish or unselfish, the interests of their class presumably get expressed. How does this happen and through what mechanisms? Is there an implicit statistical judgment that describes the behavior of most members of a class or are there representative leaders who speak for the class? These are some of the questions that remained unexplored, with the result that the concept of class interest, often invoked, appeared as vague and mystical as "national interest," "the spirit of the times," "the spirit of the people," and similar expressions.

4. The Marxist theory of the state in its simplest form asserts that the state—consisting of the legislature, courts, and armed forces—is nothing but "the executive committee of the dominant economic class." If this were so, it would be hard to explain the character of much of the criminal law or rules of evidence and procedure, which reflect either common ethical norms or professional interests not directly related to economic interests. The Marxist movement soon discovered that its economic power could be wielded in a political way to bring pressure on the state to liberalize and humanize the social relationships of men, and to reduce inequalities in living conditions. It soon discovered that with the extension of the franchise it could use the state power to redistribute social wealth through taxation, subsidies, and price supports. Under such circumstances the state, especially when it functions as a welfare state, does not act as the "executive committee" of the dominant economic class. It may do things that are bitterly opposed by that class. The state, then, becomes the instrument of that class or coalition of classes strong enough to win electoral victory. Allowing for time lags, where the democratic process prevails the state can become more responsive to those

groups that wield political power with majority electoral support, than to dominant economic interests.

5. Marxism as a movement became unfaithful to Marxism as a theory because of the success of capitalism in sustaining a relative prosperity—even if uncertain and discontinuous in times of acute crisis. Over the years, the numbers of the unemployed and poverty-stricken decreased instead of increasing. Real wages increased. Nonetheless, in order to achieve and sustain this relative affluence the state or government had to intervene in the economy with controls and plans foreign to the spirit and structure of a free market economy. The result has been a type of mixed economy—a private and public (often hidden) sector, unanticipated by the theorists both of capitalism and socialism. It turns out that the free enterprise economy of capitalism and the fully planned and planning collectivist economy of socialism are neither exclusive nor exhaustive possible social alternatives, and that in the political struggles of democracy the issue was rarely posed as a stark choice between *either* a free economy *or* a planned economy, *either* capitalism *or* socialism, but rather as a choice between *"more or less."*

6. The Marxism of the Social-Democratic movement became transformed into a broad democratic people's front in which socialist measures are the means of extending democracy, providing security, defending human dignity and freedom. It no longer speaks in the name of the working class even when the latter constitutes its mass base but instead in behalf of the common interest and common good. Despite the revolutionary rhetoric, it has become a people's socialism. Marxism is no longer the ideology of the German Social-Democratic Party whose program in broad outline (in the 1960s) barely differs from the liberal wing of the Democratic Party in the United States or the Labor Party in Great Britain. A multiplicity of problems remain to be met in order to make the welfare state truly devoted to the human welfare of all its citizens. Progress is no longer regarded as automatic but as requiring patience and hard work. But so long as the processes of freely given consent are not abridged in democratic countries and so long as large-scale war is avoided, the prospects of continued improvement are encouraging.

II

Marxism of the Bolshevik-Leninist persuasion is an extreme voluntaristic revision of the Social-Democratic variety that flourished in the period from the death of Marx (1883) to the outbreak of the First World War in 1914. The fact that it claims for itself the orthodoxy of the canonic tradition has about the same significance as the claims of Protestant leaders that they were returning to the orthodoxy of early Christianity. Even before the First World War, in Czarist Russia the Bolshevik faction of the Russian Social-Democratic movement had taken positions that evoked charges from its opponents that the leaders of the group were disciples of Bakunin and Blanqui, rather than of Marx and Engels. Their voluntarism, especially in its organizational bearings, received a classic expression in Lenin's work *What Is To Be Done?* (1902). But the emergence of Bolshevik-Leninism as a systematic reconstruction of traditional Marxism was stimulated by the failure of the Social-Democratic movement to resist the outbreak of the First World War, and the disregard of the Basle Resolutions (1912) of the Second International to call a general strike; by the Bolshevik seizure of power in the October Russian Revolution of 1917 and the consequent necessity of justifying that and subsequent events in Marxist terms; by the accession of Stalin to the supreme dictatorial post in the Soviet Union; and, finally, by the adoption of the systematic policy of building socialism in one country (the Soviet Union) marked by the collectivization of agriculture—in some ways a more revolutionary measure, and in all ways a bloodier and more terroristic one, than the October Revolution itself. The chief prophet of Marxist-Leninism was Stalin, and the doctrine bears the stigmata of his power and personality. Until his death in 1953, he played the same role in determining what the correct Marxist line was in politics, as well as in all fields of the arts and sciences, as the Pope of Rome in laying down the Catholic line in the domains of faith and morals. Although Stalin made no claim to theoretical infallibility, he exercised supreme authority to a point where disagreement with him on any controversial matter of moment might spell death.

The Bolshevik-Leninist version of Marxism got a hearing outside Russia, at first not in virtue of its doctrines, but because of its intransigent opposition to the First World War. The Social-Democratic version of Marxism was attacked as a "rationalization" of political passivity, particularly for its failure to resist the war actively. Actually there was no necessary connection between the deterministic outlook of Social Democracy and political passivity, since its electoral successes were an expression of widespread political activity albeit of a nonrevolutionary sort. Further, not only did some Social-Democratic determinists with a belief in the spontaneity of mass action, like Rosa Luxemburg, oppose the war, but even

Eduard Bernstein, the nonrevolutionary revisionist, who ardently believed that German Social Democracy should transform itself into a party of social reform, took a strong stand against the war. The attitude of Social Democracy to the First World War in most countries was more a tribute to the strength of its nationalism than a corollary of its belief in determinism. Nonetheless, the Bolsheviks on the strength of their antiwar position were able to insinuate doubts among some working class groups, not only about the courage and loyalty to internationalist ideals of Social-Democratic parties, but about their Marxist faith and socialist convictions.

After the Bolshevik Party seized power in October 1917 and then forcibly dissolved the democratically elected Constituent Assembly, whose delayed convocation had been one of the grounds offered by that Party for the October *putsch*, and in which they were a small minority (19 percent), it faced the universal condemnation of the Social-Democratic Parties affiliated with the Second Socialist International. In replying to these criticisms Lenin laid down the outlines of a more voluntaristic Marxism, that affected the meaning and emphasis of the complex of doctrines of traditional Marxism, especially its democratic commitments, in a fundamental way.

Finally with Lenin's death and the destruction of intraparty factions, which had preserved some vestigial traits of democratic dissent, the necessity of controlling public opinion in all fields led to the transformation of Marxism into a state philosophy enforced by the introduction of required courses in dialectical materialism and Marxist-Leninism on appropriate educational levels. Heretical ideas in any field ultimately fell within the purview of interest of the secret police. Censorship, open and veiled, enforced by a variety of carrots and whips, pervaded the whole of cultural life.

As a state philosophy Marxist-Leninism is marked by several important features that for purposes of expository convenience may be contrasted with earlier Social-Democratic forms of Marxist belief.

Marxism became an all-inclusive system in which its social philosophy was presented as an application and expression of the ontological laws of a universal and objective dialectic. During the heyday of Social-Democratic Marxism, the larger philosophical implications and presuppositions of its social philosophy were left undeveloped. So long as the specific party program of social action was not attacked, the widest tolerance was extended to philosophical and theological views. There was no objection even to the belief that God was a Social Democrat. Social Democrats, without losing their good standing within their movement, could be positivists, Kantians, Hegelians, mechanistic materialists, even, as in the case of Karl Liebknecht, subjectivists of a sort in their epistemology.

All this changed with the development and spread of Marxist-Leninism. The works of Engels, particularly his *Anti-Dühring* and *Dialectics of Nature*, of Lenin's *Materialism and Empirio-Criticism* and *Notebooks*, and subsequently, those of Stalin, became the sacred texts of a comprehensive system of dialectical materialism, devoted to explaining "the laws of motion in nature, society and mind." The details of the system and its inadequacies need not detain us here; but what it professed to prove was that the laws of dialectic guaranteed the victory of communist society, that no one could consistently subscribe to the ontology of dialectical materialism without being a communist and, more fateful, that no one could be a communist or a believer in communist society without being a dialectical materialist.

The comprehensiveness of this state philosophy resulted in a far flung net of new orthodox dogmas being thrown over all fields from astronomy to zoology, the development of what was in effect a two-truth theory, ordinary scientific truth and the higher dialectical truth which corrected the one-sidedness of the former, and political control of art and science. All communist parties affiliated with the Third Communist International were required to follow the lead of the Russian Communist Party. The literalness of the new orthodoxy is evidenced in the fact that the antiquated anthropological view of Engels and its primitive social evolutionism, based upon the findings of Lewis Morgan's pioneer work, *Ancient Society* (1877), were revived and aggressively defended against the criticisms of Franz Boas, Alexander Goldenweiser, Robert Lowie, and other investigators who, without any discredit to Morgan's pioneer effort, had cited mountains of evidence to show that social evolution was neither universal, unilinear, automatic, or progressive. Oddly enough the acceptance of the Engels-Morgan theory of social evolution, according to which no country can skip any important phase in its industrial development, would be hard to reconcile with the voluntarism of Bolshevik-Leninism, which transformed Russia from a backward capitalist country with strong feudal vestiges into a highly complex and modern industrial socialist state.

Reasoning from the dubious view that all things were dialectically interrelated, and the still more dubious view that a mistaken view in any field ultimately led to a mistaken view in every other field, including politics, and assuming that the party of Bolshevik-Leninism was in possession of the truth in politics, and that this therefore gave it the authority to judge the truth of any position in the arts and sciences in the light of its alleged political consequences, a continuous purge of ideas and persons, in accordance with the shifting political lines, marks the intellectual history of the Soviet Union. Here, as often elsewhere in the world, theoretical absurdities prepared the way for the moral atrocities whose pervasiveness and horror were officially partly revealed in Khrushchev's speech before the Twentieth Congress of the Russian Communist Party in 1956. Most of what Khrushchev revealed was already known in the West through the publications of escapees and defectors from the Soviet Union, and the publications of the Commission of Inquiry into the Truth of the Moscow Trials, headed by John Dewey.

1. The theory of historical materialism was invoked by all the socialist and Marxist critics of Bolshevik-Leninism since, if it were valid, a *prima facie* case could be made against Lenin and his followers for attempting to skip a stage of industrial development and introduce socialism in a backward country. Lenin and Trotsky in consequence reinterpreted the theory by asserting that the world economy had to be treated as a whole, that the world was already prepared for socialism as a result of modern science, technology, and industry, and the the *political* revolution could break out at the weakest link in the world economic system as a whole. This would serve as a spark that would set the more advanced industrial countries like England, the United States, and Germany into revolutionary motion (places where Marx and Engels had expected socialism originally to come). This meant, of course, that the theory of historical materialism could no longer explain the *specific* political act of revolution, since on the theory of the weakest link, a political revolution by a Marxist party anywhere in the world, even in the Congo, could trigger off the world socialist revolution.

On the theory of the weakest link, after the political revolution successfully took its course and spread to other countries, the world *socialist* revolution, marked by the socialization of affluence, would be initiated by advanced industrial countries, with Russia and China once more bringing up the rear because of their primitive economies. But they would be the last in a socialist world, and only temporarily, until the world socialist economy was established and strategic goods and sources flowed to areas of greatest human need.

When the theory of the "weakest link" led in practice to the fact of a severed or isolated link, in consequence of the failure of the October Russian Revolution to inspire socialist revolutions in the West, the program of "building socialism in one country" was adopted. The attempt to build socialism in one country—and in a bankrupt, war-torn, poverty-stricken country at that—flew in the face of any reasonable interpretation of historical materialism. Nonetheless, by a combination of great courage, and still greater determination and ruthlessness, and aided by the ineptitude of their political opponents, the Bolshevik-Leninists succeeded despite the theoretical veto of the doctrine of historical materialism in its classical form. There is no doubt but that a new economy had been constructed by political means. Despite this, however, the theory that the economic base determines politics and not vice versa is still canonic doctrine in all communist countries.

2. In expectation of the socialist revolution occurring in the highly industrialized countries of the West, the theorists of Marxist-Leninism have clung to the letter of Marx's critique of capitalism and his predictions. For decades they have painted a picture of mass misery and starvation in the West. They have denied that capitalism has been modified in any significant way and that the Welfare State exploits the workers any less than the more individualistic economies it replaced. On the contrary, their claim is that economically the rich get richer, and the poor become poorer—and the rest is bourgeois propaganda.

3. The concept of "class" has been quite troublesome to Marxist-Leninism particularly with Stalin's declaration that a "classless" society had been introduced in the Soviet Union with the adoption of its new constitution of 1936. If the concept of "proletariat" or "working class" is a polar one, it implies, when concretely used, a "capitalist class." But if capitalism is abolished and all social ownership is vested in the community, who or which is the exploiting class? On a functional conception of property, viz., the legal right or power to *exclude* others from the use of things and services in which property is claimed, critics have argued that the social property of the Soviet Union in effect belongs to the Communist Party considered as a corporate body. And although there is no right to individual testamentary transmission, so long as the Communist Party enjoys the privileged position assigned to it in the Soviet Constitution, in effect, one set of leaders, in the name of the Party, inherits the power over social property from its predecessors, and the differential use and privileges that power bestows. Milovan Djilas, in his *The New Class* . . . (1957), on the basis of his study and experience in Yugoslavia and the Soviet Union argued that in current communist societies the bureaucracy constituted a ruling elite enjoying social privileges which

justified calling it a "class." Subsequently other writers claimed that divisions and conflicts within the ruling elite presented a picture of greater class complexity (Albert Parry, *The New Class Divided*, 1966). It is obvious that the Marxist-Leninist concept of class cannot do justice to the Soviet, not to speak of the Chinese experience, in which peasants are often referred to as proletariat in order to give some semblance of sense to the terminological Marxist pieties of the Communist Party.

Actually the position of the worker is unique in the Soviet Union, in that it corresponds neither to the "association of free producers," envisaged by Marx nor to "the Soviet democracy" used by Lenin as a slogan to come to power. Nor is it like the position of the workers in modern capitalist societies, since the Soviet workers cannot organize free trade unions independent of the state, cannot without punitive risk leave their jobs, cannot travel without a passport and official permission, and cannot appeal to an independent judiciary if they run afoul of the authorities. Oscar Lange, the Polish communist economist, before his return to Poland, and while he was still a left-wing Socialist, characterized the Soviet economy as "an industrial serfdom" with the workers in the role of modern serfs. Like the phrases "state capitalism" and "state socialism," which have also been applied to the Soviet Union, this indicates that present-day communist economics and class relationships require a new set of economic and political categories to do justice to them. Nonetheless, that its economy is distinctive, although sharing some of the features of classical capitalism and classical socialism, is undeniable.

4. Even more embarrassing is the nature of the state in the Marxist-Leninist theory. If the state is by definition "the executive committee of the ruling class," then as classes disappear the state weakens and finally withers away. But since the Soviet Union is declared to be a classless society, how account for the existence of the state, which instead of withering away has become stronger and stronger? The conventional reply under Stalin was that so long as socialism existed within one country, which was encircled by hungry capitalist powers intent upon its dismemberment, the state functioned primarily as the guardian of *national* integrity. This failed to explain the regime of *domestic* terror, and a concentration camp economy, worse than anything that existed in czarist days. Furthermore as communism spread, and the Soviet Union became no longer encircled by capitalist nations but emerged as co-equal in nuclear power to the West, more threatening to than threatened by the countries adjoining it, the state showed

no signs of weakening. Although the domestic terror abated some-what under Khrushchev, the state still remains, after fifty years of rule, much stronger than it was under Lenin, before the Soviet Union consolidated its power.

Theoretically, the Soviet Union is a federal union of autonomous socialist republics which theoretically possess complete ethnic and national equality and with the right of secession from the Union guaranteed. In fact, it is a monolithic state that can establish or destroy its affiliated republics at will, and in which some ethnic minorities have been persecuted and subjected to severe discrimination.

5. The economy of the Soviet Union has remained a highly centralized, planned, and planning economy, primarily a command economy, functioning best in time of war and largely indifferent to the needs and demands of the consumer. The result has been the transformation within a period of fifty years of an agricultural economy into a great, modern industrial economy. The human costs in bloodshed and suffering of this transformation have been incalculable. The excessive centralization has led to inefficiency and waste, the development of a hidden market, and other abuses. To supplement the controlled economy's efforts to take care of consumers' needs, the state has tolerated a private sector in which goods and services are sold or exchanged for profit. Under the influence of E. G. Liberman and other economic reformers, some tentative steps have been taken to decentralize, and to introduce the concept of net profit in state enterprises in order to provide incentives and increase efficiency. Greeted as a return to capitalistic principles, it overlooks the limited function of profit as conceived in a socialist economy, in which prices are still controlled by the central planning authority.

What these and similar reforms do that is difficult to square with the theory of Marxist-Leninism is to increase the power of the plant manager over the workers, and to differentiate even further the incomes received. Because of differences created by advances in technology, comparisons in standards of living are difficult to make between different historical periods. With respect to per capita consumption of the material necessities of life, the workers in most of the advanced industrial economies today seem to enjoy, without the sacrifice of their freedoms, a substantially higher standard of living than the workers of the Soviet Union. But there is nothing in the structure of the socialist economy which makes it impossible to equal and even surpass the standards of living of workers in capitalist countries. An economy that can put a Sputnik in the sky before other industrial societies, can probably outproduce them, if the decision is made to do so, in the production of refrigerators or television sets. The major differences lie not in what and how much is produced, but in the freedom to choose the system of production under which to live.

6. This brings us to the major Bolshevik-Leninist revision of the Marxism of the Social-Democratic variety—viz., the abandonment of its commitment to democracy as a system of social organization, as a theory of the political process including political organization, and, finally, as the high road to socialism.

As we have already noted, until the October Russian Revolution, the phrase "the dictatorship of the proletariat" was rarely used in Marxist literature. Marx himself used the term very infrequently, and Engels pointed to the Paris Commune of 1871, in which Marx's group was a tiny minority, as an illustration of what the phrase meant. Even those who spoke of the "dictatorship of the proletariat" meant by it the class rule of the workers, presumably the majority of the population, which would democratically enact laws introducing the socialist society. That is what Engels meant when he wrote in 1891 that the democratic republic was "the *specific* form for the dictatorship of the proletariat" (Marx and Engels, *Correspondence 1846–1895*, New York [1936], p. 486). Marx and Engels also anticipated that the transition to socialism would be peaceful where democratic political institutions had developed that gave the workers the franchise. Force would be employed only to suppress armed rebellion of unreconciled *minorities* against the mandate of the majority.

The Marxist-Leninist version of "the dictatorship of the proletariat" is that it is substantially "the dictatorship of the Communist Party," which means not only a dictatorship over the bourgeoisie but *over* the proletariat as well. The Paris Commune on this view is not really a "dictatorship of the proletariat." The dictatorship of the Communist Party entailed that no other political parties, not even other working-class parties, would be tolerated if they did not accept the Leninist line. It meant that there could be no legally recognized opposition of any kind. For as Lenin put it, "Dictatorship is power based directly upon force, and unrestricted by any laws," and again "dictatorship means neither more nor less than unlimited power, resting directly on force, not limited by anything, not restricted by any laws, nor any absolute rules" (*Selected Works*, VII, 123).

This whole conception is based frankly on the assumption that armed by the insights of Marxist-Leninism, the Communist Party knows better what the true interests of the working class are than the workers know themselves; that it cannot give the workers their head but must, if necessary, restrain or compel them for their own good. Thus Lenin proclaimed "All power to the Soviets," the organs of the Russian workers and peasants after 1917, when he anticipated that they would follow the Communist (Bolshevik) Party line, but this slogan was abandoned and even opposed when there was fear the Soviets would not accept the Communist Party dictatorship. This view of the dictatorship of the Party is central to all Marxist-Leninist parties. Thus the Hungarian communist premier, Jan Kadar, in his speech before the Hungarian National Assembly on May 11, 1957, justifying the suppression by the Red Army of the Hungarian workers in the Budapest uprising of 1956, makes a distinction between "the *wishes* and *will* of the working masses" and "the *interests*" of the workers. The Communist Party, knowing the true *interests* of the workers and having these interests at heart, is therefore justified in opposing the *wishes* and *will* of the masses. This is the Leninist version of Rousseau's doctrine that the people "must be forced to be free."

The antidemocratic conception of the political party actually preceded the transformation of the dictatorship of the proletariat into the dictatorship of the party over the proletariat. Logically the two ideas are independent, since a hierarchically organized party could accept the democratic process as providing an opportunity for coming to power legitimately. The Social-Democratic conception of party organization made it a very loose-jointed affair. Marx and Engels actually assumed that in the course of its economic struggles, the working class spontaneously would develop the organizational instrumentalities necessary to win the battle. Lenin, on the other hand, thought of the political party as an *engineer* of revolution, spurring on, teaching, even lashing the working class into revolutionary political consciousness.

The political party structure devised by Lenin owes more probably to the fact that the socialist parties were underground and had to work illegally in Russia than it does to Marxist theory. The theory of "democratic centralism" was really better adapted for a resistance movement than for political democratic process. Nonetheless all of the many Communist Parties associated with the Communist International were compelled to adopt that theory as a condition for affiliation. The Central Committee of the Party was the chief organizing center, the final link in a chain of command that extended down to the party cells. The Central Committee had the power to co-opt and reject delegates to the Party Congress which nominally was the source of authority for the Central Committee. Because of its access to party funds, lists, periodicals, and control of organizers, the leadership of the "democratic centralized" party tended to be self-perpetuating. Certain maneuvers or *coups* from the top would bring one faction or another to the fore, but no broadbased movement of member opposition was possible. Until Stalin's death changes in the leadership of Communist Parties outside of the Soviet Union occurred only as a consequence of the intervention of the Russian Communist Party acting through representatives of the Communist International. Thus, to cite a typical example, the leadership of the American Communist Party which claimed to have the support of 93 percent of the rank and file was dismissed by Stalin in 1928, and the new leadership of W. Z. Foster and Earl Browder appointed. The processes of "democratic centralism" then legitimized the change. After the Second World War, Browder, based on the ostensibly unanimous support of the party membership, was unceremoniously cashiered as leader by signals communicated by Jacques Duclos of the French Communist Party at the instigation of the Kremlin.

There have been some developments in the theory and practice of Marxist-Leninism of the first political importance. Lenin and Stalin both believed that the capitalist countries were doomed to break down in a universal crisis; that because of their system of production they must expand or die, and that before they died, they would resort to all-out war against the Soviet Union. The classic statement of this view was Lenin's declaration of November 20, 1920, repeated in subsequent editions of his and Stalin's writings: "As long as capitalism and socialism exist, we cannot live in peace; in the end one or the other will triumph—a funeral dirge will be sung over the Soviet Republic or over World Capitalism" (*Selected Works*, VIII, 297). Despite the hypothetical possibility of a capitalist triumph, the victory of communism was declared to be inevitable in consequence of the inevitable war for which it was preparing. The Soviet Union and all its communist allies must consider themselves to be in a state of undeclared defensive war against the aggression being hatched against it; Communist Parties abroad must have as their first political priority "The defence of the Soviet Union"—which sometimes led to difficulties with workers who struck industrial plants in capitalist countries manufacturing goods and munitions for the use of the Soviet Union.

The doctrine of the inevitability of armed conflict between the democratic countries of the West and the Soviet Union undoubtedly played an important role in Stalin's war and postwar policy. Even though Great Britain and the United States were loyal allies in the struggle against Hitler, the war had to be fought with an eye on their capacity for the subsequent struggle against the Soviet Union. This led to an extensive development of Soviet espionage in allied countries during, and especially after, the war; the expansion of Soviet frontiers; the establishment of Communist regimes by the Red Army in adjoining territories; and a political strategy designed to split the Western alliance. Although aware of the development of nuclear weapons, Stalin was skeptical about their capacity for wholesale destruction, and remained steadfast in his belief in the inevitable victory of Communism through inevitable war.

Nikita Khrushchev, who by outmaneuvering Bulganin, Malenkov, and Beria, succeeded Stalin, had a far greater respect for the potential holocaust involved in nuclear war. Although he spurred on the development of Soviet nuclear power, he revived the notion of "peaceful coexistence," a theme originally propounded by Lenin in an interview with an American journalist in 1920, and periodically revived for propaganda purposes since. But what was highly significant in Khrushchev's emendation of the doctrine, was his declaration that although the final victory of world Communism is inevitable, world war was not inevitable; that it was possible for Communism to succeed without an international civil war. This recognized the relatively independent influence of technological factors on politics, and created an additional difficulty for the theory of historical materialism.

The second important political development since the death of Stalin has been the growth of Communist polycentrism, and the emergence of Communist China as a challenge to Soviet hegemony over the world Communist movement. Communist "polycentrism" meant the weakening of the centralized control of the Russian Communist Party over other Communist Parties, and the gradual assertion of political independence in some respects by hitherto Communist Party satellites. For the first and only time in its history the American Communist Party officially declared itself in opposition to Soviet anti-Semitism. After Khrushchev's speech exposing Stalin's terrorism, it has become impossible for Communist Parties to resume the attitude of total compliance to Kremlin demands. The degree of independence, however, varies from country to country—the Italian Communist Party manifesting the most independence and the Bulgarian Communist Party the least.

The strained relations between Communist Yugoslavia and the Soviet Union and especially between Communist China and the

Soviet Union—all invoking the theory of Marxist-Leninism—are eloquent and ironical evidence that some important social phenomena cannot be understood through the simple, explanatory categories of Marxism. After all, war was explained by Marxists as caused by economic factors directly related to the mode of economic production. That one Communist power finds itself not only engaged in military border skirmishes with another, but actually threatens, if provoked, a war of nuclear annihilation against its Communist brother-nation, as spokesmen of the Soviet Union did in the summer of 1969, is something that obviously cannot be explained in terms of their *common* modes of economic production. Once more nationalism is proving to be trumphant over Marxism.

III

The third interpretation of Marxism may be called for purposes of identification, "the existentialist view" according to which Marxism is not primarily a system of sociology or economics, but a philosophy of human liberation. It seeks to overcome human alienation, to emancipate man from repressive social institutions, especially economic institutions that frustrate his true nature, and to bring him into harmony with himself, his fellow men, and the world around him so that he can both overcome his estrangements and express his true essence through creative freedom. This view developed as a result of two things; first, the publication in 1932 of Marx's manuscripts written in 1844 before Marx had become a Marxist (according to the two previous interpretations of Marx), which the editors entitled *Economic and Philosophic Manuscripts,* and second, the revolt against Stalinism in Eastern Europe at the end of World War II among some Communists who opposed the theory and practice of Marxist-Leninism. Aware that they could only get a hearing or exercise influence if they spoke in the name of Marxism, they seized upon several formulations in these early manuscripts of Marx in which he glorifies the nature of man as a freedom-loving creature—a nature that has been distorted, cramped, and twisted by the capitalist mode of production. They were then able to protest in the name of Marxist humanism against the stifling dictatorship of Stalin and his lieutenants in their own countries, and even against the apotheosis of Lenin.

Independently of this political motivation in the reinterpretation of Marx, some socialist and nonsocialist scholars in the West have maintained that the conception of man and alienation in the early writings of Marx is the main theme of Marx's view of socialism, the aim of which is "the spiritual emancipation of man." For example, Erich Fromm writes that "it is impossible to understand Marx's concept of socialism and his criticism of capitalism as developed except on the basis of his concept of man which he developed in his early writings" (*Marx's Concept of Man* [1961], p. 79). This entails the curious consequence that Marx's thought was understood by no one before 1932 when the manuscripts were published, unless they had independently developed the theory of alienation. Robert Tucker's influential book, *Philosophy and Myth in Karl Marx* (Cambridge 1961), asserts that the significant ideas of Marx are to be found in what he calls Marx's "original Marxism" which turns out to be ethical, existentialist, anticipatory of Buber and Tillich, and profoundly different from the Marxism of Marx's immediate disciples. How far the new interpretation is prepared to go in discarding traditional Marxism, with its emphasis on scientific sociology and economics as superfluous theoretical baggage alien to the true Marx, is apparent in this typical passage from Tucker:

Capital, the product of twenty years of hard labor to which, as he [Marx] said, he sacrificed his health, his happiness in life and his family, is an intellectual museum piece for us now, whereas the sixteen page manuscript of 1844 on the future of aesthetics, which he probably wrote in a day and never even saw fit to publish, contains much that is still significant (p. 235).

Another source of the growth of this new version of Marxism flows from the writings of Jean-Paul Sartre and Maurice Merleau-Ponty, especially the former's *Critique de la raison dialectique* (Vol. I, 1960) in which despite his rejection of materialism and his exaggerated voluntarism, Sartre seeks to present his existentialist idealism as ancillary to Marxism, which he hails as "the unsurpassable philosophy of our time" (p. 9).

For various political reasons, this third version of Marxism for some time made great headway among radical and revolutionary youths in the West who disparaged or repudiated specific political programs as inhibiting action. Among those who wished to bring Marx in line with newer developments in psychology, and especially among Socialists and Communists who based their critiques of the existing social order primarily on ethical principles, the existentialist version of Marx also had a strong appeal.

The theoretical difficulties this interpretation of Marxism must face are very formidable. They are external, derived from certain methodological principles of interpretation and from textual difficulties; and internal, derived from the flat incompatibility of the key notions of existential Marxism with other published doctrines of Marx, for which Marx took public responsibility. Of the many external difficulties with the interpretation of Marxism as a philosophy of alientation, three may be mentioned.

1. The theory of alienation according to which man is a victim of the products of his own creation in an industrial society he does not consciously control, is a view that was common coin among the "true" socialists like Moses Hess, Karl Grün, and others. It was not a distinctively Marxist view. Even Ralph Waldo Emerson and Thomas Carlyle expressed similar sentiments when they complained that things were in the saddle and riding man to an end foreign to his nature and intention.

2. In the *Communist Manifesto* Marx explicitly disavows the theory of alienation as "metaphysical rubbish," as a linguistic Germanic mystification of social phenomena described by French social critics. Thus as an example of "metaphysical rubbish," Marx says, "Underneath the French critique of money and its functions, they wrote, 'alienation of the essence of mankind,' and underneath the French critique of the bourgeois State they wrote 'overthrow of the supremacy of the abstract universal' and so on" (Riazanov edition; English trans. London [1930], p. 59).

3. If Marxism is a theory of human alienation under all forms and expressions of capitalism, it becomes unintelligible why, having proclaimed the fact of human alienation at the outset of his studies, Marx should have devoted himself for almost twenty years to the systematic analysis of the mechanics of capitalist production. The existence of alienation was already established on the basis of phenomena observable whenever the free market system was introduced. Nothing in *Capital* throws any further light on the phenomenon. The section on the "Fetishism of Commodities" (*Capital*, Vol. I, Ch. I, Sec. 4) is a *sociological* analysis of commodities where private ownership of the social means of production exists, and dispenses completely with all reference to the true essence of man and his alienations of that essence. What Marx calls "the enigmatic character" of the product of labor when it assumes the form of a commodity is the result of the fact that *social* relationships among men are experienced directly by the unreflective consciousness as a *natural* property of things. The economic "value" of products that are exchanged is assumed to be of the same existential order as "the weight" of the products.

This results in the fetishism of commodities which is compared to the fetishism of objects in primitive religion in which men fail to see that the divinity attributed to the objects is their own creation. Or to use another analogy, just as what makes an object "food" ultimately depends upon the biological relationships of the digestive system, and not *merely* upon the physical-chemical properties of the object, so what makes a thing a "commodity" depends upon social relationships between men, and not merely on the physical characteristics of what objects are bought and sold. Marx's analysis here is designed to further his contention that men can control their economic and social life and should not resign themselves to be ruled by economic processes as if they were like natural forces beyond the possibility of human control. The Marxist analysis is used here to argue for the feasibility of a shorter working day and better conditions of work.

The "internal" difficulties that confront the existentialist interpretation of Marx are grave enough to be considered fatal in the absence of a politically inspired will to believe.

1. The doctrine of "alienation" runs counter to Marx's scientific materialism. Its religious origins are obvious in the idealistic tradition from Plotinus to Hegel. It is inherently dualistic since it distinguishes an original "nature" of man separate from its alienated manifestations to which men will someday return.

2. It even more obviously violates the entire historical approach of Marxism which denies that man has a natural or real or true self from which he can be alientated. Marx maintained that by acting upon the external world, nature, and society, man continually modifies his own nature (*Capital,* Eng. trans., I, 198), that history may be regarded as "the progressive modification" of human nature, and that to argue that socialism and its institutional reforms are against human nature—one of the oldest and strongest objections to the Marxist program—is to overlook the extent to which the individual with his psychological nature is a social and therefore historical creature. Many of the difficulties of the view that Marxism is a theory of alienation and a social program liberating man from his alienation are apparent as soon as we ask: *From* what self or nature is man alienated?, and then compare the implications and presuppositions of the response with other explicitly avowed doctrines of Marx. The attempt by Tucker to distinguish in Marx between a constant human nature—productive, free, and self-fulfilling—and a variable human nature—alienated in class societies—attempting to save the doctrine of alienation, fails to explain how it is possible that man's constant nature should come into existence, according to Marx, only at the end of prehistory, only when the classless society emerges. In addition, Marx like Hegel

repudiates the dualism between a constant and variable human nature to the point of denying that even man's biological nature is constant.

3. In Marx's published writing, where psychological phenomena are mentioned that have been cited as evidence of Marx's belief in the importance of the doctrine of alienation, despite his refusal to use the early language of alienation, Marx explains these phenomena as a *consequence* of private property in the instruments of production. But in his early *Economic-Philosophical Manuscripts* (written before 1847), he asserts that alienation is the *cause* of private property. This would make a psychological phenomenon responsible for the distinctive social processes of capitalism whose developments the mature Marx regarded as having causal priority in explaining social psychological change.

4. The concept of man as alienated in the early manuscripts implies that alienated man is unhappy, maladjusted, truncated, psychologically if not physically unhealthy. It does not explain the phenomenon of alienation which is active and voluntary rather than passive and coerced. Marx himself was alienated from his society but hardly from his "true" self, for he undoubtedly found fulfillment in his role as critic and social prophet. From this point of view to be alienated from a society may be a condition for the achievement of the serenity, interest, and creative effort and fulfillment that are the defining characteristics of the psychologically unalienated man. Marx's early theory of alienation could hardly do justice, aside from its inherent incoherences, to Marx's mature behavior as an integrated person alienated from his own society.

5. The existentialist interpretation of Marxism makes it primarily an ethical philosophy of life and society, very much akin to the ethical philosophies of social life that Marx and Engels scorned during most of their political career. Nonetheless this ethical dimension of social judgment and criticism constitutes a perennial source of the appeal of Marxism to generations of the young, all the more so because of the tendencies both in the Social-Democratic and, especially, in the Bolshevik-Leninist versions of Marxism to play down, if not to suppress, the ethical moment of socialism. In the canonic writings of these interpretations of Marxism, socialism is pictured as the irreversible and inescapable fulfillment of an *historical* development and moral judgments are explained, where they are recognized, as reflections of class interest, devoid of universal and objective validity. The doctrinal writings of both Marx and Engels lend color to this view—despite the fact that everything else they wrote, and even the works purportedly of a

technical and analytical character, like *Capital* itself, are pervaded by a passionate moral concern and a denunciation of social injustices in tones that sound like echoes of the Hebrew social prophets. The very word *Ausbeutung*, or "exploitation," which is central to Marx's economic analysis, is implicitly ethical although Marx seeks to disavow its ethical connotations. Even critics of Marx's economic theories and historicism, like Karl Popper, who reject his contentions recognize the ethical motivation of Marx's thought. Capitalism is condemned not only because it is unstable and generates suffering, but because uncontrolled power over the social instruments of production gives arbitrary power over the lives of those who must live by their use.

Nonetheless, despite its ethical reinterpretation of Marxism, existentialist Marxism fails to make ends meet theoretically. Either it ends up with a pale sort of humanism, a conception of the good and the good society derived from the essential nature of man and his basic needs—a lapse into the Feuerbachianisms rejected by Marx—or it denies the possibility of a universally valid norm of conduct for man or society, stresses the uniqueness of the individual moral act, makes every situation in which two or more individuals are involved an antinomic one in which right conflicts with right and self with self. If the first version generates a universalism of love or duty and brotherhood of man which Marx (and Hegel) reject as unhistorical, the second points to a Hobbesianism in which "the other" far from being "a brother" is potentially an enemy. Marx conceals from himself the necessity of developing an *explicit* positive ethics over and above his condemnations of unnecessary human cruelty and injustice. The closest he comes to such an ethic is in his utopian conception of a classless society whose institutions will be such that the freedom of each person will find in the freedom of every other person "not its limitation but its fulfillment." Many critics find this expectation an astonishingly naive conception of man and society, which does not even hold for traditional versions of the Kingdom of Heaven. But even this utopian construction can hardly absolve Marxists from the necessity of making and justifying specific ethical judgments for the City of Man.

The periodical revivals of Marxism in our age reflect moral and political interests in search of a respectable revolutionary tradition. The discovery of the social problem by phenomenologists, Neo-Thomists, positivists, and even linguistic analysts usually results in an attempted synthesis between Marx and some outstanding philosophical figure who has very little in common with him.

From the point of view of sociological and economic theories claiming objective truth, Marxism has contributed many insights that have been absorbed and developed by scholars who either do not share or are hostile to the perspective of social reform or revolution. Scientifically there is no more warrant for speaking of Marxism today in sociology than there is for speaking of Newtonianism in physics or Darwinism in biology. The fact that Marxism has become the state doctrine of industrially underdeveloped countries in Asia and Africa is testimony to the fact that his system of thought proved to be inapplicable to the Western world whose development it sought to explain. There is also a certain irony in the fact that some of the contemporary movements of sensualism, immediatism, anarchism, and romantic violence among the young in Western Europe and America which invoke Marx's name are, allowing only for slight changes in idiom, the very movements he criticized and rejected during the forties of the nineteenth century—the period in which Marx was developing his distinctive ideas. Some modes of consciousness and modes of living that marked recent New Left thought and activity Marx scornfully rejected as characteristic of the *lumpenproletariat.*

At this stage in the development of Marxism it may seem as fruitless a task to determine which, if any, version of Marxism comes closest to Marx's own doctrinal intent as to ask which conception of Christianity, if any, is closest to the vision and teachings of its founder. Nonetheless, although difficult, it is not impossible in principle to reach reliable conclusions if the inquiry is undertaken in a scientific spirit. Even if he was in some respects self-deceived, Marx after all did conceive himself as a scientific economist and sociologist. Allowing for the ambiguities and imprecision of Marx's published writings, there is greater warrant for believing that those who seek to provide scientific grounds for his conclusions are closer to his own intent and belief than are those who, whether on the basis of Marx's unpublished juvenilia or Sartre's metaphysical fantasies, would convert him to existentialism. The scientific versions of Marxism have an additional advantage: they permit of the possibility of empirical refutation, and so facilitate the winning of new and more reliable scientific truths which Marx as a scientist presumably would have been willing to accept. Existentialist versions of Marxism, where they are not purely historical, are willful and arbitrary interpretations of social and political phenomena. "Marxism," declares Sartre, "is the unsurpassable philosophy of our time," but only because he interprets it in such a way as to make it immune to empirical test. Holding to it, therefore, is not a test of one's fidelity to truth in the service of a liberal and humane civilization, but only a measure of tenacity of one's faith.

CHAPTER THREE

Spectral Marxism

To someone like myself, who was characterized for many years as the foremost Marxist among American philosophers, the resurrection of Marxism and Marxist views in Western thought, particularly in Anglo-American academic circles, has a paradoxical and even amusing side. For it comes at a time when, in the light of the historical record, most of Marx's predictions and expectations have been falsified. What passes for Marxism today is largely a mélange of doctrines that differ from Marx's leading ideas and that he would have scornfully disowned for all their sentimental socialist fervor.

When I completed the manuscript of my *Towards the Understanding of Karl Marx* in the late fall of 1932, the economic depression was at its worst; Hitler was waiting in the wings to take power; and in the thinking of many intellectuals, and in the fears of even more, a socialist revolution seemed to be a live option. That book, which appeared on the fiftieth anniversary of Marx's death, was actually published during the American "bank holiday" in 1933, when capitalism seemed finished even though no one had any idea of what was to replace it. In it I presented a version of Marx that was fundamentally empirical: I did not argue that Marxism was a science, but that it was a scientific method of achieving a socialist society.

Now that we are approaching the hundredth anniversary of Marx's death, the scene is quite different. Capitalism, despite its many crises and difficulties, is not on the verge of collapse. In most countries it has developed into a Welfare State not anticipated by Marx. The three cardinal doctrines of classical Marxism lie in ruins. The theory of historical materialism—which holds either (in its strong form) that the mode of economic production determines political change or (in its weak form) that it conditions such change—has been refuted by Lenin and Mao Tse-tung. Whether

54

the economy they and their successors built is called "socialism," or "industrial serfdom," or a new form of Asiatic despotism, they succeeded in doing what the theory of historical materialism declared could not be done. By seizing political power they built a new economic foundation under it, whereas Marx had anticipated that the economic structure of socialist society would be built antecedently to the transfer of political power to the working class.

Many of Marx's predictions about the development of the capitalist economy have been realized, but those that presumably followed from his theory of value and surplus value have not. Society has not been increasingly polarized between a handful of capitalists and the workers. The working class has not been progressively pauperized; nor has it become the overwhelming majority of the population; nor has there been a decline in the rate of profit. Despite the existence of pockets of poverty, the standards of living, as well as the longevity of members of the working class, have risen. In startling contrast to the situation that existed when Marx wrote *Capital*, the life expectancy of members of the middle class and of the proletariat do not markedly differ.

The emergence and persistence of nationalism have revealed the limitations of Marx's conception of the overriding significance and weight of the economic class struggle in understanding historical events. Certainly class antagonisms are always present, and they often erupt into open struggles—a phenomenon discovered by thinkers before Marx. But anyone who still believes that "all history is the history of class struggles" would be baffled to account for the not inconsiderable amount of class cooperation, both in ordinary times and for some great events in times of crisis. The conception of class struggle, for example, can hardly apply to World War II, when democratic capitalist powers allied to a despotic socialist power fought other despotic capitalist powers. Nor can it throw much light on the recent wars between states having socialized economies.

How, then, explain the scores of volumes whose authors have accepted the validity of Marx's analyses to a degree that is, in their minds, sufficient to justify their proclaimed allegiance to the Marxist tradition? There is a special explanation in each individual case, but in the present climate of opinion one can sense a pervasive and subtle attitude that facilitates the identification. No longer is there any danger in being known as a Marxist, especially in the elite universities. The label stamps a teacher and scholar as a man of the Left, and therefore sympathetic to the resistance of the counterculture to the establishment, however it is defined. It endears one to the student body, especially to campus organs of opinion that almost invariably are in the hands of young men and women who look back with a wistful envy to the golden and glorious era of the sixties. At the same time that it absolves one from the suspicion of being a vulgar anti-Communist, it lifts the burden of having to defend the *Gulag Archipelago.* The U.S. and the USSR can be damned with a fine impartiality, and if the brunt of criticism falls on the U.S., that is only because the U.S. is where one lives. Some revolutionary wishful thinking may enter into the desire to vindicate either Marx's overall vision or some specific analysis, but there is no doubt about the good faith of these self-denominated Marxists. Some of them even completed reputable works of scholarship before embracing the Marxist ideology—although those who knew their Marx would never call it an ideology.

Regardless of the reasons for the revival of Marxist allegiance, what all expositors and adherents have in common is a conception of Marx that makes his doctrines impervious to empirical confirmation or refutation. None of the recent Marxists—whether in history, politics, economics, psychology, or sociology—meet the criterion of scientific significance formulated a long time ago by Charles S. Peirce, the father of American pragmatism. Peirce insisted that no one could legitimately claim to possess knowledge about the world unless he could indicate what kind of objectively verifiable experience would constitute evidence of a doctrine's inadequacy or invalidity. Peirce did not mean that one should abandon a theory as false immediately on finding a single negative case. He somewhere points out that most tough-minded scientists would hold to a theory in the face of a few falsifying pieces of evidence, but insists that the difference between a scientific truth and a myth is determined by one's knowledge of what counts for and what counts against the specific hypothesis that guides one's inquiry. Despite all the epistemological refinements that show how complex the concepts of meaning and truth are, the acceptance of this criterion is crucial to any doctrine that claims to be scientifically acceptable. And if anything is indisputable in the canons of Marxism, it is the claim of both Marx and Engels that, in contradistinction to the teachings of socialists of other schools, their doctrines were scientifically valid.

In the absence of any conception of the kind of evidence that would make Marx's statements about the economy and history at least refutable in principle, any belief can be attributed to him or be characterized as Marxist. The result is that today when a person characterizes himself as a Marxist, we no more know what he really believes than we do when a person claims to be a Christian. Almost at random my eye lights on a long piece in the *New York Times Book Review* in which an academic historian discusses several books on China:

Among all the great revolutions, the Chinese Revolution of the past hundred years has been, in many ways, the most authentically Marxist. It did not take place in a rich industrial society, but revolutions have never been effected in such a society. However, it is the only revolution that, in line with Marx's prediction, moved to socialize after long periods of capitalism and with a dynamic roughly compatible to the one Marx postulated.

According to this author, the Chinese Marxist revolution must have begun in 1880, when Marx was still alive. How strange that he did not recognize it. It was "authentically Marxist" despite the fact that China was not a highly industrialized society and no revolutions have ever taken place in such a society. But does that not constitute a refutation of the authentically Marxist view that a socialist revolution can occur only in a highly industrialized society? And if China has been a capitalist country for "nearly a thousand years," as the reviewer goes on to say, does it not make nonsense of the very first sentence of Marx's *Capital,* in which capitalism is characterized by "an immense accumulation of commodities"?

One can multiply indefinitely instances of this kind of so-called Marxism. Neither Marx's texts nor the fallout of historical events serves as a sober control over what Marx said or meant. The emotive connotations of key terms have shifted with the times. When I was a student, before and during World War I, the very word "capitalism" was suspect. Only socialists and other subversives used it. The leading representatives of the existing economic order were loath to call the system under which they lived "capitalist." A vestige of that state of mind still survived in Nicholas Murray Butler, who was president of Columbia University when Louis M. Hacker published his *Triumph of American Capitalism;* Butler liked it very much except for the word "capitalism." The attitude toward Marx, not only in the press but in academic circles, was a compound of ignorance and hostility. When I carried my soapbox propaganda into my high school and college classes, to the discomfiture of my teachers, I had the advantage—not that I profited from it—that none of them, with two exceptions (M. R. Cohen and J. Salwyn Schapiro), had ever read anything of Marx firsthand. To them it was enough that the Bolsheviks called themselves Marxists, and the fact that the leading Marxists of the world were bitterly critical of the Bolsheviks was not known. Even when they noted the importance of class struggles, few professional historians concerned themselves with Marx, either on the undergraduate or the graduate level. Economists ignored him. Charles Beard, whose sympathies were always with the underdog and who professed a vague ethical socialism, never understood why those who accepted the Marxist theory of historical materialism rejected his version of it as a narrow and false view of economic self-interest, closer to Bentham than to Marx.

I

The present vogue of Marx studies and the doctrinal stance of Left-oriented intellectuals—"We are all Marxists of a sort these days"—make all the more noteworthy the publication of Leszek Kolakowski's *Main Currents of Marxism*[1]—the first volume of which is devoted to its *Founders*, the second to its *Golden Age*, and the third to its *Breakdown*. The work is an intellectual event of the first order, although the editors of some of our leading organs of opinion have not deigned to notice it. Kolakowski, who was purged for his heresies from the Communist Party of Poland and then deprived of his post as professor of philosophy at the University of Warsaw, is currently a fellow at All Souls College, Oxford. He has put all scholars and intelligent laymen interested in Marx and Marxism in his debt. Hereafter no one who undertakes to expound or criticize Marxism can afford to ignore his work. Regardless of qualifications and points of difference (and I have several major ones with him), Kolakowski's magisterial study must be acknowledged as opening a new era in Marxist criticism.

The reasons for this are many. First, it is the most comprehensive treatment of Marx, and of thinkers in the Marxist tradition, so far published. Only a few significant figures, close or distant in kinship to Marx and his ideas, have been overlooked. I was surprised to find no account of Henri de Man's profoundly interesting study, *The Psychology of Socialism*, and even more surprised at the inadequate treatment of Waclaw Machajski, who was probably the first to formulate a theory predicting the rise of a new ruling social class under socialism—the intellectuals—that would exercise a new type of exploitation. Yet his omission of Joseph Dietzgen, the proletarian philosopher, seems justified. His simplistic reflections

---

[1]Leszek Kolakowski, *Main Currents of Marxism*, 3 vols. (New York: Oxford University Press, 1980)

had no influence on subsequent socialist thought. More important, but not surprising because it reflects typical European insularity, is Kolakowski's unawareness of American critical currents of Marxist thought in the thirties that anticipated some European developments a generation later. He is also unaware of Lewis Feuer's original research on the influence of American utopian socialist colonies on Marx.

On the other hand, Kolakowski discusses interesting writers in the Marxist tradition who are unknown to me and, it is safe to surmise, to other scholars ignorant of Polish—for example, Ludwig Krzywicki, Kazimierz Kelles-Krautz, and Stanislaw Brozozowski. Their ideas, however, seem less important than those of his fellow Pole, Oskar Lange, of the University of Chicago. Lange, before he capitulated to the Kremlin (because, as he once told me, "The U.S. is not willing and prepared to fight the Russians on the River Bug"), had characterized the peculiar economy of the Soviet Union as "an industrial serfdom." He argued, together with Abba Lerner, for the feasibility of a democratic market socialism.

In addition to the comprehensiveness of the study—the chapters on Antonio Gramsci, Georg Lukács, and the Frankfurt School are outstanding—Professor Kolakowski manifests a virtue in rare supply among the fiercely polemical contenders for the legacy of Marx. This virtue is his capacity—the secret of his remarkable expository skills—for an empathetic and interpretive presentation of the views that he considers before he dissects them, although it is not in evidence in his treatment of Karl Kautsky. In some cases he is much clearer than the authors themselves. This is true not only for Lukács, with whose interpretation of Marx he is in agreement, but for the different varieties of neo-Kantianism that sought to modify and amplify the Marxist analysis and critique of the historical development of capitalism with a medley of vague ethical notions. One cannot fail to be impressed with Kolakowski's substantive scholarship. He seems at home in all fields: the sciences, philosophy, economics, the organization and strategies of political power. His methodological sophistication and capacity for drawing relevant distinctions help him and the reader to carry the burden of his erudition.

As refreshing as it is unusual in this area is Kolakowski's fair-mindedness. Even when one differs with him, one is aware of his freedom from *parti pris*, his independent judgment, his desire to recognize the truth from any quarter, and his readiness to challenge established reputations without a show of disrespect. Here is no sectarian at work. Although clearly establishing that the Marxism of Jean Jaurès was seriously flawed, Kolakowski does ample justice to Jaurès's great-souled humanism and his attachment to those universal ethical values that all Marxists themselves invoke—despite difficulty in accounting for their validity from a purely historical point of view. And Kolakowski recognizes the indisputable merits of secondary figures like Paul Lafargue, Marx's son-in-law, regarded by most critics merely as a superb propagandist.

To stop short with the list of its merits, one may note that Kolakowski's book is chock-full of arresting observations. Independent of the thrust of his analysis, these illuminate the men, movements, and events discussed in all three volumes. Almost every page contains a nugget of insight. For example, he explains why Eduard Bernstein, the first great revisionist of Marx, retained as much influence on the German workers as did Kautsky, the war-horse of orthodoxy, with a remark that sums up the situation in Germany, the home of the strongest Social Democratic party in the era of the Second International: "The revolutionary idea was much more the property of the party intellectuals than of the working masses." In one aperçu he exposes the key weakness of Jaurès's attractive social philosophy: "Like most pantheists he believed in universal salvation, the ultimate reconcilability of all things; i.e., the non-reality of evil." In dispatching the many attempts to dilute the claims of the theory of historical materialism so as to escape the absurd consequences of the monistic version in Marx, the early Engels, Kautsky, and George Plekhanov, he truly observes: "Historical materialism in such watered down terms may provide a contrast to the type of history, such as St. Augustine's, which relates everything to the design of Providence: but it does not constitute a specific method over and beyond what every historian is prepared to recognize."

Despite Marx's contumacious treatment of Moses Hess, Kolakowski observes that Hess was "the first writer to express certain ideas which proved especially important in the history of Marxism." He leaves no doubt that Marx's social ideal provides for the presence of an individuality which, in contrast with societies that call themselves socialist today, "is not diluted into colorless uniformity"—but whose authenticity does not depend on destroying the individuality of others. Regarding persistent efforts to resolve the contradiction between the first and third volumes of *Capital* by interpreting Marx's analysis to apply to "an ideal type of capitalism," he aptly remarks, "Such interpretations protect Marxism against the destructive results of experience only by depriving it of its value as an instrument of real life social analysis."

Of greater originality is Kolakowski's analysis of the concept of "exploitation" in Marx. To the mystification of followers and critics alike, Marx had claimed that it had no ethical significance in his system but that it was the corollary of a fair and legal exchange between the worker and his employer. Kolakowski shows that it can be coherently defined without invoking the doctrine of surplus value from which Marx derived it. He concludes his acute discussion with this observation: "Exploitation consists in the fact that society has no control over the use of the surplus product [which must be present in any society if it is not to dissolve into civil war], and that its distribution is in the hands of those who have an exclusive power of decision as to the use of the means of production." This analysis, if valid, is of momentous importance, for it would follow that, in the absence of democratic processes in determining social distribution, exploitation is possible even in a completely nationalized or socialized economy. Kolakowski's reading conforms with Marx's disavowal of egalitarianism. It implies that only the democratic sharing of the power to distribute the surplus product would end the exploitation of man by man. This is in perfect accord with Marx's commitment to democracy. But it is subject to the charge of utopianism on two counts. First, it assumes that fairness, regardless of the results of distribution, is only a matter of process—as if the democratic process could never result in oppression—and, second, it leaves open a likelihood that Marx seems to have persistently ignored: that there may be other forms of human exploitation which are not reducible to economic terms.

These matters may be regarded by the nonspecialist as peripheral to Marx's contributions. The general reader would probably be more concerned with Kolakowski's assessment of Marx and the Marxist tradition; the extent to which Lenin was a faithful follower of Marx; the relationship between Marxism and the Russian October Revolution of 1917; the roots of Stalinism, if any, in Leninism; and the responsibility of Marxism for Stalinism.

Before these questions are treated, however, something should be said of Kolakowski's contrasting of the Marxism of Marx with the Marxism of Engels. Here he is both original and provocative. Orthodox Marxists, whether Socialist or Communist, have looked askance at persons who, like me, have criticized Engels for his gratuitous introduction of metaphysics and ontology into Marx's scientific world view. Kolakowski believes that the gulf between Marx and Engels is even deeper than anyone has suspected and for the astonishing reason, among others, that Engels was too sympathetic to positivism. This is especially evident in Engels's view that as scientific knowledge develops, philosophy—as a discipline purporting to give verifiable knowledge about nature, society, and man—will disappear, evanescing into the study of logic and the practice of logical analysis. Such a view, although it does not speak much for Engels's consistency, is hardly to his discredit, and there is no evidence whatever that Marx believed philosophy in the traditional sense would remain an autonomous discipline. Kolakowski is on better ground in recognizing that, while both Marx and Engels are committed to an evolutionary emergent naturalism, Engels's spectator theory of knowledge and its naive correspondence-doctrine of truth cannot do justice to the activity of the human mind in knowing. But when Kolakowski, stating the difference, discusses the meaning of praxis in Marx, he rides a strange hobby horse: "Whereas Engels, broadly speaking, believed that man could be explained in terms of natural history and laws of evolution to which he was subject, and which he was capable of knowing in themselves, Marx's view was that nature, as we know it, is an extension of man, an organ of practical activity."

There is a certain ambiguity in this attribution of anthropomorphism to Marx. If it means only that "knowledge cannot be divested of the fact that it is human, social and historical knowledge," it is a commonplace which Engels certainly acknowledged. Music, literature, art, and religion are also human social and historical products; but what must be explained is that science yields knowledge whose validity transcends the social and historical context in which it is discovered. To go beyond this, to suggest that the very content of knowledge (that is, the truth of what is known) depends upon man, smacks of an idealism that ill comports with Marx's rejection of Hegel. But if Kolakowski means that the human praxis involved in the process of knowing makes a difference to the object of knowledge, then it is a very significant assertion which raises an important question: How it is possible for the mind to be active in knowing and, in virtue of that activity, to introduce changes in the situation under inquiry, and still be capable of achieving valid knowledge intersubjectively? With respect to the social scene, Kolakowski agrees with Lukács's bizarre reading of Marx, that the revolutionary consciousness of the proletariat through its praxis solves the problem—a notion I shall examine later. In passing, I note only that Kolakowski's almost total ignorance of John Dewey's theory of knowledge prevents him from seeing another and more plausible answer to the question.

II

According to Kolakowski, the whole of Marx's thought can be best interpreted in terms of three motifs: the Romantic, the Faustian-Promethean, and the rational, deterministic outlook of the Enlightenment. It is significant that Kolakowski refers to the third motif not as scientific but as "scientistic"—a disparaging term that connotes the inappropriateness of employing scientific methods to some subject matter rather than to false theories about it.

The Romantic motif is expressed in Marx's moral passion for an integrated human being in an organic society. From it flows his criticism of the phenomena of human alienation, and the main features of the Communist Utopia in which the division of labor is abolished, the state and civil society disappear, and the relationships that embrace all members of a loving family extend to all members of society, indeed the whole human race. In view of this idyllic view of the future of man, it is obvious why orthodox Marxists and orthodox Freudians must be at dagger's point with each other.

The Romantic strain is also apparent in the Marxist rejection of the traditional liberal philosophy, as expressed in Locke, Hobbes, Bentham, and Mill, and its justifications of the social contract and human rights. This philosophy, writes Kolakowski, "assumes that human conduct is necessarily governed by selfish motives and that their conflicting interests can only be reconciled by a rational system of laws which safeguards the security of all by limiting the freedom of each. This implies that men are one another's natural enemies, each one's freedom being the natural limit of everyone else's."

What Kolakowski overlooks, as does Marx, is that the philosophy of liberalism implies only that men are *potentially* one another's natural enemies—which is perfectly true and quite compatible with the view that they are *potentially* one another's friends. The considerable number of young men and women during the twentieth century who embraced Marxist Communism because they blithely assumed it was an extension of liberalism—Stephen Spender is the classic case—shows that they understood neither liberalism nor Marx's Communism.

Despite the influence of the Romantic ideal, Marx detached himself from it in at least three respects, through savage polemics against those who, he thought, were affected by its rosy glow. First, Marx had no nostalgia for the past; he was oriented exclusively toward the future. Whether or not the future is progressive, it is irreversible. The nostrums peddled by nature enthusiasts, if universalized, would return mankind to the idiocy of village life. Second, his thought was pervaded by the ideals of a secular international community. The spiritual harmonies of religion, the nation, the Volksgeist, or the imagined colorful village life celebrated by the Romantics of his time and previous times, could be idealized in art, but never realized in contemporary life. Third, Marx's attitude toward technology, if not worshipful, was enthusiastic. He lost few nights of sleep, but one of them was a consequence of the feverish intellectual excitement generated by a visit to a scientific technological exhibition in the 1850s. Marx believed, as Kolakowski succinctly puts it, that "the destructive effects of the machine cannot be cured by abolishing machines but only by perfecting them."

Kolakowski does not even mention, however, what seems to me Marx's chief difference with the Romantics. Marx did not believe that man had an original and fixed human nature from which he was necessarily alienated. Kolakowski's whole exposition of Marx is based on the uncritical assumption that Marx adhered from first to last to Ludwig Feuerbach's notion of the species nature of man. This is a fateful misreading, probably due to Kolakowski's own view about the nature of human nature. But the question here is not whether Marx is right or wrong but what he believed. Not only does he explicitly state in *Capital* that all history is a transformation of human nature; it follows from his famous critical gloss on Feuerbach that the human essence consists in the totality of man's social relationships. Since these relationships are historical in character, they change, and human nature, as distinct from its biological basis, changes too. For Marx, human psychology is social psychology. Here too Marx is at one with John Dewey, whose *Human Nature and Conduct* develops the theme in persuasive detail.

The Promethean motif in Marx's thought expresses itself in twofold fashion. First, in an impassioned defiance of all the gods of heaven and earth and, second, in a contempt for traditions and institutions that cannot justify themselves by acceptable fruits in experience. Both are preeminently embodied in his faith in human power to control our social destiny and, within limits, our natural environment too. This Promethean mood was certainly not unique to Marx. It was shared by other rebels who loathed Marx who loathed them. But it did not take the shallow form that Kolakowski implies when he imputes to Marx an indifference to the human condition, an obliviousness to the essentially tragic sense of life in the career of finite, fallible creatures against a cosmic background that conditions all that they were, are, and will be. This overlooks the fact that for Marx these features of the world, however irreducible, are irrelevant to a reasoned *social* philosophy. When they enter into human affairs, they function like a religion to distract human beings from concern with remediable evils by agonizing over first and last things. Marx was no philistine. It is unjust to say of a man who was at home with the Greek tragedies, who knew Shakespeare and Dante and Goethe by heart and cited them appositely in his work—a man whose own life was marked by intense grief, the death of loved ones, the anguish of frustrated ambition and personal betrayal—that "Evil and suffering, in his [Marx's] eyes, had no meaning except as instruments of liberation; they were purely social facts, not an essential part of the human condition." What invalidates Marx's vision of the social harmony of the classless society of the future is not death and the facts of human finitude, but his failure to recognize the likelihood of a variety of *social* evils and possibilities for human oppression in a collectivized economy. The inanities of socialist utopia-mongers, for whom the Revolution is not merely a historical but a cosmic event, should not be laid at Marx's door.

It is not the denial of death or the tragic sense of life that expresses Marx's own Utopianism but, among other things, his absurd view that in a classless society *all* division of labor would be abolished, rather than its inhuman excesses, and his failure to appreciate the Goethean insight that one of the keys to great achievement, except for the Leonardos of this world, is self-limitation. Hegel's theory of alienation was far more profound.

The third motif in Marx is one that Marx himself chiefly stressed: the rational, scientific approach to human affairs. This is apparent in most of the writings that he published when, so to speak, Marx became a Marxist. Kolakowski discounts its significance except for its tendency to breed confusion in the minds of Marx and his followers. The mischief derives from Marx's emphasis upon the presence of laws determining the structure and development of society and from his failure to do justice to the complex and difficult question of reconciling social determinism and human freedom.

Like many other natural scientists of the nineteenth century, Marx used the language of "inevitability" in describing the succession of societies, and particularly the advent of socialism. Yet he could not have meant it literally (any more than by "contradictions" he meant the relation of *logical* incompatibility). For he was no fatalist. His whole lifework was predicated on the assumption that knowledge makes a difference, that the outcome of historical events will be influenced by whether the working class accepts the truths of Marxism and has the courage to act on them. To him the rise of the workers' class *consciousness* is not undetermined, but it is not determined by the same events that give rise to class struggles. The laws that govern capitalist society do not depend upon our knowledge of them, but our knowledge of them may lead to actions that will produce a society in which they no longer operate. Other laws then take over. Just as in scientific medicine we can use our knowledge of biological laws to eliminate plague and other diseases, so we can modify social life to a point in which poverty, prostitution, unemployment, and economic exploitation disappear. Scientific physicians would never assume that when current diseases are eliminated mankind will be free of disease. Many Marxists, however, assume that when current social evils are eliminated there will be no others of any significance. The laws of nature that condition all human effort and the existence of all societies are not affected by our knowledge of them. Marx would have agreed with Spinoza that we can change nature only by natural means. Nor is the validity of social laws, if any, affected by our knowledge of them—only their scope.

Kolakowski disputes this analysis of Marx's scientific motif. He asserts that for Marx the questions of "determinism or human freedom, belief in historical laws or human initiative have no meaning," on the grounds that Marx had overcome the dualism between fact and value, between what is and what ought to be. How Marx did it he leaves completely unclear, despite some obfuscatory pages in which he tries to explicate Lukács's ideas.

As must be apparent, Kolakowski's assessment of Marx is not a conventional one. With respect to almost all the scientific predictions that Marx ever made, Kolakowski concludes that they are false, that at best they have heuristic value in calling attention to the pervasive effects of the underlying economy on the structure of social and cultural life, and the alternatives of action and belief which they frame. What he regards as distinctive to Marx, in contrast to Engels's simplistic scientific naturalism, is a view of human knowledge in which understanding and transforming the world are integral to the process by which the working class acquires the consciousness that leads to socialism. Although he is severely critical of Georg Lukács for his Stalinist allegiance and contemptible personal behavior, he claims that Lukács's indisputable merit is his recognition of this "essential feature of Marxism"—something all the Marxists during Marx's own and later generations failed to see. He seems unaware of how utterly bizarre is the notion that no one truly understood Marx until Lukács wrote.

III

Before evaluating Kolakowski's assessment of Marx, something should be said of his treatment of the post-Marxists to whom two of the three volumes are devoted. Kolakowski rejects the German Social-Democratic tradition, as expressed in Kautsky's interpretation, as unfaithful to the soul of the dialectic revolutionary principle in Marx and as too naive in its reliance on the immanent laws of capitalism and its collapse to bring about a socialist society. He underplays both the intellectual significance of Eduard Bernstein and the vindication of Bernstein's criticisms of Marxist orthodoxy by events. Bernstein is the true father of the Bad Godesberg program of present-day German Social Democracy.

In a fascinating chapter that should be prescribed reading for literary intellectuals who have been beguiled by Leon Trotsky's tragic fate and by his rhetorical brilliance, Kolakowski shows that in all essential matters Trotsky's doctrines—and, when he was in power, his practices—were no different from those of Stalin. Trotsky's passion for party democracy arose when he and his followers were victimized by Stalin. It did not extend to the far greater multitudes of non-Communists, innocent of any crimes, who experienced an earlier, if not worse, fate.

Less controversial today—after Solzhenitsyn's searing history of the Gulag Archipelago, which traces its justifications to Lenin—is Kolakowski's analysis of Lenin. It is a clinical annihilation of those who would dispute the evidence that Stalin, despite Lenin's testament urging that he be removed as party secretary, was Lenin's legitimate ideological heir. By judicious citation Kolakowski leads the reader to the inescapable conclusion that "There is absolutely nothing in the worst excesses of the worst years of Stalinism that cannot be justified on Leninist principles if only it can be shown that Soviet power was increased thereby." Still, Kolakowski does recognize some difference between Lenin and Stalin. For one thing, Lenin called his oppressions by their right names, whereas Stalin was a master of mendacity.

This well-fortified conclusion about Lenin's responsibility for creating the system that bred Stalin will bring cold comfort to those in the American radical movement who anticipated that judgment forty years ago. I recall an article by James Burnham in a *Partisan Review* of 1939 in which he declared Stalin to be "Lenin's heir" and which provoked a loud outcry on both sides of the Atlantic. George Orwell, who was by then a confirmed anti-Stalinist, found this bitter truth so unpalatable that he denounced Burnham as "a Fascist" for daring to see in Stalin's deeds the harvest of Lenin's seed. At the time he never used such an epithet to characterize Stalin.

Concerning the much more difficult question of the relationship between Marxism and Leninism, Kolakowski offers an ambiguous and highly qualified answer. On his reading, the Leninist version of socialism in theory and practice is a possible interpretation of Marx, although certainly not the only possible one. But if Leninism is a *legitimate* possible interpretation of Marx, that is indeed a devastating judgment. For what he is really saying is that the historically unprecedented system of totalitarianism which Lenin ushered into the world is implicit in Marx's basic ideas and ideals. But if the conception of a truly democratic socialist society is also implicit in Marx, as Kolakowski acknowledges, then Marx's social and political writings must be considered basically incoherent.

Kolakowski, it seems to me, goes astray here. Although he notes Lenin's lack of fidelity to the Marxist tradition in his early advocacy of an alliance between the working class and the peasantry, and in his exploitation of nationalism as integral to the strategy of the conquest of power, he does not sufficiently stress the chief difference between Marx and Lenin. This is to be found in Lenin's identification of "the dictatorship of the proletariat" with "the dictatorship of the party," which is literally a dictatorship over the proletariat and everyone else. That identification proved to be the poisoned premise from which all the multiple tyrannies of the Soviet Union flowed—and there is not a line in the enormous corpus of Marx's work that warrants attributing this view to Marx himself. If anything, Marx erred in his emphasis on the spontaneity of the working-class revolutionary movement, affirming and reaffirming that the emancipation of the working class can be achieved only by that class itself. No exegesis of Marx's statement about Communists serving as a "vanguard" of the working class can be used as a source of Lenin's theory of the party. In 1904, before Trotsky became a Leninist, he denounced that theory in words which are uncannily appropriate for the dictatorship of the Politburo and the dictatorship of Stalin. After all, the government of the Paris Commune—to which Engels pointed as illustrating what Marx meant by "the dictatorship of the proletariat"—was a coalition of many political tendencies in which no party exercised a dictatorship and in which Marx's own political faction was not officially represented. Before he died, Marx, like Engels, admitted that the dictatorship of the proletariat could be brought into being through the democratic parliamentary process.

IV

One can say with reasonable confidence that as scholars come to grips with Kolakowski's three massive volumes they will find little to take issue with in more than two thirds of the work: the second and third volumes. It is with Kolakowski's treatment of Marx that major difficulties can be raised, and these involve his assumption that there is no essential difference between the early Marx and the Marx of his major published writings. There are enormous difficulties in this view, which cannot be overcome by pointing out some linguistic continuities between the young and the mature Marx. The crucial question is, When did Marx become a "Marxist"? Until the *Economic and Philosophic* manuscripts were published, the almost universal answer was that he became a Marxist when he promulgated the theory of historical materialism. This doctrine and its corollaries are completely at odds with the Feuerbachian and "true socialist" standpoint of the manuscripts. The whole doctrine of "self-alienation" presupposes logically an essential and perduring self from which man can be alienated—a notion foreign to both Hegel and Marx and, when it was taken over by French socialists, Marx characterized it in the *Communist Manifesto* as "metaphysical rubbish." The question is of more than biographical interest; depending upon how one answers it, Marx will be considered either a muddleheaded philosopher or a pioneering scientific sociologist.

A second major difficulty in Kolakowski's exposition of Marx is his view that the development of the forces of production, or technology in its broad sense, is the driving force of history. "The message of historical materialism would seem to be that a given technology is a sufficient cause of particular relations of production provided certain other conditions of geography or demography are present." Here, it seems to me, Kolakowski's position is very questionable, although other highly regarded scholars share it. This view is not only incompatible with Marx's texts, except where he is using metaphors, but runs counter to the central notion of the relations of production and their organic development, in which technology plays a role. Whether a technology is used and how it is used depends upon the state of the relations of production. Once isolated as the basic variable in social change, as Kolakowski understands it, the same technology may be found in two different social systems—that is, systems with different relations of production. In this sense, slaves liberated from slavery can still employ the same technology as freemen, just as in many respects the technology of the U.S. and the USSR today is the same. Here the older Marxist schools were justified in stressing the *mode* or *relations* of economic production as the basis of social organization and development. (It is even reflected in Lenin's odd definition of communism as "Soviets plus electrification," where the term "Soviets" refers in the historic context to a new, collectivist mode of production.) Further, behind every technological development is an idea. It has been argued that the industrial revolution is primarily a scientific revolution. Before long, the technological interpretation of history now put forward to explicate the materialistic interpretation of history is transformed into the traditional idealistic interpretation that Marx explicitly rejected. The obvious retort to this is that ideas, especially when applied, do not develop in a historical vacuum. They are always found in a social context. They are inspired by social needs. Even when they modify, they fit into the net of social relations or the dominant mode of economic production.

The third and most questionable of Kolakowski's positions is his conception of Marx's theory of knowledge. He correctly divines that Marx rejects the contemplative theory of knowledge for a view that makes knowing an activity, a form of practice that must leave the world somewhat altered. But the character of that practice is rather mystifying because of Kolakowski's tendency to identify the activity with revolutionary action—though obviously not all knowledge is related to revolutionary practice. Sometimes he identifies Marx's theory of knowledge with knowledge of social and historical affairs, solving the problem of how we can predict events that we try to influence or bring about. "The act of foreseeing coincides with the act of effecting what is foreseen; the proletariat knows the future in the act of creating it, not after the fashion of a weather forecaster when the changes that actually happen are unaffected by anything the forecaster can do." This is a form of magical idealism. Even in social affairs many events can—in the short run, at least—be foreseen but cannot be effected, certainly not by the proletariat. Considered as a general theory of knowledge, the whole view runs into absurdity in the claim that "cognition signifies taking possession of the world in a process of revolutionary changes"—as if knowing something were like eating it, as if all processes of change were revolutionary, and as if Marx were proclaiming truths about social development that could be valid only for the proletariat.

Another conception of knowledge suggested by Marx's fragmentary comments is ignored by Kolakowski: this view recognizes that an element of activity or praxis enters into every instance of knowledge—from truths of perception to truths about the world, physical or social, outside us. In this view all reliable or tested knowledge involves praxis, not as something practical or useful, but as an activity comparable to what is done in an experiment and one which always involves interaction between the knower and the field he is cognitively exploring. In this sense it entails a rearrangement of the field. We do not learn merely by opening our eyes but by doing, though not all doing is learning. Knowing changes the world in some way, so we may read conclusions that test the anticipated consequences of that change. This does not mean that we change the moon when we learn something about it; it means that to learn something about the moon (or about any other object), we must do something to elements in the field even if we only alter the position of our bodies. Such activity will vary with different disciplines and with different problems, but if knowledge is won, it will be valid independent of who or what class knows it.

This theory of knowledge is embryonic in Marx and is incompatible with Engels's crude view that our ideas are images or copies of things, and therefore objects of knowledge that serve as a screen between things and their knowers. The theory is more plausible than Lukács's reading of Marx and, despite its internal difficulties, closer to Marx's naturalistic outlook.

Regardless of the validity of one or another interpretation of Marx, it is clear that Marx's contributions, in whatever modified form, have entered the consciousness of our time, affected the idiom of our language and understanding, and left an ineradicable imprint on the world of scholarship. All this is hardly sufficient to justify anyone's calling himself a Marxist unless he wishes to break out a flag of political allegiance. Just as no scientific biologist, in discussing the genetic aspects of evolution, would call himself a Darwinian today, so no scientific sociologist, if he were concerned only with the truth of his statements, would call himself a Marxist. Even with respect to those scholars who avow Marxism in order to declare their political faith, the spectrum of their beliefs runs from some forms of Leninism to a Third World tribal Maoism. The only thing one can be certain about is their unalterable hostility to the democratic welfare state of the Western world, especially of the United States.

CHAPTER FOUR

Lenin and the Communist International

Lenin and the Comintern is a remarkable study of a remarkable man who was the chief architect of one of the most remarkable organizations in human history.[1] It is a paradigm of scholarship in a field in which passion and *parti pris*, fortified by wisdom after the event, have been more concerned to plead a cause than to establish the truth. Although a treasure trove for specialists, it is a book from which many others can learn, not only those who wish to understand history but those who are intent on making it. Above all, it is indispensable to those of large theoretical and philosophical interests, concerned with unravelling the tangles of causal connection between personality and social-economic forces, for it expounds and illuminates a cluster of paradoxes centered around the life work of a professed disciple of Marx who in *interpreting* the legacy of Marx's thought not only *changes* the world but definitively refutes Marx's central doctrines.

That Lenin is among the greatest architects of the twentieth century can only be contested by those who deny that leadership plays a distinctive role in determining the alternatives of political and social development or who refuse the title of architect to one whose plans when executed have consequences far different from what originally had been intended. Although Marx himself uses the architectural metaphor in a thumbnail sketch of his philosophy of history, he allows no place for any architect, secular or divine, in his account. Lenin's claim to the title of master architect of the twentieth century, as the authors of this volume establish, rests

---

[1]Branko Lazitch and Milorad M. Drachkovitch, *Lenin and the Comintern* (Stanford, Ca: Hoover Institution Press, 1972)

upon three achievements of which he was the guiding spirit. The first was the organization of the Russian Communist Party into a new and unique political party having little to do with any socialist organizations of the past. Without Lenin, there would have been no party of this kind. The second was the conquest of political power in Russia by this new and unique party in violation of Marxist theory, in defiance of universal expectation, and in the face of overwhelming odds. The third was the organization of the Third, or Communist, International, the fashioning of its program and structure, and its gradual transformation into an instrument of Soviet foreign policy.

This first volume of the study by Drs. Lazitch and Drachkovitch is devoted to the early history of the Communist International and Lenin's role in it. It begins with a consideration of proletarian internationalism during World War I, Lenin's critical stance toward and subsequent break with the Zimmerwald Movement, and the founding of the Third International on March 2, 1919 at which Lenin proclaimed: "By order of the Central Committee of the Communist Party of Russia, I declare this first International Communist Congress to be in session," thus jumping the gun on delegates unable to be present and in opposition to those who thought they were merely attending a conference to explore the possibilities of organization. The book continues with a detailed and fascinating account of the organization, programs, proceedings, and personalities of the two Congresses and treats with clarity and insight Lenin's relations with "Left Communism." It then traces the checkered course of the Comintern in engineering splits and defections in the European socialist parties, whose high point is the crucial and disastrous insurrectionary action in Germany of March 1921. It concludes with the change of course that was to initiate the tactics of the so-called united front. The first volume spans the period which began with a proletarian revolutionism prepared to subordinate the interests of the newly born Soviet Union to the revolutionary world struggle and which ended in July 1921 at the Third World Congress, where it was proclaimed that "unqualified support of Soviet Russia remains, as before, the prime duty of Communists in all countries." The phrase "as before" was a transparent ruse to cover up and make acceptable the reversal of policy.

This volume possesses so many scholarly virtues that one is confronted by an embarrassment of riches in enumerating them. Among them is the authors' capacity to make illuminating distinctions. Recognizing Lenin's titanic role in determining events, they point out with justification that his greatness as a strategist cannot be established merely by the historical events he acted upon. Things worked out to save the Bolshevik Revolution but not in the way he anticipated them. To the extent that his predictions came true, they were not the consequence of his strategy or tactics but of events he did not himself initiate as well as to the ineptitude and blunders of his opponents both before and after the Bolsheviks, at his urging, seized power. His judgments were prophecies rather than genuine predictions. Thus, much has been made of Lenin's wisdom at the time of Brest-Litovsk in trading space for time. But what motivated him was his fanatical belief that a socialist revolution in the West would cancel the capitulation and territorial losses to German imperialism. In arguing for the acceptance of the harsh terms of the German high command at the Seventh Congress of the Bolshevik Party (March 7, 1918), he admitted: "It is an absolute truth that without a German Revolution we are doomed." But neither this revolution nor the other military and political events that resulted in the nullification of the treaty was what Lenin had actually anticipated. It was the wrong kind of revolution and not even a social revolution. As the authors point out:

The unfolding of these events, however, was not the result of the proletarian revolution in Europe which Lenin prophesied but of the victory of the Entente powers, which Lenin did not desire and which indeed he made more difficult, first by staging his coup in Petrograd in November 1917, and then by concluding the Brest-Litovsk Treaty in March 1918 (pp. 37–38).

One may conclude from this and other important episodes treated in the volume that although without Lenin there would in all likelihood have been neither a Bolshevik party so completely different from all previous socialist parties nor the Bolshevik seizure of political power in the fall of 1917 nor the Communist International, nonetheless his presence did not make the events inevitable. As event-making as he was, Lenin was not a Carlylean hero. He did not create the situations he exploited. Had Russia not entered World War I, had Kerensky taken Russia out of the war after the attempted Kornilov *putsch* (which he regretted not doing in his final evaluation of his own role), had the German military staff not provided Lenin with the means of returning to Russia—few people would have heard of Lenin. Lenin was certainly a master in exploiting historical contingencies whose significance his own simplistic views of history could not account for.

A balanced history of Lenin and the Comintern must do justice to the factors that explain the relative success of the Bolshevik party and the Comintern in winning adherents in the West despite the fact that they constituted such a small minority among the Russian masses. After all, here was a minuscular group employing a language and a vocabulary foreign to the cultures and political history of the Western world, openly proclaiming (concealment came later) that its agents were actively intervening in the internal affairs of other countries in order to help organize the revolutionary overthrow of the governments regardless of whether they were hostile, friendly, or neutral toward Soviet Russia, and at the same time insisting that the traditionally democratic socialist and labor ogranizations in those countries accept the insurrectionary tactics of Bolshevism "as a model of tactics for all" in their struggles. Wherein lay its appeal? How could Lenin succeed in organizing a Communist International *before* Communist Parties existed in most countries and succeed by no external sanctions in splitting the socialist and labor movement almost everywhere and founding large and influential Communist Parties?

The authors of this volume offer an explanation that is very persuasive. The appeal of the Bolsheviks and of the Comintern was not to schooled Marxists and socialists who had labored in the vineyards of social reform and progressive labor movements and who were quick to detect a continuity between Bolshevik doctrine and tactics with Bakuninist tendencies that had plagued them in their past activities. The most militant Communists in all countries and their mass base were drawn to Bolshevism by virtue of two things. First, their opposition to war after the most exhausting and bloodiest conflict in human history which produced a great revulsion even in the victorious countries. Secondly, not the program of the Bolsheviks but the emotional euphoria of their conquest of power, the mystique of the revolution triumphant, the promise blazoned forth in their slogans and rhetoric of a new world for the underprivileged and the oppressed.

After all, it required a powerful pull to overcome the negative reactions toward the antidemocratic ideology of Bolshevism and the news of its early excesses. This powerful pull was the tide of antiwar sentiment on which the Bolsheviks rode to popularity among a new generation of idealists impatient with the hair-splitting criticisms of the socialist critics of the concept of "the dictatorship of the proletariat." Even in America, which was comparatively untouched by the war, sentiment in the socialist movement crystallized in favor of Bolshevism among members of the most militant antiwar faction despite their almost total ignorance of the Bolshevik program. In war-torn and war-weary Europe the answering response was heaviest in the defeated countries but also very powerful among the victorious ones. Louis-Oscar Frossard, one of the founders of the French Communist Party, frankly admits that it was not doctrine but disgust and hatred of the war that swelled the ranks of the party.

Only their hatred of the war brought these young recruits to us. They reached us filled with a terrible bitterness, built up over the tragic years. The war had cruelly marked them and the odor of death still clung to their martyred flesh. The spirit of revolt was awake in them. Returning from the immense massacre mutilated and battered, they hungered for quick revenge. They blamed the system that had made them suffer, and were ready to overthrow it (p. 215).

That system had already been overthrown in Russia, whose leaders urged revolutionary violence in order to usher in a world without war. The Bolsheviks rode that line hard. The ends and costs of revolution were in the first flush of revolutionary enthusiasm regarded as inconsequential compared to the evils and costs of the wars that the system "inevitably" bred.

Nor can the influence of the mystique of the successful revolution be overestimated in its influence upon those who were already wedded to the ideals of socialism that until then had appeared to be only a dream. But now the dream was about to be realized. The largest country in the world flaunted the banner of socialism, whose device proclaimed the abolition of human exploitation. Like the sun, the rays of social salvation were coming from the East, and the tender-minded among the socialist leaders in most countries basked in their promise. I still recall the electric effect when, as a very young socialist, I heard the declaration of Eugene V. Debs, the grand old man of the American Socialist Party, who was more of a populist democrat than a Marxist. "From the crown of my head to the soles of my feet, I am a Bolshevik, and proud of it," he proclaimed when the first news of the October *coup d'état* percolated to the United States. At the time, Debs had not the foggiest notion of what Bolshevism represented. He had never read anything by Lenin and Trotsky or even heard of them. Although his democratic instincts led him in a few years to reject the intrigues and dictatorial policies of the Comintern, to the end of his days he saw the Russian revolution through the rose-colored illusions created in his mind by its early libertarian rhetoric and, above all, by the act itself. The same was true of socialists in other countries who if not as great-hearted as Debs were more sophisticated. Typical of them was Bohumir Smeral, the Czech "social-patriot" converted to communism by the revolutionary act.

"I did not know a word of Russian, had read hardly any of the Bolshevik literature, but the October Revolution had greatly impressed me." Niggling doubts seemed petty to those caught up in the poetry and passion of great events. For some individuals nothing succeeds like success. The longer the Bolsheviks remained in power, the greater became the hypnotic influence of the realized ideas of the Revolution even upon some of its original critics.

Allowing for all the contributing factors, historical, economic, psychological, of Lenin's successful achievements, the authors nonetheless do full justice to Lenin's distinctive role. They themselves do not in this volume undertake an independent analysis of Lenin's character and personality. These are vividly portrayed through the documentation of Lenin's words and actions and by the vignettes of him penned by his colleagues, comrades, and disciples during the stormy years of political struggle. What emerges is a picture of Lenin as the totally dedicated political person without any indication of the presence of an internal spiritual or cultural landscape so manifest in his erstwhile rivals and subsequent allies— Rosa Luxemburg and Leon Trotsky. There is no evidence that Lenin ever had an unpolitical thought or entertained a speculative idea irrelevant to the political task at hand at the moment.

Lenin's total political dedication was of a distinctive kind. The documentary history of his activity, the tributes and accolades to him, and the jeremiads against him all show a person in whom was fused an absolute fanaticism of goal with a maximum flexibility and opportunism in strategy and tactics. Lenin was not a fanatic in Santayana's sense of a man who "having forgotten his goals redoubles his efforts." Lenin never forgot his goal. It was not expressed in the ritualistic ideals of socialism that appeared to him as no more relevant to the next political step than invocations to the brotherhood of man. Lenin's goal was the conquest and retention of political power first in Russia and then in other countries of the world. Beyond that, he never permitted his mind to go, except to dispute doctrinal orthodoxies he believed—mistakenly in many instances—were crucial to the struggle for political power. He was a fanatic in that he was prepared to use any means to achieve that goal regardless of the consequences of those means on the traditional ideals of socialism. And although Trotsky implies that toward the end of his life Lenin had second thoughts about whether the gains of the Revolution had been worth the agony, there is no convincing evidence that Lenin actually had such thoughts. Such retrospective and introspective judgments were altogether out of keeping with his extrovert character.

Lenin was a master of political improvisation. There was no point in the Bolshevik program that could not be abandoned if it furthered the conquest of political power and its retention. "All Power to the Soviets!" Yes, but not if the Soviets were in the hands of the Mensheviks or Social Revolutionaries. "Nationalization of all land by the State!" No, if this will alienate the peasants whose temporary support was required to seize and keep power. Usually Lenin made no bones about his opportunism. He gloried in it except when its avowal in a specific situation would defeat his immediate purpose. "The victorious Bolsheviks," he lectured his fellow Communists abroad, "wrote into their land decree not a single word of their own true thoughts but copied letter for letter the demands on behalf of the peasants printed in the newspapers of the Social Revolutionaries." Slogans of peace? Of course, if it will help disarm the enemy. Pacifism? By no means if it will erode the revolutionary fervor of the masses or interfere with preparations for military insurrection. No man in Lenin's eyes had a moral character independent of his political line of the moment. Trotsky is a "swine" early in 1917 but the very model of a Bolshevik before the year is out. And the same is true of Lenin's judgments of Radek, Zinoviev, Kamenev, Gorky, Plekhanov, and countless others. Lenin never respected a person as a human being with whom he politically disagreed. What was true of persons was true of parties, organizations, and classes. This was the source of his cruelty—all the more dangerous for being so unconscious— a cruelty which is not properly documented in this volume. But Lenin had the virtue of his defects. To those who capitulated politically, even if he had previously cursed them as social patriots or traitors to class or party, he was magnanimous. It was enough that they came to Canossa. They did not have to crawl. He always remembered but he bore no grudge. He was no Stalin. Everyone could be useful provided he was willing to play the role Lenin assigned him. Woe to him, however, if he persisted in playing an active political role in opposition to Lenin's purposes. Unlike Stalin he drew the line at execution of erring party comrades. But he was merciless to all others. He had one stock recipe for taking care of them, whether they were czarists or social democrats or Kronstadt sailors who wanted Soviets without Communists: "You shoot them," as he repeatedly advised the French Socialists ne-gotiating for admission to the Communist International, on how to take care of their Social Democrats (p. 283).

There was an impressive consistency in Lenin's character whether in planning the seizure of power in Russia or in planning a much lesser task, the organization of the Comintern. He was no believer in spontaneity or inevitability, although his rhetoric sometimes invokes them. He would plan to the last detail. Whenever he could, he, so to speak, would examine the very nails in the shoes of the horses of the riders he was sending into battle with his sealed dispatches. And he sent riders abroad not only to organize Communist Parties but to infiltrate and split socialist parties. The authors present with painstaking documentation Lenin's mode of operation at the various Congresses of the Comintern and the meetings of its Executive Committee. They quote a passage from Jacques Sadoul, a sympathetic French officer who as a convert to Communism was present at the founding of the Comintern. This passage reveals Lenin the tactician:

Twenty years of furious struggle in the forefront of the Russian Social Democratic Party; uninterrupted leadership of its Bolshevik faction, conceived, nurtured, then ushered by him to its present apotheosis; experiences in the ways of international congresses; an awesome knowledge of the human heart and mind; an unparalleled political flair; bulldog tenacity strangely combined with a natural propensity to expediency—he seems to venerate the will to power in all its forms, and the leisurely force of guile as well as the quick might of battle—all of this and many other qualities, which have been many times analyzed before, make of Lenin, notwithstanding his legendary reputation as a sectarian and fanatic, an inspired opportunist—intransigent when it is opportune to be so—craftiest of the jousters at a congress session, most dazzling among the schemers in the back room (p. 84).

This volume throws light on another complex issue, namely the extent to which Bolshevik-Leninism constitutes a major revision of, or a creative advance on Marxism. This question is of some moment today among some pundits of the New Left who, having regurgitated Stalinism and neo-Stalinism, wish to preserve their allegiance to Lenin as an orthodox Marxist. It would be tempting to say that the authors let the facts speak for themselves. But facts never really speak for themselves. They must be interpreted in order to have significance. What this volume records in fascinating detail are the struggles among the Marxists of Western countries to define their position with respect to the demands Bolshevik-Leninism or Lenin was making on them—demands that required heroic action, basic reorganization, and new articles of faith. One must recall that the period described by the authors precedes the one in which the doctrine of "socialism in one country" became canonic in Bolshevik theory and practice. Although Marxists knew that Marx had predicted that socialism would arrive first in the highly industrialized countries of the West, by stretching a point they could swallow the notion that the political signal, so to speak, could be sounded elsewhere. In Europe, at any event, political phenomena have always had a tendency to spread by contagion. Sparks, struck off on the borders of industrialized areas, could ignite the revolutionary potential force stored in their socio-economic structure. What then was the sticking point, or more accurately, the nature of Bolshevism at which they gagged? The evidence of this volume suggests it was the ruthless elitism, the undisguised practice of dictatorship in state, society, and party, which outraged Marxists who were prepared to overlook other departures from the Marxist tradition as expressions of a crotchety Russian idiom. In a sense European social democracy at the time of the Russian Revolution was more democratic than socialist and was hopeful of using the democratic political parliamentary process of extending or achieving socialism in the way Engels had explicitly approved.

The acceptance of this view was a betrayal of Marxism in the eyes of Lenin and the Bolshevik Party. The rejection of this view was a betrayal of Marxism to most of the socialists who still considered themselves Marxists. It is true that some of those who were critical of Lenin on democratic grounds swallowed their doubts in hopes that the participation of the masses would introduce a kind of control from below. Somewhat in the spirit of the convert to Christianity who prays, "Oh Lord, I believe. Help Thou my unbelief," they joined forces for a time with the Bolsheviks, only to experience a rapid disillusionment. But some of their early insights were extremely perceptive. Thus Boris Souvarine in November 1917 wrote: "One fears that with Lenin and his friends the 'dictatorship of the proletariat' means a dictatorship of the Bolsheviks and their chief, which could prove disastrous for the Russian working class, hence for the world proletariat" (p. 211). Even when these Marxist critics of Bolshevism moulted their Marxist feathers and irreversibly transformed themselves into good Bolsheviks, their words remained to embarrass and rebuke them. Thus the *doyen* of French Marxists who subsequently became one of the leaders of the French Communist Party, Charles Rappaport, was moved by the brutal suppression of the Constituent Assembly, the result of the only democratic election held after the Bolshevik *coup d'état*, to write in the socialist *Journal du Peuple*:

By an act of force, Lenin has just overthrown not only the Constituent Assembly but also and, above all, his own doctrine, the International Socialist program. The Lenin-Trotsky Red Guard have just shot Karl Marx, whom they are always hailing as their patron saint against the militarist opportunists. It is a mad dash for the abyss! Blanquism with Tartar sauce! The suicide of the Revolution. One does not toy like that with the basic laws of a free country (p. 434).

The contention that Lenin revised Marxism to a point of abandoning its central doctrines while preserving its phrases and rituals with a dogged linguistic piety is, of course, far from original despite the surprise with which this is greeted among revolutionary neophytes today, especially in underdeveloped countries. Nor is the authors' illuminating analysis of Lenin's career as one which began with the project of Westernizing Russian socialism and ended with Russianizing Western socialism altogether novel although presented as one of the many historical ironies and paradoxes of the twentieth century. What is both arresting and original in the authors' juxtaposition of Marx and Lenin is the contrast they draw between Marx's reliance upon the proletariat as the chief if not exclusive antagonistic force to established society, and Lenin's political opportunism—it would not be too strong to call it Machiavellianism! To Marx the petty-bourgeoisie, the peasantry, even the hordes that constituted the *lumpenproletariat* were not historically fit to be the carriers of the revolutionary idea. He scorned appeals to nationalism, to pacifism, to populism. He was even reluctant to invoke the ethical ideals of justice and the rights of man for fear that they would be misleading. Lenin, on the other hand, was willing to exploit any kind of antagonism, provided only he could direct the course and political goal of the agitation. He was prepared to sacrifice doctrinal purity for organizational priority if it brought the Party closer to the masses and enhanced its political influence among them. He would make a united front with anyone, provided he gained in virtue of that front.

"Whereas," write Lazitch and Drachkovitch, "Marx reduced the history of the Western world to a single dominant antagonism, Lenin built his revolutionary policy around the exploitation of a multitude of antagonisms, emphasizing first one, then another, depending on which seemed most useful for the moment" (p. 232). Here was the source of the great agitational strength of the Bolsheviks. The realities of political struggle liberated them from the inhibitions of their dogmas about *the* class struggle. Unlike the New Left today, Lenin never repudiated the working class, no matter whom it supported, as the ideological carrier of the revolutionary idea. He assumed that wherever *he* was, was the vanguard of the proletariat, regardless of the numbers behind him. But like the New Left today, Lenin was extremely catholic in appealing to and in politically using those who felt oppressed. "With Lenin, Communism on the plane of revolutionary strategy became identified with the exploitation of all contradictions, and on the plane of revolutionary organization it became the great haven for the disaffected" (p. 232).

There is an apocryphal story, not related by the authors, which testifies to the catholicity of Lenin's approach. In reporting the organization of German Soviets (*Rätezellen*), Clara Zetkin informed Lenin that the first successful organization had been of the prostitutes of Berlin. The only objection Lenin made was to the priority given to the task. He preferred that organizational efforts be directed to the Berlin housewives and female factory operatives, not on grounds of morality but of political effectiveness.

Although this first volume documents the change of course that Lenin laid down for the Comintern when he saw that the tactics of revolutionary offensive for Communist Parties struggling to be born had failed, the authors present convincing evidence that, by the time Lenin had come to this realization, his policies had shattered the Italian labor and socialist movement so badly that it was unable to combat effectively the rise and victory of fascism. Indeed, Lenin had defined the issue in Italy as one of "an imminent death-struggle . . . between the Communist proletarian revolution and capitalist society (including capitalism's supported arch-henchmen, the social democrats) whereas the real battle shaping up was between parliamentary democracy which safeguarded the existence of all parties . . . and a fascist dictatorship" (p. 460). The Leghorn split that Lenin engineered made impossible the cooperation required to defeat Mussolini. The Kremlin consequently bears a heavy responsibility for the triumph of Italian fascism. The second volume presumably will document the role of the Kremlin and its theory of social fascism and the practices flowing from it in helping Hitler and German nazism to come to power.

In summing up this masterly study, it would be accurate to say that it is notable not so much for the novelty of any of its specific conclusions as for the manner of reaching and stating them, not so much for what is said but how it is said. The patience of detail, its cumulative force, the choice quotations from the memoirs and reminiscences of the principal and peripheral figures of the early revolutionary years, its apt summaries, and its arresting comparisons—all contribute to make this a very readable, and in places, an exciting work of scholarship. The paragraph in which the change in the meaning of the party in the comprehension of non-Russian Communists is traced, is particularly felicitous both in insight and expression and conveys the quality of the writing:

After the Second Congress, first for non-Russian Communists, then for the outside world, the word *party* began to take on a new meaning, though retaining the old spelling and pronounciation. Until that time, for the Marxists of the Second International, their *party* was a political organization, regarded as somewhat more important perhaps than their trade unions, cooperatives, parliamentary activities, and so on, but a political entity nonetheless. After the Second Congress, however, for Communists of the entire world the *party* became what it had earlier come to be for Russian Communists, a synonym and surrogate for History, the Army, the Church. The party was equated with History because it was seen as the instrument of an unstoppable process leading inexorably first to world revolution and then to a Socialist world order—an enterprise without precedent in human annals. It was equated with the Army because to wage a successful revolutionary war one had to have a high command (the party Politburo and Comintern Executive Committee or Presidium), soldiers (the party rank and file), officers (party cadres), battle plans (revolutionary strategy and tactics), discipline ("democratic centralism"), and of course, as in any army, deserters (party renegades). It was equated with the Church because one needed a faith and gospel (Marxism according to the Bolsheviks), saints (Marx and Engels), a pope (Lenin), canons (the Comintern's decisions, resolutions, theses), and, to complete the tableau, heretics and excommunications (the party's dissidents and purges). This total concept of *the party* naturally eventuated in party totalitarianism (pp. 322–23).

CHAPTER FIVE

Communism and the American Intellectuals from the Thirties to the Eighties

In the fall of 1932, an interesting event occurred of profound symbolic significance for the development of radical political thought and activity in the United States. A pamphlet was published entitled *Culture and the Crisis*, in which about thirty leading literary and cultural figures, of whom perhaps Edmund Wilson, Sherwood Anderson, and John Dos Passos were the best known, endorsed the candidacy of William Z. Foster and James W. Ford, the presidential and vice-presidential nominees of the American Communist Party. This was the first time in the history of American thought that an organized group of intellectuals had committed themselves to the support of a social philosophy totally at variance with the American democratic system. To be sure, early in the century a number of literary figures had associated themselves with the Intercollegiate Socialist Society, which later developed into the League for Industrial Democracy. But they were not regarded as fundamentally alien to American radical traditions and did not suffer from association with a foreign country whose openly declared purpose was the overthrow of democratic regimes.

The direct political effects of *Culture and the Crisis*, together with the League for Professional Groups that grew out of it, which generously estimated numbered several hundred members, was negligible. But it did establish a pattern of cultural organization and penetration of American life in the mid-thirties. To the leaders of the American Communist Party, it meant that their movement had broken out of its isolation from American cultural life.

The American Communist Party was a small sectarian party embracing hardly a hundred thousand men and women in its heyday. Nonetheless, through a network of organizations like the League of American Writers, the American Artists Congress, the Theatre Arts Union, and the League Against War and Fascism, renamed the League for Peace and Democracy after the Seventh Congress of the Communist International, it was able to dominate the cultural life of the country, split the socialist and labor movement, and make a shambles of the union of liberal forces in the nation. More indicative of the deceptive way they operated than symbolic of their influence was the fact that they were able, through fellow-traveling intermediaries, according to Donald Ogden Stewart, to line up none other than Franklin Delano Roosevelt as a member of the League of American Writers. The Communists and their vast peripheral organizations suffered a severe setback during the period of the Nazi-Soviet Pact, but after Hitler invaded the Soviet Union on June 22, 1941, and after Pearl Harbor, they regrouped and regained much of their influence among a new generation of intellectuals. Their second setback occurred when the Kremlin ditched Earl Browder, the American Communist leader who had served it faithfully, when Stalin openly resumed the cold war against the West. It was finally eclipsed after the butchery of the Hungarian revolutionists and Khrushchev's revelations of the monstrous crimes of Stalin, which exceeded by far the worst accusations of the severest critics of the Soviet Union.

From the very outset, the American Communist movement was not a mass movement of the working class but primarily, after it overcame its factional struggles and immigrant base, a movement of lower- and middle-class intellectuals and professionals. The questions one must ask are: What were the appeals of the Communist movement to American intellectuals? What were the sources or grounds of its influence at a time when it was not safe or respectable to profess Communist allegiance or to enter into associations with Communists?

To begin with, it must be pointed out that there was something rather anomalous from the conventional ideological point of view about the identification of the intellectuals with the interests of the working class. Marx and Engels, in the *Communist Manifesto,* had proclaimed that consciousness does not determine social existence but that social existence determines consciousness. But no more than in the case of Marx and Engels and the leaders of the working classes throughout the world did the social existence or professional status of the American intellectuals determine their political allegiance.

1. This brings me to my first major point about the intellectuals'

conversion to the Communist faith. They were not moved by narrow self-interest. If Communism is an aberration or a disease, it is a disease of idealism. Originally, what inspired the political orientation of these intellecturals was the mass misery and suffering produced by the greatest economic crisis in American history— the most prolonged period of widespread disasters, culminating in 16 million unemployed—at a time when there were no social welfare programs to serve as a safety net for those who through no fault of their own found themselves bereft of the means to keep themselves and their families from the breadlines. Nineteen-thirty-two was a year of mass despair, one without hope. Everything had apparently been tried. Few seem to recall that the electoral programs of *both* the Republican and the Democratic parties in 1932 called for the balancing of the federal budget. During the week after Roosevelt's inauguration in 1933—a period I remember well because my book *Towards the Understanding of Karl Marx* came from the press that week with no buyers in view—a bank holiday was declared. Everyone thought that capitalism was finished. I am convinced that, if Roosevelt had decided to nationalize the banks or even some major industries at that time, there would have been no strong opposition. The situation was absolutely unprecedented—and extremely difficult for anyone who did not directly experience it to understand.[1]

2. A second reason for the political option of the intellectuals who supported the Communist position was their belief that there was a viable alternative to the anarchy and chaos of the capitalist system. This was their conception of a planned and planning society that made full use of the resources of society and which avoided the periodic boom and bust of the market economy. It was an alternative presumably illustrated in the functioning of the Soviet Union. The perception of Soviet society was largely based on illusion, cultivated by tales of visitors who judged Soviet society by its programs and propaganda, not by the realities that were carefully shielded from their eyes by supervised tours and a succession of Potemkin Village effects. Actually, during the very years in which American intellectuals were crying up the virutes

---

[1] John Kenneth Galbraith observes that "Communists were not remarkable in the [early] 1930s. To be immune to doubts as to the excellence and success of capitalism in that dismal decade was to be unusually insensitive to the world. For those who thought they responded [with] an uncluttered, unfearful, forthright mind, communism was the obvious answer" ("Alger Hiss and Liberal Anxiety," *Atlantic Monthly.* [May, 1978]).

of the Soviet economic system over those of the American system, Russia was in the throes of a mass famine that resulted from the enforced collectivization of agriculture. When Lincoln Steffens announced with respect to the Soviet Union that he had seen the future and that it worked, he soon showed that he had not the slightest inkling of *how* it worked. Confronted by the evidence of savage cultural and political repression in the USSR, he dismissed it as the cost of progress. In addition, by 1932–1933, the menace of Nazism had become very grave and was threatening another world war. The future appeared as a choice between Communism, with all its drawbacks, and the barbarities of Fascism. There were some, like myself, who although critical of the doctrinal orthodoxies of Marxism-Leninism were prepared to swallow their political doubts in the hope that the Communists would prevent Hitler from coming to power and unleashing the program of war and conquest that he had outlined in *Mein Kampf.*

The dominant mood of the intellectuals at the time was one of impatience. This explained their allergy and hostility to a whole array of reform movements—technocracy, the single tax, state capitalism, consumer cooperatives, democratic socialism—with their programs of piecemeal change. All were characterized and rejected as half-hearted. Communism as a system of total opposition had an emotional and romantic appeal. It was against religion, against the class system in all its expressions, against the existing family, and against the profit system and the vulgarities of mass culture that the profit motive allegedly bred. Every intellectual's pet peeve and spite against the system found gratification in the expectation of a total and permanent revolution. The English language itself would be purged of its class bias!

3. The third source of the attraction of Communism was the ideology, or mythology, of Marxism that prided itself on its scientific grasp of the laws of development in society and history and which in the dogmatic form it was propagated provided an easy explanation for anything that happened. It sought to unravel the secrets not only of politics but of art, literature, religion, even of science, by reference to the roles of the social classes in the mode of production and to the struggle between classes that these roles generated.

The relations between Marxism and Communism, as we have seen are quite complex, and I have argued for the thesis that the Communism of the Soviet Union (and, for that matter, of every other Communist country today) is incompatible with the principles and predictions of classical Marxism. But the American intellectuals as a whole were devoid of any knowledge of Marxist theory. They accepted their Marxism as it was interpreted for them by the Kremlin and its official representatives in the United States. They were impatient with scholars, even those politically sympathetic, who sought actually to test Marx's analysis and predictions by the scientific methods that Marx himself proudly professed to follow when he stressed the scientific character of his Socialism. Most of these intellectuals took Marx's economic analysis on faith. It was sufficient for them to observe the collapse of the capitalist economic system, a collapse that they assumed confirmed the truth not only of Marx's economic theories but of his theories of history and of the state as well. They read that the state was the executive committee of the ruling dominant economic class. That was enough for them. They refused to make an empirical analysis of how the state actually operated. If the U.S. government issued injunctions against the organization of labor unions, that revealed its class character. On the other hand when it facilitated such organization through the Wagner Labor Relations Act, it did so out of fear of revolution. In either case, it was serving the interests of the dominant economic class.

4. Another factor that contributed to American intellectuals' support of the Communist cause was the optimistic assurance—central to the Communist faith—that the struggle for human betterment and the fulfillment of age-old dreams of universal peace and prosperity would be victorious. It breathed hope and confidence that things would get better at a time of widespread despair. It taught that science and history and the laws of dialectic were on the side of the emerging worldwide classless society in which the division of labor would disappear and a new age of new men and women would appear. Although opposed to supernaturalism, Communism functioned more and more as a religion in the lives of its intellectual adherents, in that they believed that there was a kind of historical and cosmic support for their generous ideals. The language of "inevitability" was not metaphorical for the intellectual true believers. The advent of Communism was inevitable regardless of the evidence of its setbacks.

5. Finally, I want to stress the presence and importance of these generous ideals among the intellectuals drawn to the Communist movement, partly because of their subsequent erosion among those who remained faithful to the Communist Party and partly because of the subsequent disaffection from the Communist Party and all its works by those who remained faithful to their ideals. What were these ideals? Briefly, a strong sense of social justice and a

passionate opposition to social inequalities rooted in irrational tradition and arbitrary power. And underlying this complex of ideals was a vague but strong commitment to equal opportunity and to the belief that all human beings had a right to develop themselves to the full reach of their potential power to live a life of individual freedom under just laws.

There are some who will say that I have left out one of the most powerful sources of the attraction of Communism for intellectuals, namely, the prospect that the triumph of Communism would give them the opportunity to exercise power as a new managerial ruling class or as bureaucratic aides to such a class. My own experience gives little warrant for such a view. It may have been true for those few intellectuals who joined the Communist Party, but most intellectuals did not join. The best among them already enjoyed status, reputation, influence, and a comfortable standard of living, which were placed in jeopardy by their new allegiances. Perhaps if they had sought political power more avidly they would have been cured of their political illusions more readily. If they had been better schooled in the social philosophy of Marx, they would have been more sensitive to the realities of power in the new societies calling themselves socialist.

The great tragedy of the American intellectuals drawn to Communism was that in the intensity of their faith they ceased to function as intellectuals. The Communist Party very cleverly built up within them a sense of their relative unworthiness as authentic revolutionaries because of their nonproletarian class origins. They were made to believe and to feel that any intellectual doubt was the occupational stigmata of the petty bourgeoisie. The proletariat, disciplined by its work, was predisposed to accept the intellectual discipline of party directives. The intellectual, pursuing his wayward course, tended toward egocentricity and anarchism. The result was that the intellectuals who remained in the ambience of the Communist Party and its multiple peripheral organizations became eloquent, articulate, and *completely uncritical* spokesmen for the Communist Party line. The transformation was startling. They no longer thought as professional intellectuals. They turned with indignation against fellow intellectuals who raised doubts or questions about the validity or wisdom of any position taken by the Communist Party. "Who are you," I would be heatedly rebuked, "to take issue with William Foster on dual trade unions?" I recall variations of this question on a number of other occasions by individuals who had been proud of their independent judgment before they had seen the great light from the East. To question the leaders of the American Communist Party might be overlooked as an excusable temporary lapse in the process of Communist acculturation. But to question or criticize Stalin or Lenin on any subject on which they had taken a stand was to put oneself forever beyond the pale. "Only a Social Fascist would disagree with Stalin's thesis that Social Fascism and Fascism were equally dangerous to the working class," I was solemnly told. And, since I was one who disagreed, this made me a Social Fascist, too.

Those American intellectuals who tried to function as intellectuals in pursuit of their revolutionary faith—a comparative handful—soon found themselves in opposition to the Communist Party and the major body of Communist-oriented intellectuals on a succession of issues. In time, because of the developments of the American economy and of the Soviet Union, these individuals modified their views but not their ideals.

The mass of the American intellectuals who followed the American Communist Party line soon made the startling discovery that there was no American Communist Party line; that the line in every field was laid down by the Kremlin, whose leaders relayed it to their subordinates in the United States. In their blind faith in the Kremlin, the credulous American intellectuals overlooked the fact that whatever the ultimate purposes of the leaders of the Soviet Union were, they in fact were using the Communist Parties of the world as "fifth-columns" in their own countries, making them serve as border guards of the Soviet Union to resist its alleged encirclement. "Defend the Soviet Union at all costs by any means" became the operating maxim. The result was to transform a group of idealistic heretics into fanatical and, in time, cynical conspirators.

Many illustrations of the slavish dependence of the American Communist Party on the Kremlin can be cited. For example, the revolutionary strategists of the Kremlin discovered that the American Negroes were an ethnic minority like their own minorities. (When I was in Moscow in 1929, leading Communists kept pressing me to tell them what the native language of the American Negro was!) In order to exploit this revolutionary potential, they commanded the American Communists to make a central political demand for "self-determination for the Black Belt," i.e., the right of a block of southern American states with black majorities to secede from the Union and to establish their own Black Confederate Republic—as if the American Civil War were to be fought all over again. In their rigorous piety, the American intellectual proletariat went along. Stalin could do no wrong. Nor could his representatives!

Much more serious in its consequences was the uncritical acceptance of the theory of Social Fascism, according to which the socialists were just as much an enemy of the workers as the Fascists. This split the working class, in Germany especially, where it enabled Hitler to come to power. In this country it led to the Communists' breaking up a Socialist protest meeting, at Madison Square Garden, against the suppression of the Austrian Socialists in 1934. We were able to split away a handful of distinguished intellectuals at that time, but the bulk remained faithful.

Perhaps the nadir in the spiritual degradation and Byzantine servility of American intellectuals was reached at the time of the Moscow Trials, when together with a few others I helped organize the John Dewey Commission of Inquiry into the Truth of the Moscow Trials. Not only did hundreds of fellow-traveling American intellectuals—many of them distinguished in their professional fields—unqualifiedly endorse the verdicts of the Moscow Trials, according to which all of Lenin's lieutenants and trusted companions, with the exception of Stalin, were from the very beginning of the October Revolution agents of foreign powers who ended up as collaborators of Hitler, they viciously attacked even the effort to make an inquiry into the evidence in order to give Leon Trotsky a hearing and a chance to state his case. The very efforts to discover the truth were dubbed activities of "Trotskyite Fascists."

After that there was no infamy committed by Stalin within or without the Soviet Union that the American intellectuals did not swallow. The shock of the Nazi-Soviet Pact and the intimate collaboration between Hitler and Stalin, until Hitler double-crossed his partner, restored many American intellectuals to some semblance of political sobriety. They faded out of public activities only to be replaced by a new crop of intellectual political innocents who regarded the heroic resistance of Russian soldiers at Stalingrad and the military defeat of Hitler as evidence of the superiority of the Soviet social system. This made as much sense as the contention that the defeat of Napoleon's army by the czarist troops in 1812 demonstrated the progressive character of Russian serfdom!

Meanwhile, there were changes going on in the social fabric of both the non-Communist and the Communist worlds that should have been the primary concern of intellectuals professionally interested in general ideas and the realities they reflected and partly modified. These intellectuals failed to observe that historical events more and more called into question the adequacy of the Marxist analysis. The capitalist economy had recovered from its crisis and by virtue of the effects of political democracy on that economy a new form of society—neither purely capitalist nor purely socialist—had developed that became known as the welfare state. This had not been anticipated by Marx. Nor had Marx foreseen the rise of fascism, which in turn contributed to undermining the validity of his monistic view of historical materialism. The spectacle of capitalist nations like England, France, and the United States aligned with the Soviet Union and its socialized economy against capitalist nations like Germany, Japan, and Italy suggested that in the twentieth century the mode of political decision was as decisive in determining the character of our time and culture—if not more decisive—as the mode of economic production. If this were true, then the basic issue of our time was not to choose between capitalism and socialism but to choose *more* or *less* of either as the means of furthering the complex of human freedoms that constitutes democracy as a way of life. Not only were these events and the continuing relative prosperity challenging the principles of Marxism, but the renewed growth and intensification of nationalism were fatal to the old Marxist contention that the workers had no fatherland.

The developments within the Soviet Union instead of confirming the Marxist theory of history actually had invalidated it. Marx had maintained that a Socialist society could develop only when all the material, technological, and psychological presuppositions for it had been established under capitalism. That is why he predicted that socialism would come first in England and the United States and that the attempt to introduce it in a backward economy of scarcity would socialize poverty. Instead, his followers seized power in one of the most backward and primitive countries in the world and built by terrorist political means a materialist, collectivist economic foundation under its culture. Truly we are confronted here by one of the great ironies of history: Marxism in key respects has been refuted by those claiming to be its pious heirs.

Further, the glorification and cult of Lenin was a recognition of his indispensable role in the transition to the new society. Even Leon Trotsky, whose Marxist orthodoxy few could doubt on scholarly grounds, reluctantly admitted that without Lenin there would have been no October Revolution. But this was attributing to the role of personality a causal influence in history utterly incompatible with historical materialism. The "greatest phenomenon in human history" could hardly be attributed to the contingency or chance of an event-making personality being present on the Russian scene in 1917. In passing, it should be noted that the attempt of Soviet apologists, after Khrushchev's speech, to explain away the horrendous evils of the Soviet system as due to the cult of Stalin's personality likewise departs from strict Marxist historical principles, which explain the limits and achievements of historical characters by the social and economic forces operating at the time. The system that produced Stalin, or made it possible for him to emerge, cannot be absolved of responsibility for his horrible misdeeds.

Even more striking was the American intellectuals' obliviousness to what was developing within the social structure of the Soviet Union itself—the transformation of the dream of a new commonwealth into a nightmare of total terror. In area after area, from art to zoology, the iron clamp of suppression was screwed down more tightly by a Political Committee utterly unqualified to pronounce judgment. A new Soviet class emerged with differential living standards equaling or surpassing in their invidious dimensions that of the West. Step by step the American intellectuals who remained within the orbit of the Communist Party became apologists for the power structure of the Soviet regime, slandering the defectors from the system who bore witness to the existence of inhuman concentration camps in which millions of innocent human beings perished. Gone were their idealist pretensions; the fine flowers of their rhetoric withered before the grim realities of the Gulag Archipelago. They became defenders of the most oppressive police state in the postwar world, perhaps in all history. What Camus wrote about Sartre and the French intellectuals whose talents had been put at the service of the Kremlin remained true for them, too: "The will to power came to take the place of the will to justice, pretending at first to be identified with it and then relegating it to a place somewhere at the end of history, waiting until such time as nothing remains on earth to dominate."

Communism in its Soviet form lost its attractiveness for American intellectuals after Khrushchev's speech, the suppression of the Hungarian Revolution, and the invasion of Czechoslovakia. For a while, some of the disillusioned American intellectuals pinned their hopes on Mao, then Castro, and then Ho Chi Minh: Peking, Havana, and Hanoi became the new intellectual Meccas, but not for long. With minor variations, the same police state patterns appeared in all the Communist states—the greatest difference being the outpouring of refugees in such numbers that even the apologists for these regimes have lapsed into silence, leaving it to Noam Chomsky—who heralded Hanoi's victory in Vietnam as a new birth of freedom—to contest the exact number of the hapless victims of the Communist dictatorships. (His initial response was to dismiss the report of Communist atrocities in Vietnam and Cambodia as mere propaganda.)

As for the future, there is no danger that American intellectuals will be lured by the promise of Soviet Communism again. The roadblocks typified by the fate of Solzhenitsyn, Sakharov, and Soviet anti-Semitism stand in the way—not to mention Afghanistan and Poland. However, the disillusioned fellow-traveling American intellectuals have bequeathed anti-Americanism rather than pro-Communism to the contemporary generation of disaffected intellectuals. This anti-Americanism is manifest on every issue in which there is a conflict between the Soviet Union or one of its proxies and American national interests, whether in Central America, Africa, or Western Europe. This anti-American animus, which systematically ignores the geopolitical and ideological threats of Soviet Communism, is the dominant mood on American campuses, or at least among its most articulate spokesmen. This raises another theme that cannot be pursued here. But I would like to conclude with a few words about the role of intellectuals who are dedicated to political and cultural freedom in our troubled world today.

To begin with, the function of intellectuals is never to serve as poet laureates of the status quo. They are, or should be, always a part of the "adversary culture," exercising their critical judgment with courage and responsibility to further human freedom. There is always a gap between what things are and what they should be, since the tasks of defending and extending human freedom are never completed. But there is a tendency, when we keep our eyes only on what should be, to overlook the extent of the progress that has been made by progressive incremental steps in the past. There is a danger that we take for granted the democratic system that has made progress possible and, in the light of the absolute ideals of what should be, turn against the system itself or become indifferent to the challengers who would destroy it.

Today, by and large, the mainstream of American intellectuals is either indifferent to the challenges of the Communist world to the relatively free world of the West or hostile to the very conception of such a challenge as a manifestation of cold war sentiment. Some even maintain that in the light of Vietnam and Watergate the United States represents a mode of life and civilization not worth defending. In effect, they have become neutralists in the global struggle between democracy and totalitarianism.

This is very strange when we consider the attitude of American intellectuals to the threat of Fascism forty or fifty years ago, at a time when, with respect to civil, social, and economic rights, and especially the freedom of dissent, conditions in the United States were far worse, far more removed from the decencies of a humane society than they are today. I remember Goebbels and other Nazi Gauleiters mocking America's hypocrisy in criticizing Nazi racialism in the light of its own racist practices. Reference would be made to lynchings in America in an attempt to stop the mouths of critics of Nazi crimes. Nonetheless, American intellectuals, except for a minuscule obsessed minority, repudiated the attempt to undermine the struggle against Fascism because of the imperfection and betrayals of America's own democratic ideals. Today, compared with what existed forty years ago and despite the evils that still exist, the culture of the United States and the culture of the West are far healthier and contain more promise, not of realization, but of approximation to the ideals of equality and freedom under law. Why, then, should American intellectuals be more alienated from the critical defense of Western culture and the open society in the looming presence of the totalitarian Communist threat than they were before the hovering threat of Fascism a generation or two ago?

Until now, peace has been kept by virtue of the balance of terror. But, in the long run, more important than potential fire power is the will and resolution to defend the basic values of the society its weapons are supposed to defend. The responsibility of intellectuals today in the United States and the West, as they remain critical of the functioning of their institutions, is to rethink the significance of these values, the alternatives opposed to them, the costs of upholding them, and the methods of ensuring their survival.

CHAPTER SIX

The Twilight of Capitalism: A Marxian Epitaph

Karl Marx has been revised many times and in many different ways. Michael Harrington in his book, *The Twilight of Capitalism*, has the unique distinction of revising Marx by the cool assertion that Marx "misunderstood" himself, and therefore "misrepresented" Marxism to the world.[1] In consequence he not only confused himself but Kautsky, Plechanov, Lenin, and shoals of lesser disciples except Harrington who is confident that he knows what Marx really meant better than Marx apparently did himself. He dedicates himself to restating Marx's genial insights free of the blundering and inept words in which Marx obscured them. This goes much further than C. Wright Mills who called himself "a plain Marxist," as distinct from the vulgar and sophisticated varieties, listed seventeen key propositions of Marx, and rejected all but one—and that a truism!—as "confused," "unclear," or "quite clearly wrong."

Were Harrington's book not so long and labored, one would be tempted to interpret its first part as an elaborate spoof. But since he is obviously serious and humorless, his procedure must be characterized as intellectually scandalous. He performs not a lobotomy on Marx but a brain transplant, substituting for Marx's closely knit grey matter a diffuse Hegelian mess. In the course of the operation, he abandons the best known text of Marx on historical materialism, the preface to the *Critique of Political Economy, 1859*, in which Marx asserts that "the mode of economic production in material life determines the general character of the social, political and spiritual processes of life."

---

[1]Michael Harrington, *The Twilight of Capitalism* (New York: Simon & Schuster, 1976)

The key sentences of the Preface and the varying, graphic metaphors Marx uses to convey his meaning have been critically evaluated for more than a hundred years in the light of the historical evidence. Harrington dismisses the entire Preface in which the mode of economic production is given primary but not exclusive causal importance, as the most vulgar expression of vulgar Marxism. He insists that a few sentences from an *unpublished* manuscript written earlier about the process of production in a market society, and which are irrelevant to the question of how the economy is causally related to the rest of the culture, give Marx's true meaning. That true meaning denies that economic base or foundation determines the general character of the political and ideological superstructure. Rather, it asserts that the culture of a society is an "organic whole" in which all parts interact (dialectically, of course!) and mutually determine each other. The mode of economic production on this view is no more basic or ultimately determining than the mode of dress, war or marriage. It would follow from this that Marx also misspoke himself in the famous sentence immediately following the one quoted from the published Preface: "It is not the consciousness of men that determines their existence but, on the contrary, their social existence determines their consciousness." Marx really meant, if we are to believe Harrington, that consciousness does determine social existence—as if Marx had not outgrown his Hegelian diapers. Harrington's reading brings to mind that Yiddish production of Shakespeare's *King Lear*, subtitled, *"erganzt und verbessert"* ("completed and improved").

Having dubbed Marx's Preface an indiscretion of his mature years, consistency requires that Harrington judge *The Communist Manifesto* an indiscretion of Marx's earlier years since it formulates the theory of historical materialism in even simpler terms. He must also jettison Marx's analysis of class. For Marx defined a class fundamentally by its role in the mode of production. Since Harrington denies that the mode of production played a decisive role in slave and feudal societies—he is somewhat ambiguous about capitalist society—he must regard Marx's statement that "The history of all hitherto existing society is the history of class struggles" as another absent-minded aberration. The statement, to be sure, in its unqualified form is mistaken but it is no mistake that Marx believed it. He kept on republishing it in edition after edition to his dying day. His only modification was to exempt some primitive societies, after he became aware of Lewis H. Morgan's pioneer but misleading research.

Aware of the extremism of his operation on Marx, Harrington

makes a desperate effort to save the characteristic Marxist emphasis on the mode of production by distinguishing between "the determinant" and "the dominant." The economy is always "determinant"; it is "dominant" only under capitalism. However in any genuinely organic system, causally this is a distinction without a significant difference. The economy, Harrington asserts, is determinant in two senses. First, it is "a sine qua non of life itself." But so is oxygen. Second, it is the source of a "light" or color or odor that pervades the entire society. But this obviously cannot be what Marx means by "basic" or primary because such phenomenal qualities have no executive character or causal effect in bringing about social change. It is not the color of the flash of an explosion that kills; it is not the odor of bitter almonds that is fatal but the chemical effect of the cyanide.

Harrington takes the human body as a paradigm of an organic system. Human society is far from being as organic because of the greater influence of physical factors on it. Even in the human body not all aspects are "dialectically" interrelated. But regardless of the degree of interrelation it is downright silly to ask, what is the most decisive or dominant or determinant aspect in the functioning of the body—its digestive, nervous, circulatory, reproductive, or skeletal system? Only in relation to some problem or difficulty or purpose is such a question meaningful and answerable. Similarly with society. The relevant causal factor is that which must be altered or controlled to achieve a desirable result.

Engels was right in proclaiming that above all Marx was a revolutionist. His theory and practice of social revolution was animated by a moral purpose Marx's own doctrines couldn't adequately explain. He made some discoveries whose validity was independent of his purposes. To that extent some of his contributions may be considered scientific in a broad sense. But with respect to his central predictions, events have proved most of them wrong. In any case we must sharply distinguish between the meaning of Marx's assertions and their truth or falsity, and not pretend when an assertion turns out to be false, that Marx couldn't really have meant it.

There is hardly a page in Harrington's book that does not invite correction or critical comment. In general whenever he ventures into philosophy, he is in water over his head. Although he seems to have taken a crash course in Hegel to help him understand Marx, he fails to see the difficulties and defects of the Hegelian logic which is an ontology rather than a theory of inquiry or scientific proof. Indeed, since it finds truth in the ineffable Whole it is incompatible with the methods of scientific experiment or abstraction which presuppose that *not* all things are interrelated. He disregards Marx's explicit statement that he was "coquetting" with Hegel's terminology, that his findings were derived "scientifically," independently of Hegel, and therefore must be judged by the historical, empirical evidence.

It is precisely that critical assessment of Marx's theories in the light of the empirical evidence that Harrington wishes to avoid. Although he admits that some specific predictions of Marx, and especially their timing, were disastrously wrong, he still fervently affirms the validity of Marx's analysis of capitalist development. He nowhere indicates what empirical evidence would falsify Marx's central contentions, and at what point in time. After all, it was not merely the timing of the revolutionary overthrow of capitalism that Marx got wrong. He failed to predict the rise of the welfare state, fascism in all its varieties, bureaucratic collectivism (or Communism), the triumphs of nationalism, and the impressive absolute gains in living standards of the working class under capitalism. In Harrington's eyes this in no way affects the basic validity of Marxism. Though History slay him yet will he trust and maintain his ways before It. No matter how long the twilight years of capitalism drag on, darkness will surely fall. He is not so confident as Marx was that it will be followed by a true socialist dawn. That is definitely to his credit.

Karl Marx's contributions, modified, qualified and corrected, are great enough to have entered into the mainstream of modern sociology and history. It is the rare sociologist or historian who doesn't acknowledge, regardless of his political faith, the heuristic fruitfulness of Marx's approach. Despite Harrington's contention to the contrary, the mode of production under feudalism and slavery did determine to a considerable extent the realities of political power and the distribution of goods and services although it does not explain, among other things, the *differences* between European Christian feudalism and Japanese Buddhist feudalism. But Marxism as a system may be laid to rest except as the state philosophy of totalitarian despotisms that call themselves socialist and as the religion of heretical Marxist sects.

Rejecting the classical Marxist positions on historical materialism and the class struggle, Harrington clings all the more fiercely to Marx's theory of surplus value and the economic analysis of *Capital*. His argument is somewhat obscure: he seems to believe that because Marx was aware of the contradiction between the first and third volumes of *Capital* that therefore there is no contradiction.

Here, too, he ignores Marx's text by denying that Marx predicted the progressive pauperization of the working classes because he made allowance for local, limited and temporary improvements in their condition. Where Marx speaks of the workers' "growing mass of misery, oppression, slavery, degradation, exploitation," Harrington insists that Marx was referring only to the *relative* difference in income and standards of living between workers and capitalists. On Harrington's view of Marx's meaning, even if workers were to enjoy real wages and fringe benefits of $50,000 annually in uninflated dollars, so long as there were a small group of millionaires, the workers would still be degraded paupers and Marx's account of their lot true.

Harrington does in places seek to soften the stark meaning of Marx's words especially when Marx speaks of "inevitability." This may be legitimate in view of Marx's occasional recognition of historical alternatives. But even so Marx was more wrong than right in charting the future of capitalism because he underestimated the effects of political democracy on its evolution. In the twentieth century the mode of political decision is as important for many aspects of daily life as the mode of economic production, and in some respects even more important. In *Capital* Marx says of the natural laws of capitalist production that "these laws or tendencies are working with iron necessity towards inevitable results. The country that is more developed industrially only shows, to the less developed, the image of its own future." From which it follows that in 1914 the United States and England were showing Russia, then the less developed capitalist country, the image of its own inevitable future! Actually, Lenin had more to do with that future than any economic law. His event-making role in the October Russian Revolution, together with the party he forged, succeeded in doing what on Marx's theory was historically impossible. They used political means to transform their primitive economy. The iron necessity was more in their ruthless will than in the laws of capitalist economy.

To me the first part of this volume is an additional argument against immortality. For if the human spirit survived the death of the body, Marx would have risen from his grave at Highgate in thundering protest. In life his fury exploded at lesser provocations.

The second half of Harrington's book is an attempt to show that the welfare state in no way refutes Marx's economic predictions. It merely postpones the inevitable day of reckoning. Harrington insists that the welfare state in the United States and elsewhere is still a capitalist society. In one sense it is. But it is also true that the size of the public sector, the power of free trade unions, the scope of regulatory agencies, makes capitalist society of 1976 more different from that of 1876, than 1876 is from 1776. The relevant questions are those of degree, direction, and the possibility of transition to more democratic and socially responsible forms of economic investment and control. Once rational and more equitable tax laws, especially of inheritance, are legislated and enforced, it will become clearer that as I have argued on many occasions, our choice is not between capitalism or socialism but between *more or less* of either. We do not and cannot now live under the capitalism of Adam Smith—but there are other forms of socialism than those envisaged by Karl Marx, whose true utopianism is expressed in his views about the withering away of the state. The state will not disappear. The administration of things will never replace administration by human beings. The democratic task is to make the state more responsive to the public interest as it protects basic human civil liberties.

The second section contains some well-founded criticisms of current tax and energy policies. Their failure is attributed to the capitalist nature of the welfare state. To establish this Harrington abandons the notion of society as an "organic" totality in which there is reciprocal causation among plural factors and reverts to reliance upon the "primary" or ultimate cause—the capitalist structure—that cannot explain differential, specific effects. For him it is not the Vietnam war nor the cowardly and foolish tax policies of the Johnson administration nor the failure of Nixon's half-hearted price and wage controls nor the boycott of the OPEC countries that caused the crisis of unemployment and inflation, but the "profound limitations of capitalist society." Regardless of the problem, it seems as if it is always cpaitalism that in the last analysis is responsible for our failure to solve it. But since welfare state capitalism is certainly compatible with tax, energy and income policies that more equitably redistribute the burdens of the recession, if only enough citizens can be persuaded of it, capitalism cannot be the decisive factor in explaining the choice among policy alternatives. Our mixed economy does not preclude the possibility of a guaranteed family income at a decent level or a comprehensive national health insurance plan any more than it did the Civil Rights Act of the nineteen-sixties.

Harrington's analysis is as enlightening as the observation on the death by lung cancer of a heavily addicted smoker, that his death was not merely the result of his addiction but also of "the profound limitations" of the human organism.

A scientific approach to social as well as medical problems deals only in proximate causes. The limitations of capitalist society are much more modifiable than those of the human organism. In *Capital* Marx blamed capitalism for the fact that the life expectancy of the workers of Manchester was 17 years. Today it is close to 70. By the same token capitalism should be given credit for that. One would have expected someone as partial to Hegel as Harrington to be more sympathetic to the possibility that a gradual "quantitative" change in the powers of the capitalistic welfare state through greater consumer and labor representation may result in a "qualitative" change. To facilitate this it may be necessary among other things to find another vocabulary. Those who put freedom or democracy first may lose their allegiance to "capitalism" when they discover that when human welfare is at stake, it puts profits first. But they may have good reason for fearing "socialism" more. Harrington quite properly judges capitalism not by its ideals and theory but by its historical practices. One must therefore judge socialism equally not by its rhetoric but by its historical practices. Any reasoned comparison of the historical fruits of both will conclude that the prospects for a humane, prosperous and free society are far greater under the democratic welfare state than under any current socialist alternative. Workers who cherish their free trade unions know this best of all.

CHAPTER SEVEN

Marx for All Seasons

Marxism: For and Against is an intriguing title: it arouses expectations of a judicious and balanced evaluation of the specific doctrines of Marx and Marxism from a scholarly and nonpartisan point of view.[1] Unfortunately, there is a fundamental ambiguity in the way the author, Robert Heilbroner, understands the terms "for" and "against." They do not mean so much "true" or "valid" and "false" or "invalid" as *for* revolutionary change or *against* revolutionary change. But should not one's attitude toward the revolutionary change urged by Marxism depend largely upon the truth or falsity of its major doctrines?

Heilbroner does not really convey his own position on Marxism when he says that it is "beyond that of total embrace or rejection." Except for pious dolts or fanatics, could we not say this of any great thinker in human history—Plato, Kant, Kierkegaard? Who embraces or rejects them totally? I know of no reputable historian, regardless of his attitude toward revolutionary change, who *totally* rejects all of Marx's views. The relevant questions are: which specific doctrines or propositions are valid, and to what extent?

Heilbroner defines Marxism in terms of four elements: (1) a dialectical approach to knowledge itself; (2) a materialist approach to history; (3) a social analysis of capitalism—Marx's theory of value and surplus value; and (4) a commitment to socialism. This last element is confusing since it is not logically related to the other three. For Marx believed that his economic and historical doctrines were true regardless of whether one was committed to socialism. He held that they were as objective as the findings of natural science, valid regardless of anyone's commitment.

---

[1]Robert Heilbroner, *Marxism: For and Against* (New York: W. W. Norton & Co., Inc., 1980)

Before assessing Heilbroner's evaluation of Marx's contributions one must say something of how he goes about his inquiry. Instead of testing Marx's statements about history and economics in the light of the empirical evidence, he considers them in relation to what capitalism essentially is. "We read *Capital* not merely to discover how capitalism works . . . but to learn what capitalism *is*." This essentialist approach is quite foreign to Marx's outlook, as it is to every scientific analysis. What a thing, system, or process is cannot be unrelated to how it behaves. "By their fruits ye shall know them" and "the proof of the pudding is in the eating" are customary Marxist maxims. Not so for Heilbroner, "I find it imaginable," he writes, "that the next century will declare Marx to have been completely mistaken about the future course of capitalism; but as long as capitalism exists, I do not believe that we will ever be able to declare that he was mistaken in his identification of its inner nature." On this view, no matter what happens Marx is right! It is doubtful whether Marx or any sensible Marxist made such a claim, yet it pervades Heilbroner's discussion of all the defining elements of Marxism.

1. According to Heilbroner, "a dialectical approach yields a rich harvest for the imagination but a scanty one for exact analysis." How can it then enable us to distinguish between fantasies and truths? Marx speaks of the dialectic *method*, not of the dialectical vision or imagination, and rightly or wrongly, identifies it with the scientific method which he thought he was applying in his inquiry into the nature and development of capitalism. For Heilbroner, by contrast, the dialectic goes beyond ordinary scientific method by correcting its limitations, although it is not clear how it does that. He does not tell us what specific truths reached by the dialectic are beyond the reach of the ordinary empirical methods of scientific investigation, and how we know they are true. Are we dealing here with a doctrine of two truths, with the dialectic serving as the higher truth with all the awesome and noisome consequences illustrated in the history of Soviet physics, biology, and historiography?

"Dialectics," Heilbroner writes, "seeks to expand the conception of the scientist's work beyond the borders of a positivist approach." The evil of positivism, in Heilbroner's eyes, is its emphasis upon prediction. Prediction, of course, is not everything in science, but on any coherent philosophy of science a theory that makes false predictions cannot be true. Heilbroner is happy to cite some of Marx's economic predictions that have been confirmed but is averse to considering the devastating implications of those that have been falsified. The dialectic functions in his thought to sustain the will to believe.

2. Even more unsatisfactory is Heilbroner's discussion of historical materialism. The "mode of economic production" functions, according to him, only as a limiting condition on a culture (like climate?), and far from determining the legal, political, and religious institutions of society, as Marx clearly says, is itself determined by them. Heilbroner simply does not confront the evidence that, however it may have been in some previous periods, in the twentieth century the political mode of decision is more decisive for historical events than is the economic mode of production. On the theory of historical materialism how would one explain, for instance, the fact that the United States and Great Britain, with their capitalist modes of production, joined the Soviet Union, with its socialist mode of production, in a war against Nazi Germany, another capitalist power? How would one explain the October Russian Revolution and the emergence of a socialist economy in an under-developed country with undemocratic traditions? The answer is that, having seized political power, the Bolsheviks then built an economic base beneath it.

Neither does Heilbroner judge the theory of historical materialism in the light of the emergence of the democratic welfare state, the rise of fascism, or the recurrent strength of nationalist sentiment, all completely unanticipated by the theory. He ignores completely the role of personality in history. Even Leon Trotsky admitted before he died that without Lenin there would have been no October Revolution—and, one can add, probably no Mussolini in Italy or Hitler in Germany because, among other reasons, the Bolsheviks split the working-class resistance to fascism. One can recognize and applaud the heuristic value of the theory of historical materialism in historical inquiry and reject, on the basis of the evidence, the current claims to its validity.

3. Surprisingly, in the light of modern economic theory with which he is quite familiar, Heilbroner accepts without qualification Marx's theory of value and surplus value, admitting at the same time that is is an "unprovable proposition." He does nothing, however, to meet the standard difficulties that call it into question. On Marx's theory, in an industry in which there is intensive use of labor (a window-cleaning firm, for example) there should be a higher rate of profit than in an industry in which highly developed technology is used (a power plant). Yet a more or less uniform rate of profit prevails. Heilbroner brings in the market to explain that the prices of production must diverge from the true values

of the commodities produced. This makes value irrelevant to any specific question of price and what determines it, and to the rate of profit in any specific industry.

Although willing to credit Marx for successfully predicting "the rise of large-scale industry, the internationalization of capital, . . . and the centralization of capital"—which are not necessarily implied by the theory of surplus value and can be explained independently—he dismisses phenomena that invalidate even more important predictions of Marx like the progressive impoverishment of the working class, the disappearance of the middle class, and the growing reserve army of the unemployed. Heilbroner's treatment of the "immiseration" of the working class is very peculiar. He cannot deny that with respect to "the material conditions" of life, workers today are far better off than in Marx's time, but he artfully suggests that in some non-material way the workers are no better off—the factory robs labor of "its human rhythm and meaning." Nothing is more obvious that that Marx, in speaking of the growing "mass of misery, oppression, slavery, degradation, and exploitation" of the workers, was addressing the quality of life of the English proletariat of his own time. Who can seriously deny the tremendous difference in the quality of life of the English working class in Marx's time—when their life expectancy was (according to Marx himself) seventeen in Manchester, fifteen in Birmingham—and their life today?

Under the guise of a balanced inquiry, Heilbroner has given us an apologia for Marx's main tenets. Where the evidence is overwhelmingly against Marx, he tempers his criticism to make the error appear minor. Thus, nothing is more central to Marx's political philosophy than his view that the state is the executive committee of the dominant economic class. The theory, strategy, and even tactics of current Communist theory depend on this false notion. But to Heilbroner it is merely an "incautious" statement.

Where Heilbroner departs from Marx is at the point of Marx's perennial appeal. Marx was a fighter for human freedom, for whom socialism meant not an abridgement of the political and cultural freedoms of bourgeois society but their expansion. Heilbroner's view is that "it is unlikely that a socialist civilization will be fundamentally interested in what we call liberty. . . ." He may be right! But that was not Marx's view.

Heilbroner keeps referring to the "Marxist" regimes of Cuba and other Communist and Third World countries, but never asks what makes them Marxist, aside from their self-characterization. Are they dictatorships of the proletariat? However the term is conceived, Marx never identified the dictatorship of the proletariat with the dictatorship of a party, and a minority one at that, over the proletariat and the entire population. Heilbroner can hardly be unaware of this. In his view, however, Marx's commitment to human freedom and his faith in the prospects of a democratic society are utopian fantasies. Even so, moral and intellectual hygiene would require that he use the term Marxist with greater precision. Even if one rejects the Marxist prospect as ill-conceived and ultimately unworkable is it fair to saddle him with the systems of organized terror in Communist states today?

CHAPTER EIGHT

Disremembering the Thirties

Two virtues are clearly possessed by this well-written memoir of the tumultuous thirties, of the rise of an influential radical intellectual movement and of Malcolm Cowley's role in it.[1] First, it provides an absorbing account of the cultural and social climate generated during the years of the Depression and of the New Deal, particularly as they affected the consciousness of the middle class and professions. Although Cowley's account lacks the vividness of Edmund Wilson's *American Jitters*, it does communicate something of the alternating moods of bewilderment, frustration, despair, and hope that swept through those whose moorings had been cut loose by social phenomena beyond their intellectual grasp.

Second, Cowley recognizes that the allegiance of the vast majority of intellectuals attracted to the Communist Party and its peripheral organizations was more religious than political: their commitment was total, based more on an emotional need to believe than on argument or comparative evidence. This led them to swallow infamies and outrages by the Soviet Union, always enthusiastically endorsed by the Communist Party, that far transcended evils in American society—actions which when attributed to other totalitarian regimes reinforced the zealotry and orthodoxy of the Communist faithful.

However, with respect to the actual history of the radical intellectual movement of the thirties, the ways in which the Communist Party exercised its influence and control over it, the attempts of various individuals and groups to contest, in the name of a more liberal and pluralistic conception of communism, the extremism and opportunism of the Party, their bruising conflicts

---

[1]Malcolm Cowley, *The Dream of the Golden Mountains: Remembering the 1930s* (New York: The Viking Press, 1980)

with the orthodox, and their resolute attempts to tell the truth about the Soviet Union—with respect to all this, and particularly Malcolm Cowley's own activity during the decade, this book is from first to last a self-serving exercise in apologetics. Historians interested in compiling an accurate record of the period will be ill served if they accept its assertions on their face. For example, Cowley would have us believe that the reasons he did not join the Communist Party, despite the extent and intensity of his agreement with its ideals and program, were his literary reservations in 1932 and his political reservations in 1935. To be sure, he was always uncomfortable with the Party's rhetoric but, judging by his writings at the time—which are accessible to those interested— there is not a trace of any political reservations. If anything, his enthusiasm for the Soviet Union and its American agents reached a higher pitch in 1935 when he helped organize the League of American Writers than when he helped organize the League of Professional Groups for Foster and Ford in 1932.

There is no evidence to show that Malcolm Cowley was ever asked to join the Communist Party. Nor, I am convinced, would he have been accepted had he applied. For the truth of the matter is that he served the Communist Party and what it represented better by not joining it and by functioning where he was, as literary editor of the *New Republic,* a post he could not have kept had he officially become a Party member. Already in early 1937 John Dewey, who had been one of the pillars of the *New Republic,* resigned as a contributing editor on the ground that the *New Republic* had betrayed the principles of liberalism, and, among other criticisms, had cited the tendentious way Cowley ran the book review section. By the end of the thirties, despite Cowley's alleged political reservations about the Soviet Union, Edmund Wilson, his friend and patron, wrote to him in protest: "You have been carrying on in a way that matches *The New Masses* at its worst. . . . You write better than the people on the regular Stalinist press but what you are writing is simply Stalinist character assassination of the most reckless and libelous sort" (*Letters on Literature and Politics*). Coming from Wilson who, according to Cowley, was above the battle of factions, this is weighty testimony. Actually, from the Communist Party's point of view, the fact that Cowley was not an official member was very helpful. It could cite his judgments on the Moscow trials and attacks on Communist critics and defectors as the findings of an independent non-Party thinker.

Before examining some of these judgments, it is necessary in the interest of the truth to correct Cowley's account of the League of Professional Groups—the most prestigious of the Party's fellow-traveling groups before the popular front. Despite my own doctrinal differences with the official Communist line, I played a leading role in its organization in the utopian hope of being able to influence Communist Party thinking from without. No sooner was the election of 1932 over, when, together with Lewis Corey and about a dozen other members, I suggested a series of membership meetings to consider some of the dogmas that we believed were contributing to the growth of reaction—nationally and internationally. When Hitler came to power we were more forthright in our criticism because we were convinced that these dogmas had heavily contributed to Hitler's victory. Our most impassioned opponent was Malcolm Cowley, who worked hand in glove with Joseph Pass and Joseph Freeman, the heads of the Party fraction in the League. Cowley implies that we were all Trotskyists. Only two of the group had such connections. Although I was unaware of it at the time, Corey was a secret member of the Lovestone Communist Opposition. The rest of us had no affiliation. Instead of reporting that the Party had decided to liquidate the League to prevent critical discussion of its dogmas, Cowley suggests that the League was killed off by "its dreary meetings," where he "listened impatiently to speeches about the betrayal of the Chinese Revolution of 1927." Cowley's memory here, as elsewhere, is seriously at fault. China was one topic that was never on the agenda. What he was impatiently listening to was our sustained critique of the theory of social fascism, according to which the socialists were the twins of fascists—a horrendous view that split the German working class and prevented a united front and resistance against the Nazis. What he also heard, with more than impatience, was a criticism of the communist theory and practice of dual trade unionism. I recall his turning to me and asking indignantly, "Who are *you* to criticize William Foster on trade union policy?" That was not the role of intellectuals according to the Party. Cowley must also have heard, if he attended that meeting, questions about the political wisdom of the Communist Party slogan: "Self-determination for the Black Belt."

In his current retrospective account of the early thirties, Cowley claims to have harbored strong doubts about these very points (except the last, which he does not mention). He is particularly vehement in his claim to have been unhappy about the doctrine of social fascism which the Kremlin abandoned in 1935. Yet early in 1934, when the Communist Party forcibly broke up the meeting of the Socialist Party in Madison Square Garden that was called in support of the cause of the Austrian workers shot down by Dollfuss's Heimwehr, Cowley refused to sign the letter of protest sent by Dos Passos and others to the *New Masses*. Cowley explains: "I kept out of the dispute not having attended the meeting. . . ." This is disingenuous on its face. None of the other signers had attended the meeting. There was no dispute but an organized Communist riot. And was any Communist meeting ever broken up that Cowley failed to protest on the ground that he had not attended it? His claim that he was critical of the theory of social fascism at any time before the Kremlin abandoned it is, I submit, false. Likewise false is his statement that toward the end of the thirties, when he thought of the impending war, he "came to feel" that America "must" enter it. Like his colleagues at the *New Republic*, he definitely did not feel that way at the time.

Malcolm Cowley in a previous work sought to explain his differences with those of us who were critical of the Comintern line by saying that whereas we feared only Stalin, he feared Hitler. No one who listened to us even with half an ear—"this New York bunch of Jewish intellectuals," as we were contemptuously referred to by Communist Party officials (although Lewis Corey, James Rorty, and John McDonald were not Jewish)—could have believed this. The main point of our indictment of the Party line was that it was helping Hitler to come to power and to stay in power.

The greatest service Cowley performed for the Communist Party was his defense of the Moscow trials. His was the most extended and persistent attack on the defendants and was based, so he claimed, on a careful reading of the official proceedings. He dismisses the lack of any material evidence at the trials on the ground that it is contained in many volumes not made available to him but to the prosecution! He asserts that "the most improbable crimes, like the murder of Maxim Gorky and his son, are the best motivated and the most thoroughly substantiated." But the only evidence was poor Dr. Levin's confession. He accepts Tukhachevsky's guilt on the ground of "widely accepted rumor [sic]" from non-Soviet sources. Not only does he swallow whole Stalin's charge that Trotsky, Bukharin, and most of Lenin's other lieutenants were guilty of treasonable dealings with Germany, Poland, Japan, and the British intelligence service; he holds them responsible for such "mean and repulsive" crimes as "pouring nails and broken glass into eighty car-loads of butter, spreading corn beetles in the granaries, infecting horses with anthrax or cholera, and hogs with erysipelas. . . ." Even Communist Party hacks were fearful of repeating these fantasies of Vyshinsky lest they provoke hilarity. Already in the case of his jeering review of George Kitchin's book on his experiences at the hands of the Soviet secret police, Cowley had endorsed its draconian policy against its victims. He acknowledges the innocence of Kitchin, the use of torture by his captors, and the essential truth of his story. But he dismisses this truth as "of a special sort"—the truth of a parasite (*New Republic*, 9/11/35). In going beyond the bounds formally observed by the Kremlin's inquisitors, who always insisted that their victims were guilty of the charges against them, Cowley reveals how total was his commitment to the Stalinist faith. He could serve it both as policeman and as poet.

Malcolm Cowley now confesses that he no longer accepts the validity of the Moscow trials. But he does not tell us when he changed his mind, and on the basis of what new evidence. This is most curious. Khrushchev's speech before the Twentieth Congress of the Russian Communist Party on Stalin's crimes made no explicit mention of the Moscow trials. To this day there has been no rehabilitation of its numerous defendants, not even of Bukharin. As far as the public record goes, there is no more evidence available today on the guilt or innocence of the defendants than when Cowley reviewed the verbatim testimony. That testimony, however, was examined by the Commission of Inquiry into the Truth of the Moscow Trials, headed by John Dewey. On December 12, 1937, at the Hotel Center in New York, Dewey made a preliminary public report of the findings of the commission, which revealed the complete baselessness of the charges against the defendants. He subsequently instructed me to send a copy of that report to George Soule, Bruce Bliven, and Malcolm Cowley, with whom he had corresponded when he resigned from the *New Republic* earlier in the year.

Although that report was in Cowley's hands before the end of 1937, on May 3, 1938, he defended the Moscow trials in the *New Masses* and impugned the integrity of the commission. Then on May 18 and May 25 he repeated and endorsed, in the *New Republic*, the substance of Vyshinsky's accusations.

Could he have finally read the report of the Dewey Commission? However that may be, his memoir is not a true account of the intellectual life and struggles of the thirties. Among its many failings, it does not begin to explain the role of the Moscow trials in polarizing the American liberal community, their fallout in the Hiss case a decade later, and why "the dream of the golden mountain"—the universal brotherhood of workers and thinkers—turned into a totalitarian nightmare.

The question is not one of reliving the radical political conflicts of the thirties. All the embattled participants were guilty of failing to realize the promise of American democracy despite its imperfections—especially those who went whoring after false gods on whose bloodied altars millions of human beings had already been sacrificed. The question is one of historical truth, and why its continued distortion over the decades has gone unrebuked. Those who, like Alfred Kazin, have hailed Cowley's book as authentic history have become accomplices in that distortion.

CHAPTER NINE

Home Truths About Marx

There are many virtues in this comprehensive and scholarly biography of Eleanor Marx, the most likable member of Karl Marx's family, and the only one who did not renounce her Jewish heritage.[1] Through her sympathetic account of Eleanor Marx's life and letters, Yvonne Kapp succeeds in vivifying all of the Marxes, as well as the large circle of their friends, personal and political. Everyone is humanized when seen through Eleanor Marx's loving and compassionate eyes—except, strangely enough, Edward Aveling, her common-law husband, whose actions drove her to a tragic death by suicide at the age of forty-three under mysterious circumstances that to this day have not been cleared up. At the same time, we are provided with a veritable encyclopedia of information about relevant and irrelevant details of the working-class movement in Western Europe, especially England.

Nonetheless, for all its virtues, it is hard to understand the chorus of unqualified critical praise this book has received. For as a biography it seems to me to leave more questions unanswered than answered, especially when it comes to Edward Aveling. In 1929 I met the socialist leader Eduard Bernstein in Berlin. Bernstein was approaching senility at the time, but the mention of two names roused him to passionate outbursts of lucid denunication. The first was that of David Riazanov, the head of the Marx-Engels Institute of Moscow, whom Bernstein accused of stealing manuscripts from the Social Democratic archives. The second was Edward Aveling. To Bernstein's mind, Aveling was an unmitigated scoundrel, accused not merely of leaving Eleanor but by implication of doing away with her.

Yet the only thing that was indisputably established about

---

[1]Yvonne Kapp, *Eleanor Marx*, 2 vols. (New York: Pantheon Books, Inc., 1976)

Aveling was his infidelity—an old story in those rather uncon-
ventional circles. Aveling himself was a paragon of political orthodoxy in the inner group of Marxist socialists, someone who
had sacrificed a distinguished professional career for the uncertain
life of a labor educator and organizer, with an unsavory reputation
that was a result partly of factional hostility among socialists and
anarchists opposed to parliamentary action, and partly of insin-
uations by Eleanor's friends about his life as a Lothario despite
his unprepossessing appearance and his persistent ill health. Aveling
was in fact a man of admirable intellectual courage, not only a
"dangerous" socialist but a militant atheist at a time when persons
of his outspoken views were liable to be jailed for blasphemy.

Despite his background, his wide learning, and his oratorical
gifts, Yvonne Kapp portrays Aveling as little better than a fraud
and a dead beat, "a gasbag whom time has rudely deflated . . .
so far as posterity is concerned a thundering bore." Perhaps; but
this makes it all the more incumbent upon a biographer to explain
why such a man could profoundly move contemporary audiences.
A tough English labor veteran acclaimed him as "one of the greatest
orators this country ever heard." The more one accepts the author's
assessment of Aveling's personality and intellectual legacy—"his
voice is not merely without character: it is muted, dead. Nothing
rings through the words. Nothing at all"—the more puzzling is
the fascination he exerted over the vibrant, loving, yet level-headed
Eleanor, who slavishly devoted herself to him. "My last word to
you," reads the farewell note she penned in the moments before
her death, "is the same that I have said during all these long,
sad years—love." There must have been something about Aveling
to account for a love so prolonged, profound, and desperate. We
must conclude that the biographer who has not found it has not
understood something central in Eleanor Marx's life.

Even more surprising in a book which is to a considerable extent
a biography of Marx himself is the absence of any intellectual
analysis of Marx's leading ideas, or of the criticisms made of them.
Miss Kapp's own Marxism is orthodox Old Left and theoretically
primitive. She believes that Marx had a "scientific philosophy"
that explains "the processes by which societies develop, applicable
at all times and in all places," and scornfully says of the Fabian
society that it "had no more earthly chance to supersede Marx
than to reverse the laws of gravity." What we would like to know
is whether Eleanor Marx, whose orthodoxy was as unquestioning
as that of Engels, ever confronted the challenges to Marx's ideas.
Miss Kapp's account pictures her primarily as a tireless and effective

popular propagandist. Her letters concerning Eduard Bernstein's first tentative steps toward revisionism, which now seems scientifically more justified than the traditional orthodox view, reveal pious horror but little understanding.

More regrettably, Miss Kapp has missed a golden opportunity to explore and evaluate Marx's treatment of the "Jewish question," although she does devote a few pages to Eleanor Marx's gallant identification of herself as a Jew despite the fact that she was born of a Christian mother and a baptized Jewish father. "I am the only one of my family," she remarked to Max Beer, the historian of the socialist movement, "who felt drawn to the Jewish people." This came about as a result of her observing the grinding poverty under which immigrant Jewish workers lived and the birth of socialist consciousness among them; it also arose out of her characteristic impulse to identify with the insulted and injured, and probably too out of a sense of personal guilt over the thoughtless anti-Semitism endemic to the early socialist and labor movement in Europe.

It must be remembered that the concept of a Jewish proletariat was quite foreign to Europeans of the day, who associated Jews with commerce and huckstering. (As late as 1928, German students were incredulous about the existence of a Jewish proletariat in the United States.) Miss Kapp believes that Eleanor Marx's declaration, "I am a Jewess," at the time of the Dreyfus affair undid "in four words her paternal grandfather's years of cogitation and eventual baptism." If so, only in her own case. It did not undo the effects of her father's treatment of the Jewish question, of whose drift she could hardly have been unaware. Eleanor idolized her father: there is no evidence that she questioned any of his views about anything.

This is not the place to consider in detail Marx's discussion of the Jewish question. In the light of what happened to European Jewry after Marx's time, his views strike one not only as extremely biased but as horrendous. Yet a certain injustice has been done to him in downplaying the fact that his writings on the subject do argue for the extension of all political rights to observant Jews—this, before the era of Jewish political emancipation, and despite his identification of Judaism with money-grubbing, rapacious usury, and the worship of Mammon. One of the current translations of Marx's *Zur Judenfrage* is entitled *A World Without Jews*. This is a distortion that borders on falsification. It would have been more truthful to entitle it, *A World Without Jews and Christians*. For its animus is more against religion as such than against Judaism. It sins against both the historical approach of Hegel and the universalistic humanism of Feuerbach. And worst of all, it fails to apply to the Jewish question what is sound in the theory of historical materialism toward which Marx himself was groping at the time. It did not require any esoteric scholarship to recognize that the objectionable aspects of the vocational activities of the Jews had been forced upon them by Christian communities. And although the essay belongs to Marx's younger years, there were ample opportunities to modify his judgment subsequently. The czarist pogroms had begun before he died, and anti-Semitic literature was not uncommon. Yet scurrilous references to Jews not only persist in his personal correspondence but are echoed in the letters of his daughters.

It is hardly a mitigation of Marx's insensitivity to the plight of the European Jews that anti-Semitism was rife in almost all varieties of socialism, and that insulting references to his own Jewish origins occasionally appeared in the polemical writings of socialist sects. The man who could sympathize with the exploited masses of India and China, whose compassion was aroused by the sufferings of English workers and Irish peasants, whose imagination was stirred by the heroic resistance of the Poles, seemed utterly indifferent to the periodic excesses against his own people. No one knew better than this omnivorous reader of the annals of the past that his kinsmen had for centuries lived on sufferance beyond the protection of the laws, victims both of arbitrary spoliation by oppressive rulers and of the popular fury of their subjects, the perpetual outsiders and scapegoats whose present condition could not be understood or judged without reference to their fateful legacy. Marx's utopian internationalism and universal outlook had not blinded him to the realities of European national struggles in their concrete historical contexts. Why had they obscured his vision where the Jews were concerned?

It was certainly not out of moral cowardice or a desire to ingratiate himself with others or to avoid polemical attacks. At the time of the Paris Commune, Marx had braved the obloquy of an outraged European public opinion. We can only guess at the unconscious psychological motivations that underlay his thoughtless and harsh judgments concerning the Jews and Judaism and that inhibited him from reacting as Eleanor did to the pathetic plight of those harried by persecution and living in large part on the margins of society.

At any rate, no man is all of a piece. Those not already familiar with some of the incidents in Marx's life that seem to diminish his stature as a human being will find them here as they relate to Eleanor and other members of his family. Some of them have their amusing sides. Miss Kapp reproduces Marx's letter to Paul Lafargue, who was paying court to his daughter Laura, in which Marx appears in the role of a heavy-handed Victorian father protesting Lafargue's unseemly public displays of ardor and warning him off the premises if in his daughter's presence he is unable "to love her in a manner that conforms with the latitude of London."

More important and self-revealing was Marx's demand that Lafargue offer some guarantees of his economic prospects; and— since "as regards your family, I know nothing"—that he furnish information about his parents' social and economic status. Fear of poverty and a bad conscience over having imposed poverty on his wife accounted for Marx's concern. "You know that I have sacrificed my whole fortune to the revolutionary struggle. I do not regret it. On the contrary. Had I my career to start again, I should do the same. But I would not marry. As far as lies in my power, I intend to save my daughter from the reefs on which her mother's life has been wrecked." Marx refused to give his daughters the freedom to make their own choice. He succeeded in breaking up Eleanor's engagement to Lissageray, one of the heroes of the Paris Commune, despite Eleanor's deep emotional attachment to him. In all likelihood, despite "the shortcomings of French husbands," on which all the members of the Marx household seem to have been agreed, had Eleanor married Lissageray she would have escaped her tragic entanglement with Aveling.

Other incongruities between the social ideals of Marx, his family, and his intimate circle and their social behavior are observed by Miss Kapp with a suppressed inquietude. Their attitude toward servants, for example, was hardly different from that of their unenlightened English neighbors. And although one cannot expect socialists to abolish or even to modify the institutions under which they have been brought up, still one does expect them to exhibit a certain fraternity of spirit in relation to their fellow humans regardless of station or birth.

There was something positively feudal in the Marxes' relationship to Helene Demuth, Mrs. Marx's old family retainer, who did indeed become a member of the family, so to speak, as did so many old servants at the time who had no life of their own. The fact that Helene Demuth bore an illegitimate son to Marx is not as significant as the way in which the child, and necessarily the mother, were treated. The child never crossed the threshold of the Marx domicile after he was sent out to foster parents, never met Marx, saw his mother only clandestinely, and enjoyed none of the cultural advantages of the other Marx children. He had a rather rough time growing up and was treated with aversion by Engels even after Helene Demuth became Engels's housekeeper upon Marx's death. He became friendly only with Eleanor, from whom the knowledge that he was her illegitimate half-brother was kept until shortly before Engels died.

It is not altogether clear whether Mrs. Marx was aware of all the facts, although it is difficult to believe that the situation could have escaped her notice. Here, too, what may be shrugged off as customary behavior when ordinary mortals are involved, seems odd and unseemly on the part of those heralding a new era in human relationships. One cannot but sympathize with Eleanor Marx's shock and incredulity when apprised of Freddie Demuth's parentage, not because her father was involved, but because of the ignorance in which she had been kept and the cowardly truckling to the cruel social conventions of the time by those who, like Marx himself on many occasions, had denounced the hypocrisies of bourgeois morality.

Eleanor Marx herself seems in every way to have been an admirable person, capable only of small spites and jealousies, and overburdened by too great a piety toward her father and his work. The world was too much for her partly because she approached it with the oversimple determinism derived from the Marxist tradition. Moral evil appeared to her to be no more than a physiological defect remediable perhaps by medical and social means. Shortly before her death she wrote to Freddie Demuth:

In some a certain *moral* sense is wanting just as some are deaf or have bad sight or are otherwise unhealthy. And I begin to understand that one has no more right to blame the one disease than the other. We must try and cure and if no cure is possible, do our best. I have learned this through long suffering.

Such a view makes the concepts of moral good and evil unintelligible, and the quest for social justice the pursuit of a chimera. It fails to do justice to what inspired Karl Marx and his followers as well as to the life of Eleanor Marx herself.

CHAPTER TEN

Reflections on the Frankfurt School

One of the most important currents of Marxist revisionism (or Marxist interpretation, if one rejects the term "revisionism") is the Frankfurt School. It is comprised of a number of writers of whom the most notable are Max Horkheimer, Frederich Pollack, Theodor Wiesengrund-Adorno, Herbert Marcuse, and Erich Fromm. Despite important variations among them, they are unified by a set of doctrines that certainly differentiates them from the traditional Social-Democratic Kautskian and the Marxist-Lenin schools.

There are two main questions that can be asked of the Frankfurt School: (1) to what extent can it be considered Marxist—without obvious question-begging conceptions of Marx's meaning; and (2) regardless of whether it is Marxist or not, has this school made important contributions to the understanding of man and society? With respect to the first question: there is no doubt that the leading members of the school regard themselves as Marxists. During the first two decades of its existence, the Frankfurt School preserved a carefully ambiguous position toward Marxist-Leninism and the social organization of the Soviet Union. Only after World War II were there any explicit criticisms of Soviet Marxism and society in connection with the criticism of the role of technology in industrial society. But at no time, as far as I am aware, have leading members of the Frankfurt School explicitly disavowed Marx or Marxism.

Nonetheless, it seems to me that with respect to at least five doctrines central to Marx—namely, his historical materialism, his naturalism, his conception of scientific socialism, his reliance on the working class as the carrier of revolutionary social change, and his commitment to basic democratic values—the Frankfurt School has so Hegelianized Marx that it represents a form of revisionism more radical than that of Eduard Bernstein. Because

120

of the limitations of space, I shall restrict myself primarily to the views of Max Horkheimer, the leading figure of the Frankfurt School.

1. In one of his introductions to *Capital*, Marx wrote that he "coquetted" with Hegel's terminology but it is clear that he regards the political economy of capitalism as an organic system in which terms like capital, wage labor, profit, rent, and other basic economic categories are related to each other, so that an adequate understanding of one involves an understanding of the others. The systematic aspect of the economy is regarded as the primary object of economic analysis rather than separate individual economic transactions considered as units that are elements of a complex structure. Where Marx discusses the exchange value of labor power or the Money-Commodity-Money cycle, he regards it as the seed which already contains within itself the systematic pattern of the developed economy. It is only with respect to the economy that Marx believes that relations are internal as they are normally considered in any organic system.

What Horkheimer and almost all so-called latter-day Marxists have done is to apply this organic relationship that holds for the economy in which parts mutually determine each other, to society and culture as a whole. This is how Hegel, and some of his bastard offspring like Spengler, conceived of society—in which the economy, law, education, philosophy, religion, and art mutually determine each other—a relationship that can be grasped by the categories of totality and reciprocity.

Whether or not such an extension of the logic of organic systems to the whole of society and culture is valid, it makes the theory of historical materialism unintelligible. No matter how we attempt to modify Marx's formulation to avoid reductionism and to accommodate the empirical facts of the influence of law and politics on the economy, it can hardly be denied that, according to the theory of historical materialism, the mode of production must function as the independent variable, changes in which determine the changes in the dependent variables. Horkheimer's Hegelianized transformation of Marx makes utterly incomprehensible Marx's basic metaphor of foundation and superstructure in his Preface to the *Critique of Political Economy*, the locus classicus of the doctrine. Many have been the attempts to explain away the significance of Marx's statement and Engels's restatement of the theory of historical materialism. The most bizarre is Michael Harrington's view, previously discussed, in *The Twilight of Capitalism*. He dubs the Preface an indiscretion of Marx's mature years, an expression of "vulgar Marxism." Once we dismiss the causal priority of the mode of production in considering the structure of society and its changes, we eviscerate the theory of historical materialism beyond recognition.

2. What is even more startling in any school of thought that considers itself Marxist, is its apparent rejection of naturalism. Marx wrote no systematic philosophy and together with Engels predicted the end of philosophy as an autonomous discipline that could give us truths about nature, society and man. We know that he believed the critique of religion to be the basis of all criticism, and when Darwin's *Origin of Species* appeared, he declared in a letter to Engels that it constituted the basis of their world view in that it made man continuous with nature, even if he was a distinctive part of nature. According to the explicit statements of Max Horkheimer in his *The Eclipse of Reason* any attempt to assign priority to matter or nature is self-defeating because it presupposes an intellectual activity that implies the existence of something different from or prior to nature. "Thus," he says, "even the assertion of the primacy of nature conceals within itself the assertion of the absolute sovereignty of spirit, because it is spirit that conceives this primacy of nature and subordinates everything to it" (p. 169). As an argument this is singularly unpersuasive if by spirit is meant human intellection whose exercise depends upon the functioning of the human organism. As well argue that we could never conclude that there was a time when we were not present in the world since the inference must be made in the present—a short and easy proof of immortality! At any rate, the reference to the "absolute sovereignty of the spirit" is pure Hegel. We do not have to resolve the question of whether naturalism or any or all varieties of idealism are valid to characterize Horkheimer's view as non-Marxist, On several occasions, Marx explicitly asserted that Hegel's philosophy, certainly his ontology, is a sophisticated, and to him a sophistical, expression of the Judaic-Christian theology.

3. The most distinctive feature of the Frankfurt School is its emphasis upon "critical method," its invocation of Reason, and its reference to the dialectic by which Reason and the critical method discover truth. It is in the eclipse of Reason that the crisis of civilization lies. I have elsewhere reported my failure during two extensive seminar discussions in the thirties with Horkeimer and his colleagues to clarify how Reason or the dialectic method functions concretely to reach any truths about the world. Suffice it to say when requested to give a specific illustration of some truth discovered by Reason or the dialectic which was beyond the reach of scientific method or a conclusion reached by scientific

method in any field that required correction by Reason or the dialectic, they were unable to do so. Instead they delivered themselves of a criticism, sustained in the writings of all members of the School, of positivism. By positivism they meant not merely the historic expression of the doctrine by Comte and his followers but also the intellectually more rigorous philosophy of logical empiricism and in addition the scientific pragmatism of Peirce and Dewey, disregarding the important differences among them, most notably the pragmatic contention that judgments of value in the specific historical contexts in which they are formulated are cognitively meaningful and therefore can be assessed as valid or invalid. Any belief that maintained that the rationale of any of the natural sciences, was a paradigm of reliable thinking about the world, they dismissed as scientism, as the worship of the methods of the natural sciences which, they alleged, reduced human beings to things. They invoked Reason as a special faculty, distinguished from intelligence or understanding, that in some mysterious way grasped "the inherent meaning of things."

Here is not the place to uncover the ambiguities and confusions in this apotheosis of Reason and its spectator theory of mind that harks back to Plato and Aristotle. It is sufficient to point out that it fails to recognize the activity of mind in the process of knowledge, an activity disclosed not only in every scientific inquiry of how the mind works, but required to explain how thinking can be practical, how thinking can ever make a difference to the world. The Frankfurt School's characterization of positivism and pragmatism is a caricature. Of positivism it says that it regards science as "philosophical technocracy" as "the automatic champion of progress," and as "exclusive faith in mathematics" (*op. cit.*, p. 59)—which is certainly odd, considering the positivist view that pure mathematics consists of tautologous propositions. The pragmatic opposition to any dogma from, or in, any field that threatens to block the road to inquiry, expressed in Justice Holmes' dictum as belief in "a free market in the world of ideas," according to Horkeimer, "reflects a businesslike attitude towards matters of the spirit, a preoccupation with success" (*op. cit.*, p. 71). This is on all fours with Ludwig Stein's proof that pragmatism is merely the ideology of capitalism, for did not William James say that an idea is comparable to a check drawn on future experience whose validity is ultimately determined by its cash value? Such interpretations suggest a will not to understand, a willful failure to see that a belief in a free market of ideas is a belief in intellectual freedom, a freedom not necessarily dependent on a free market in commodities from which it is being distinguished.

In connection with the legitimacy of the Frankfurt School to be considered Marxist, two considerations are relevant here. Its acceptance of psychoanalysis as a key to the explanation of personal or social behavior, even, overlooking its scientific difficulties, is very dubious from Marx's point of view. Marx seeks to derive individual psychological needs and desires from social psychological norms. This would make the study of habit and habit formation more congenial to Marxism than burrowing in the recesses of the unconscious to uncover the causes of normal as well as neurotic behavior. For Marx, once he shed his Feuerbachian concept of species-man, there is no such thing as man's essential nature assumed by Horkheimer to be fulfilled by the contemplative life. "By acting on the external world and changing it," says Marx, "Man changes his own nature" (*Capital*, I, Kerr, trans., p. 198)— where the external world is not so much the physical world but the social-historical world. For Freud and his disciples, on the other hand, in any social system, the Oedipus complex would still operate as well as the aggressions of the id. If psychoanalysis is valid, especially in the claims made by Freud in *Civilization and Its Discontents*, Marxism is not, especially with respect to its social psychology. Of course both could be invalid.

Horkheimer has a strange conception of the nature of scientific method and philosophies like pragmatism that regard scientific method as the most reliable way of reaching truths. He charges that it glorifies "fact" and therefore must be a partisan of the *status-quo*, not understanding that any competent approach to "fact" must realize that facts by themselves have no significance except as related or relevant to a theory, or an hypothesis; and that every proposed experiment to test a theory involves a change in the given, an attempt to discover what might or may result from a rearrangement of the *status quo*. Whatever the difficulties and imperfections of the scientific approach, its achievements in pushing back the borders of human ignorance are *incontestable*. Even if there is no guarantee of success in its continued employment, there is some warrant in using its pattern of inquiry in exploring new phenomena and problems. What alternative method does Horkheimer propose that has not already been tried—Hegelian Reason? According to Marcuse in his *Hegel and the Revolution*, Reason fled from Berlin to Moscow in 1933. But even Marcuse, before he died, discovered that either Reason had found no asylum there or was transformed into the Unreason of absolute political terror.

The second consideration is the proud claim by Marx that his socialism was scientific. Marx's conception of scientific method may have been primitive, expressed as it was in the language of the time that used terms like "necessity" and "inevitability" loosely. But there is no doubt that Marx regarded his method as continuous with the methods of the natural sciences, and capable of reaching conclusions of the same type but not degree of objectivity as in other disciplines. Accepting the test of consequences, many of his key statements about historical and social developments have been proved wrong, and some have been substantiated. Nor can it reasonably be denied that Marx believed that his vision of the good society, in which the exploitation of man by man is abolished and the planned use of all natural and social resources, made the basis from which man is to leap into the kingdom of greater freedom, is possible only by the application of scientific method. Why, then, does Marx himself not come under the positivist ban of the Frankfurt School? Because of his progressive ideals? But Comte, Mach, and Dewey, not to mention lesser figures in the condemned positivist and pragmatic tradition, were no less progressive.

4. So far as I am aware, only on one explicit point have leading members of the Frankfurt School repudiated Marx. As everyone knows, Marx taught that the carrier of revolutionary ideals was to be the proletariat since it could not universalize the values it was struggling to achieve without transforming existing class society and therewith establishing, after a short transitional period, a classless society. "The emancipation of the working class can only be achieved through the working class," proclaimed Marx, and certainly not by philanthropists, charismatic religious leaders, intellectuals, and independent, critical thinkers who regarded themselves as free from any vested or class interest.

But the development of industrial society in the capitalist countries of the West has resulted, despite the existence of class antagonisms and class struggles, in a relatively homogeneous culture. Not only have the ideas of the dominant economic class become the dominant ideas of society, but the values, tastes, and aspirations of the dominant class, particularly in its frenzied preoccupation with consumption and transitory sensual excitement, have become dominant throughout society. The working class has become *bourgeoisified* and no longer—one may question whether it ever did—lives up to the heroic ideals of a class-conscious proletariat struggling to bring into birth a new socialist society forming within the shell of the old, a society in which "the free development of each is the condition of the free development of all." Contrast the ideals of the working class as Marx saw them—a working class which, he says, "regards its courage, self-confidence, independence, and sense of personal dignity as more necessary than its daily bread"—with the ideals of today's working class, whether organized or unorganized, in any capitalist country. According to the Frankfurt School, and here Marcuse is the most eloquent among them, the working classes have been corrupted by the ethics of consumption arising from the needs of a market economy to clear its stocks in the quest for ever renewed pursuit of profit.

There is no hope, according to Marcuse, for revolutionary change by a bourgeoisified proletariat. Instead, one must look for revolutionary action through a coalition of the outcasts and oppressed—those whom Marx called the *lumpenproletariat*, the racial and ethnic minorities, feminists with raised consciousness of male chauvinism, and intellectuals who have not been co-opted by the system. This resistance movement is to develop the counterculture to protest the philistinism and vulgarity of the dominant culture, and to prepare by educational means, including demonstrations and civil disobedience, for the new society. The appearance of tolerance in bourgeois society is basically repressive against genuine social change. Within the universities, violence is to be eschewed, but intense agitation and demonstration should be made for the strategy of a new, different and enlightened kind of "repressive tolerance." (This position seems to be uniquely Marcuse's.) Not only in the future but now, the coalition that constitutes the resistance, especially the students among them, must urge a policy of enlightened repressive tolerance. This consists of two main principles. First an attack on false tolerance. Marcuse admits that within the existing university structure supported by subsidies from the state and the dominant economic class, tolerance exists for right and left, for Fascist and Communist, for black and white, for Marcuse and Marcuse's critics. But he denounces this tolerance as false because it is impartial. Impartiality and neutrality in the presentation of all sides can result only in the triumph of the worse over the better because the consumer-oriented minds of students cannot grasp the imperatives of Reason. True tolerance he contends "would include the withdrawal of toleration of speech and assembly from groups and movements which promote aggressive policies, armaments, chauvinism, discrimination on grounds of race and religion, or which oppose the extension of public services, social security or medical care, etc." This policy is to hold within the university as well as without. Moreover, "the restoration of freedom of thought may necessitate new and rigid restrictions on teaching and practice in educational institutions."

There is something ironical about the fact that under the protection of the false doctrine of tolerance which he has denounced, Marcuse has led a flourishing life in the university instead of becoming a victim of a reverse policy of repressive tolerance that would have denied academic freedom to others. To Marcuse, however, there was no irony in this situation but merely *die List der Vernunft.*

5. Regardless of the validity of Marx's historical and economic analyses and predictions, sober scholarship will show that he consistently defended individual freedom and the democratic principles of a self-governing community. Some of his other doctrines may have implications that threaten the principles of freedom and democracy, but this would only prove, if that turned out to be the case, not that Marx did not hold these principles but only that like some other thinkers, he was inconsistent. Marx was an ardent proponent of popular sovereignty through universal suffrage. He lived long enough to modify his call for forcible overthrow in the *Manifesto,* written at a time when the vast majority of the working class, if not the general population, was politically disenfranchised, and to maintain together with Engels that socialism could be achieved through the constitutional means of universal suffrage. If anything, there was a kind of utopianism in Marx's pious faith in the spontaneity and ultimate validity of the judgment of the working class, and in his belief that even when it followed wrong paths—i.e., different from those he urged—it would learn from its own experience, and that the unenlightened majority would in time become the enlightened majority and introduce socialism. He was not prepared to force socialism down the throats of the working class and denounced others who proposed dictatorial seizure of power by enlightened minorities for the sake of others.

The attitude that pervades the entire corpus of writings of the members of the Frankfurt School is different from that of Marx. Rather it is one of contempt for the choice of the masses from the standpoint of a privileged cultural élite. This is illustrated especially in the unbridled attack on popular or mass culture. I am not objecting to the criticism of the shoddiness and tawdriness of popular culture even when it assumes the guise of modernity. To hold up standards of quality, to cultivate the forms and models of the best of what has been thought and achieved in past cultures and to compare them invidiously with the cult of thrills and sensation in the popular arts is always legitimate. But what is objectionable is to contest the right of the masses to make their own choices in choosing modes of experience and ways of life uncongenial to those who regard themselves as the cultural élite. At most, the élite can offer examples of high culture, and often as in the case of music, museum attendance, and fine films there has been a perceptible growth in the quality of popular appreciations. But the masses have a right to their own cultural preferences even if they are being deceived by the tinsel in which the cultural goods are sold to them. There is an arrogance in Horkheimer's contention that mass culture "sells people a way of life in which they are fixed and which they unconsciously abhor but overtly acclaim." If, after listening to Horkheimer and his colleagues denounce their way of life, people still overtly acclaim mass culture and persist in their cults of consumption and immediate gratification, how does Horkheimer know that they unconsciously abhor them? How easy is it to go on to a policy that would consciously deny the right of the masses to choose what they unconsciously abhor?

The extent to which this antidemocratic attitude pervades the political thinking of the Frankfurt School was revealed in the course of a public discussion between Marcuse and myself during the *Partisan Review* Seminar on "The Idea of the Future" at Rutgers University in June 1965. Marcuse had delivered himself of his customary litany of denunciation of the low cultural level of the population, its tolerance of injustice and indifference to the deprivation of the materially distressed, as well as to the sufferings of the politically and spiritually oppressed. I objected to the unrelieved grimness of the black on black picture Marcuse was drawing and called attention to the significance of the Civil Rights Acts Congress had passed and which already had made a heartening difference in improving the political and social life of the blacks and which promised even more. "What's the good of all that," Marcuse countered, "since the politically liberated blacks are choosing the same dismal values and life-styles of the white workers, seduced by the opportunities to consume shoddy goods and wallow in the degrading excitements of the popular art?"

I then directed the following question to him: "Which situation would you prefer: one in which the blacks had no political freedom to vote or to choose the cultural values they pleased, or one in which they had these freedoms but chose unwisely?" After a moment's hesitation, he replied "Well, since I have already gone out on a limb, I may as well go all the way. I would prefer that the blacks did not have the right to choose wrongly."[1] And who

---

[1] I reported this exchange in a letter to *The New York Sunday Times Magazine*, Nov. 10, 1968. In a public address on May 18, 1969, Marcuse criticized the American

would make the determination of what a wrong choice was? Naturally, Marcuse and the other partisans of Reason. This undisguised paternalism is incompatible with any conception of a democratic policy. It is reminiscent of the tradition of enlightened despotism from Plato to modern totalitarianism according to which the rulers are better judges of the true interests of those over whom they rule than the people themselves.

I conclude that although not everything the Frankfurt School stands for is false, it cannot be regarded as a legitimate Marxist school; nor can any of its non-Marxist analyses of our culture solve any of the problems that Marx himself failed to do.

Civil Liberties Union of Southern California, which had defended *his* right to speak and teach from attacks by cultural vigilantes, for its stand on free speech (*New York Times*, May 19, 1969).

CHAPTER ELEVEN

John Reed, Romantic

John Reed became a legendary figure in the Pantheon of revolutionary heroes not in virtue of any deeds but of the publication of his *Ten Days That Shook the World*. Lenin in a short introduction hailed the book as "a truthful and vivid exposition of the events" that culminated in the Bolshevik seizure of power in October 1917. Its vividness is unquestionable; its truthfulness something else again. Even when its truthfulness is in doubt, there is no deliberate deception. The bias enters into the selectivity of the things and words recorded, the tone and mood of the writing, the adjectives applied to those who appear to him as congenial or sinister. It certainly is a faithful rendering of Reed's impressions of what was going on around him.

The book had millions of readers in multiple translations until the advent of Stalin. It was then suppressed by the Communist presses of the world because of the key role attributed to Trotsky who loomed all the larger because his Georgian rival was barely mentioned. Regardless, however, of the historian's judgment of John Reed's objectivity, were it not for his book on the Russian October Revolution, neither he nor his wife, Louise Bryant, would be the subject of any great biographical interest.

So Short a Time,[1] by Barbara Gelb, a biography of John Reed and Louise Bryant, is a sensitive and compassionately written account of the short, frenetic careers of two courageous and mildly talented persons caught up in a vast historical transformation which they romanticized without understanding its costs and fateful consequences. If Reed achieved distinction through his book, Louise Bryant achieved distinction only through her relations with Reed. His life, ending with the onset of his disillusion, can be considered

---

[1]Barbara Gelb, *So Short a Time* (New York: W. W. Norton & Co., Inc., 1973)

tragic. Hers was pathetic. In her own right she would never have been noticed. She was completely dependent upon the men she knew—and deceived. After the shock of Reed's death and an ill-starred marriage to William Bullitt, left only with her memories she lost herself in drugs and alcohol. They were of an age. Reed died when he was 33; Louise Bryant 16 years later at the age of 49.

Upton Sinclair once referred to John Reed as "the playboy of the Revolution"—an unjust remark which he lived to regret. No playboy ever evinced Reed's moral courage in defending unpopular causes; nor his physical courage when threatened with death by an illiterate soldiery; nor endured hardships so uncomplainingly. He was capable of great personal sacrifice, was free of snobbery, and although burdened with a sense of guilt as a social parasite before he found his vocation, never took himself too seriously. At the same time he was an incurable romantic with a craving for risk and adventure, politically naive despite an air of sophistication, theoretically unprepared to understand the significance of what appeared to him as merely esoteric controversies which divided the revolutionary ranks.

It is hard to see how Mrs. Gelb could have improved her biography of this oddly matched pair of Bohemian acolytes of love, poetry and revolution without going much more deeply into the events of the October Revolution on whose interpretation John Reed rode to fame. She has uncovered some new details in the lives of Reed and his wife, especially the latter's strange interlude with Eugene O'Neill. The book is likely to have a greater effect at second remove. It invites readers with memories of the original impact of *Ten Days That Shook the World* to revisit the scene, so to speak, and assess the insights and qualities of writing that made the volume a revolutionary source book and classic.

Reed made no pretense of scholarly qualification. He wrote as a "conscientious reporter." His knowledge of Russian was scanty, and he was confessedly dependent upon handouts, hearsay, and inside explanations he could not control. Nonetheless he was eminently successful in communicating the color, excitement, confusion, danger, and agonies of the crucial days when power changed hands. The reader sometimes feels he is an eyewitness of the events described. Reed's sympathies from the moment of his arrival were with the Bolsheviks with whose history and political strategy he was completely unfamiliar. Their dynamism, opportunism, and willingness to gamble their lives and the fate of the revolution against overwhelming odds appealed to his own reckless nature.

He accepted their version of the July days when they sought to overthrow Kerensky as a spontaneous mass action. He swallowed their demagogic rhetoric at face value but disregarded the warnings of their socialist critics who invoked Marx against Lenin, and whose dire predictions were soon to be confirmed, as irrelevant Talmudic exegesis.

Reed was a master of the anecdotal method using it deftly to convey an impression to the reader of the authenticity of mass moods. He did this by projecting his own emotional reactions to some incident or speech on the encompassing political horizon. Thus when *Pravda* printed Lenin's denunciation of some of his erstwhile disciples who charged the Bolsheviks with establishing a dictatorship not *of* the proletariat but *over* the proletariat as well as over other classes, Reed wrote: "The response from the whole country was like a blast of hot air [against the insurgents]." When the Military Revolutionary Committee placarded the walls of Petrograd threatening extreme terrorist measures against government functionaries on strike, Reed wrote: "The masses of workers and soldiers responded [in support] by a savage tremor of rage, which swept all Russia." All this was poetic invention. Reed was never in a position to canvass the sentiment of "all Russia" or "the whole country."

However the one great central insight of Reed's book was confirmed by subsequent events and by later chroniclers of almost all shades of opinion—an insight which explains not only the Bolshevik triumph but why the Provisional Government lost out and could not rally a successful counterthrust to the coup at Petrograd. This was the complete and utter war weariness of the Russian masses and the technical inability of any Russian regime to continue the war against Germany. It was not as Marxists, Socialists, or Communists that the Bolsheviks won but chiefly as resolute opponents of the war. This was also the source of their subsequent influence in Western countries. Before he died Kerensky admitted in a poignant conversation with me that his greatest error was not the policy of relative moderation he pursued toward the Bolsheviks but his failure to take Russia out of the war after Kornilov's revolt. Reed's perception of this situation was sharpened by his own passionate antiwar sentiment and his earlier bitter experiences reporting the carnage in war-torn Europe.

With respect to almost everything else, although a first-rate reporter of the surface of events, Reed's naiveté was apparent as soon as he ventured on political analysis. Bertram Wolfe in his masterly introduction to the 1960 edition of *Ten Days That*

Shook the World (New York: Vintage Books) quotes an unnamed participant in the dramatic events at Petrograd to the effect that Reed "did not know whether he was celebrating a marriage or a funeral." Reed would have replied that it was a double celebration by and about different historical personae. In justice to him one must acknowledge that when he penned his book there was not the slightest sign of any canker of doubt or skepticism in his attitude. (That was to come later after he returned to Soviet Russia and became embroiled in the politics of the Comintern.) His mood was euphoric. The concluding pages express an intense faith in the October Revolution as the harbinger of a new society of justice, peace, and freedom.

The thinking behind that faith was pathetic. He was capable of writing to his wife, advising her on how to present the Bolshevik takeover persuasively to American farmers, that although all private property in land had been abolished, the Russian peasants need fear no interference with their freedom to farm the land, "since the government owned the land and the farmers and workers *were* the government. They object, of course, to anything which takes the ownership of their land away from them; but they should understand that private property in land is just a means of being secure in possession of it, which public ownership under Bolshevism makes them automatically."

Most disheartening is the evidence that Reed's will to believe eroded his faith in democracy. When his commitment to revolution was challenged, he justified it on the ground that the revolution expressed "the will of the great majority." He plays up on many pages the Bolshevik demand for the convocation of the Constituent Assembly as the most authoritative institution of the new Russian democracy. Yet when Reed completed his book on New Year's Day 1919, he knew that the Bolsheviks had already bayoneted it out of existence the previous January. They had garnered less than 20 percent of the vote. Even in Petrograd which the Bolsheviks tightly controlled they received less than 50 percent of the votes cast. Yet Reed swallowed without any compunction the forcible suppression of the Constituent Assembly—an act that led Rosa Luxemburg to a final break with Bolshevism, and which prepared the way for Leninist terror and Stalinist totalitarianism.

According to Balabanoff, Gitlow, and Eastman, John Reed died a bitterly disappointed rebel. Had he lived and escaped from the Soviet Union would he have disavowed his book to prevent it from nurturing similar illusions in others? He certainly would have scorned Stalin and all his works. But would he have acknowledged—as Trotsky and other Leninists refused to do—that the system which made Stalin possible was not built by Stalin alone? One would have liked Mrs. Gelb to have explored the question. As it stands it is a highly creditable account of two lives illuminated by the incandescence of a great historical event.

CHAPTER TWELVE

Out of the Depths

The informed reader may wonder about the justification of including a discussion of the conditions existing under the Stalinist Soviet regime in a volume dedicated to Marxist studies. As we have already noted, one can plead in extenuation that like the term "Christian," the term "Marxist" has become so elastic in its historical connotations that such a discussion should not occasion wonder or intellectual discomfort. If it is legitimate to consider the history of the Spanish Inquisition in the history of Christianity, it certainly is legitimate to consider the development of Stalinism in the historical assessment of Marxism broadly understood.

There are other reasons that give an even greater plausibility to this discussion. Few scholars would deny that Stalin was the ideological and organizational heir of Lenin, provided this did not entail a belief in the complete identity of their doctrines and practices. There is a certain ambiguity in Lenin's attitude toward the doctrine of socialism in one country. But concerning the role of the Communist Party in taking and keeping political power, the structure of the Communist Party itself, the meaning and functioning of Party dictatorship there is little difference between Lenin and Stalin (and Trotsky, too).

It may be objected that precisely at this point there is a sharp cleavage between Marx and Lenin, including all of Lenin's epigoni. There is not a line in Marx that identifies the rule of the working class with the dictatorship of a minority party not only over the proletariat but over all society. This would exclude a study of Stalin and Stalinism from a volume devoted to a critical analysis of Marx's ideas but not from a study of Marxism as an historical *movement*.

Ernest Renan, the great French historian and philologist, is reputed to have said, "Happy is a people who have inherited a revolution, woe to those who make it." This is certainly not true

135

for all revolutions. The February (1917) Revolution against the Czarist regime was almost bloodless. The Bolshevik October Revolution against the Kerensky regime has left a legacy of suffering and oppression much worse than the bloodshed and terror that spawned its birth. Anton Antonov-Ovseyenko, the author of *The Time of Stalin: A Portrait of a Tyranny*,[1] was born after the October Revolution. His father, the famous revolutionary, Vladimir Antonov-Ovseyenko, headed the Bolshevik forces that stormed the Winter Palace in 1917, and was chief political commissar of the Red Army from 1922 to 1924, a position next in importance to that of Leon Trotsky. The father died in Stalin's blood purges of 1938, accused of having been a secret agent of Western imperialists from the very outset of his career. The mother committed suicide in one of Stalin's prisons. The son, for no other reason than his relationship, spent twelve years in the Gulag Archipelago from which he emerged blind and in shattered health a few years after Stalin's death.

According to Anton Antonov-Ovseyenko, although his father was posthumously exonerated under Khrushchev's leadership, his name and memory are still being defamed by the cowed servitors of the existing regime whose principals have halted the progress made in the process of destalinization. The son has devoted himself to telling the truth, as he knows it and feels it, about the time of Stalin. The original Russian edition from which this English translation was made was published not in the USSR but in New York. Stephen Cohen, the biographer of Bukharin, tells us in his introduction that Anton Antonov-Ovseyenko "is the only child of a martyred Soviet founding father to emerge as both a witness and historian of Stalinism." He has been able to learn a great many things by virtue of his parentage and his own fate as a victim and from descriptions in unpublished memoirs and letters of observers and survivors of his period for which there is no public documentary record.

This is a book whose study should be mandatory for all students interested in the history of the Soviet Union under Stalin's rule. It contains material hitherto not revealed outside the Soviet Union, and its authenticity will have to be assessed by scholars in the years to come. For example, Antonov-Ovseyenko makes reference to the existence of a letter—on the strength of the testimony of an unnamed witness—from Tito to Stalin that reads: "Stalin, you've

---

[1] Anton Antonov-Ovseyenko, *The Time of Stalin: A Portrait of a Tyranny*, trans. George Saunders (New York & London: Harper & Row, 1981)

sent seven men after me—with pistols, grenades and poison. If I send one, I won't have to send another. Josip Tito." Many other reports sound plausible, but the plausible is not necessarily true. Without other evidence no critical historian can accept this purported letter from Tito as authentic.

For the general reader, however, this is a book only for those with strong nerves. I have been a close reader of the voluminous literature published by the victims of Soviet terror ever since Tchernavin's *I Speak for the Silent*. But I have never read anything as searing as Antonov-Ovseyenko's account. It is like being present in a chamber where a person is being tortured. Its impact is more devastating than Aleksandr Solzhenitsyn's three volumes on the Gulag Archipelago. The author's pain and frustration, his sense of outrage at the brutalities and indignities visited upon the innocent, including children, his indignation with the fellow travelers abroad and other "useful idiots" (Lenin's phrase) who denied or apologized for Soviet terror rise from almost every page. His graphic description of the mood of terror and its effects on the populace read like pages out of Orwell's *1984*. It is not surprising that his passionate hatred of Stalin, whom he regards as the chief architect of the Soviet structure of terror, would make him somewhat credulous to reports concerning Stalin's early career as "an intriguer and provocateur." He goes so far as to suggest that since Stalin was capable of having acted as an agent of the czarist secret police, there may be something in the hitherto unsubstantiated charges of Isaac Don Levine and Alexander Orlov.

However, Antonov-Ovseyenko does establish some things. Stalin, Trotsky to the contrary notwithstanding, was no mediocrity. He was a man of powerful character, actually "a genius of evil," as Ronald Hingley characterizes him in his recent biography. The astonishing thing is that Stalin was able to conceal this from those who were politically so close to him, Lenin and his lieutenants, and also from the statesmen of the Western world who readily judged Hitler by his deeds but refused to make appropriate inferences from Stalin's political behavior. Neither Churchill nor Roosevelt had a glimmer of the man they were dealing with, one who, in turn, suspected them of deep duplicity since their naiveté was incredible to him. Nothing speaks more eloquently of the pathetic unawareness of the statesmen of the Western world than Canadian Prime Minister Mackenzie King's reaction to Gouzenko's defection from the Soviet embassy in Ottawa with documents revealing the vast Soviet espionage operation against its wartime allies. Reporting to the House of Commons, King said:

I told the man Gouzenko he should go back and put it into the Soviet files, that we did not want it. And the reason I did it . . . I did not want to complicate relations with Russia. From what I have heard and know about Premier Stalin, I am confident that the Russian leader would not countenance or condone such action in one of his country's Embassies.

With views such as this influencing the perception of post-World War II realities by allied leaders, it is difficult to resist the notion that Providence played a benevolent role in directing the outcome of Western and American foreign policy. But the inhabitants of the Baltic and East European states must have bitterly wondered why He did not extend his protection to them.

There are other puzzling phenomena that Antonov-Ovseyenko clarifies in heartrending detail. Why did innocent men and women confess to deeds that they could not possibly have committed and fabricate, at the instigation of their interrogators, fantastic tales involving other completely innocent persons? After reading this book no one can doubt that it was torture, actual and threatened, to themselves and their loved ones that explains the confessions— torture both brutal and refined, sustained until the victim capitulated or collapsed. Even so, many unsung and until now unhonored heroes withstood this torture. Some survived. But the great majority yielded. The extraction of confessions became a fine art. Interrogators vied with each other in the achievement of results. In addition, "an investigator earned a bonus of two thousand rubles for each confession." Sadism became a well-paid habit.

Here we also have an explanation of why Khrushchev's program of destalinization was stopped in its tracks. It was not because, after Solzhenitsyn's *One Day in the Life of Ivan Denisovich*, the Soviet presses were overwhelmed by a Niagara of personal memoirs of similar and worse days. Rather it was because destalinization, if continued, would have required the exposure, if not the punishment, of at least a half-million officials and bureaucrats, great and small, who conscientiously and often enthusiastically had participated in the destruction of the innocent. Torture had become a way of life for so many that the only thing that mattered to them was survival and the natural fear that they would meet the fate of Lavrenti Beria, who, after Stalin, was the head of the apparatus of repression. It is clear that genuine repentance had not moved Khrushchev to make his revelations before the Twentieth Congress of the Soviet Communist Party; rather, it was the necessity of outmaneuvering Georgi Malenkov, Vyacheslav Molotov, and the other hard-liners. In the apocryphal pages of *Khrushchev Remembers*, the former premier writes, "It would have been better to tell everything. Murder will always out." Antonov-Ovseyenko laments that murder is not yet out in the Soviet Union, that its perpetrators sit enthroned in comfort.

Ignorance can be criminal but unpunished crime is doubly criminal. There is no adequate punishment for the fanatical bigotry and cruelty of the Stalinschina, but at least Stalin's thugs should not be left in comfort, prosperity, and obscurity. The butchers of Ravensburg, Auschwitz, and Dachau have been punished. Why haven't the butchers of Solovki, Kolyma, and Bamlag ever been named? I'm not asking for punishment. Simply that their names be published.

Even the most sympathetic reader will not fail to note that Antonov-Ovseyenko's answers to some of the key questions he poses are hardly adequate. If Stalin was such a monstrous and corrupt creature even before he schemed his way into power, how was it that his closest comrades, especially Lenin, did not recognize the true lineaments of his character? Consummate artistry on Stalin's part? Hardly. He did not conceal his rudeness from Lenin, but neither Lenin nor Trotsky nor any of Stalin's future victims discerned the bloodthirsty lust for total power behind the smiling mask. Antonov-Ovseyenko treats Lenin's responsibility for Stalin very gingerly. In one place he recognizes that "Lenin's doctrine of the dictatorship of the proletariat contributed to the usurpation of power by a dictator more than anything else." But he is silent about the dictatorial methods that Lenin himself employed against non-Communists. It was not simply the belief in the dictatorship of the proletariat—which can be construed as it was by Friedrich Engels and others as referring to the economic program of a legally and democratically elected government of the entire population— that constituted the poisoned premise from which the theorems of totalitarianism were derived. It was Lenin's dogma, shared equally by Trotsky and Stalin, that the dictatorship of the proletariat could be exercised only through the dictatorship of the minority Communist Party *over* the proletariat and the entire population which set in train the fearful consequences.

Nor have we an adequate explanation of why Stalin spared such figures as Tarlé, Maisky, Pavlov, Jaffe, and Litvinov, who by history and conviction were further removed from him than many of his victims. Antonov-Ovseyenko opines that Stalin thought they could be useful for his purposes. But thousands of those he sent to their cruel deaths were potentially of greater use to him.

One crucial question Antonov-Ovseyenko does not discuss at all. Why in the light of Stalin's oppressive terror was there no organized opposition to him? Why no effort by colleagues, friends, and admirers of those Stalin crushed to overthrow him instead of passively waiting their turn to be liquidated? After all, Hitler's domestic regime was not as oppressive to the majority of his subjects as Stalin's was to the great mass of Soviet peasants and workers. Yet there were plots against Hitler and at least one failed effort. But there is no objective evidence of any movement directed against Stalin. The notion that Stalin "had to play rough" because there was a conspiracy against him—the line handed out by spokesmen for the Kremlin to soothe the sensibilities of their supporters abroad who were shocked by wholesale murder—is properly dismissed by Antonov-Ovseyenko as "unholy nonsense." Granted—but why no opposition despite the century-old traditions of revolutionary opposition to despotism?

The only plausible explanation I have heard came from General Walter Krivitsky of Soviet military intelligence, who defected to the West in the late 1930s. He told me that the government, through the secret police, organized its own opposition. It recruited tens of thousands of agents and informers who were sent out into the population. Like magnets attracting steel filings, these individuals attracted all elements who for one reason or another were discontented and critical. Periodically they were gathered in. Most of them were severely punished. Many rendered contrite by the magnanimity of the government—which promised to suspend punishment, subject to their future behavior—willingly accepted the role of magnet of other dissidents. Under such circumstances it is hard to see how a genuine opposition movement could be organized. Even the apparently spontaneous expression of dissatisfaction by a person's fellow worker could be a provocation. Safety could only lie in denouncing him.

Today in the Soviet Union the worst of Stalin's excesses have been limited; the concentration camps still exist, but not on such a vast scale. Refinements of torture have been introduced that escaped Stalin's ingenuity: sentencing dissidents to insane asylums where they are demoralized by drugs, for example. The system that spawned Stalin is still intact. Although it is improbable that the Stalinschina will recur in the same form, it is not precluded that something similar—or worse—may still arise in the future. The prospects of a democratic revolution from below are bleak. Perhaps if there is a falling-out among Leonid Brezhnev's successors, one of the contenders for popular support may seek to liberalize the system from above. But whatever happens, it will have little to do with Marx's conception of a free and classless society.

CHAPTER THIRTEEN

Some Fables of
American "Fear & Terror"

It is a well known phenomenon that without containing a single falsehood, a description of an historical situation, personage or event can still be a lying account. Indeed, every statement made may be literally true, and yet the drift and impact of the whole story egregiously false. This approach is the stock in trade of clever and unscrupulous attorneys in an adversary procedure more concerned with saving a client than in seeing justice done. Dishonest journalists under the pretext of advocacy-reporting resort to similar techniques. And it is an old story that political demagogues out to smear an opponent or to make the worse appear the better cause are adept in using some truths to conceal or distort the facts. But whatever the circumstances of the use of such methods, there is absolutely no place for it in any undertaking that professes to be a contribution to scholarly understanding.

David Caute's *The Great Fear*[1] is a massive volume that has the appearance of a scholarly work that has been meticulously researched with more than a hundred pages of notes, references and bibliographical items. The appearance is deceptive. It is an impassioned political attack by a British author against the policy of the United States at the end of the Second World War when with the resumption of Communist aggression against the West and the revelations of the pervasive nature of Soviet espionage, a loyalty and security program was introduced by the government. The period covered includes the Hiss, Rosenberg, and Coplon trials, and the conviction of the leaders of the Communist Party

---

[1]David Caute, *The Great Fear: The Anti-Communist Purge under Truman and Eisenhower* (New York: Simon & Schuster, 1978)

under the Smith Act, as well as the Korean War, McCarthy's demagogic crusade and the entire era of "the Cold War." The villains are *not* the Communists, all of whom were staunch Stalinists who supported without qualification every infamy of the Kremlin. They are gently chided by Caute for not standing up on occasion more firmly for their principles. Nor is it Joseph McCarthy and his disciples whose role, for all its irresponsible demagogy, Caute regards as "historically healthy" because its very extremism shocked the public into awareness that liberty was "not easily divisible." The real villains were the "Cold War liberals" or "liberal anti-Communists" who detested both the Communists and McCarthy's methods of combating them. Caute's moral indignation is directed mainly against them. Because as liberals they believed in principled opposition to Communism as well as to Fascism, they prepared the way, according to Caute, for reactionaries who, like McCarthy, found difficulty in distinguishing between socialists and Communists, between heretics and conspirators. From Caute's position, Harry Truman is more to blame than Joe McCarthy, and those who defended "the vital centre" against totalitarianism of every cut and colour were a greater threat to genuine freedom and democracy than the Communists.

Throughout the volume, Caute seeks to establish an equation between the American security program under Truman and the Stalinist terror regime while admitting that the first resulted in tears, the second in rivers of blood. He sees what happened in America as the logical consequence of a struggle to impose the *Pax Americana* on the world in the struggle against the *Pax Sovietica*.

Both Washington and Moscow were now committed not merely to a Manichaean struggle for the allegiance (or subservience) of the world, but also to absolute conformity [*sic!*] among their own citizens.

Caute doesn't bother to explain what American actions in Europe in 1948 corresponded to the Communist coup in Czechoslovakia, the merciless Soviet repressions in the Baltic countries, and the seizure of power in Poland and other Eastern European nations. Nor does he point to any Soviet analogue of the Marshall Plan and of the American willingness to surrender its monopoly of atomic weapons (the Baruch-Lilienthal proposals) to an international authority. And as for the American desire to impose "absolute conformity" on its citizens, it is a pity that he does not cite the decrees of the U.S. Cabinet or Congress laying down the proper American party line in all fields from art and astronomy to zoology which presumably parallel the decrees of the Central Committee of the Russian Communist Party in these areas, violations of which often resulted in imprisonment and sometimes death.

That Caute can bring himself to write this way is some indication of how far his obsessions can take him. They soon show themselves to be beyond any rational control.

The result of Caute's survey of the period is a fantasy picture of a nation swept by hysterias of fear synthetically contrived by its political leaders. A reader unfamiliar with the political climate of these years would never guess from Caute's account that there was an objective danger of war with the Soviet Union and that from June 1950 on the United States was actually involved in an undeclared war with Communist North Korea, and shortly later with Communist China, that threatened to burst into a world conflagration. To compare this period with the genuine reign of terror in the United States that existed immediately after World War I—when there was not the slightest threat to the security of the United States and when most excesses by law enforcement authorities were of an extra-legal character—is to abuse language. Caute echoes the declaration of a Communist fellow-travelling organization that the measures taken to prevent Communist infiltration into government and to expose Communist activities in American cultural life constituted "the most serious threat to civil liberties in our [US] history." Even granting the absurdity of some of these measures, the judgment is clear evidence not only of historical ignorance but of political animus.

The gravest intellectual deficiency in Caute's work is its failure to state fairly and come to grips with the arguments and evidence of those whom he denounces. He doesn't argue—he merely jeers. The books and speeches of the leading cold war liberals and socialists who waged energetic campaigns against *both* Communism and McCarthyism—of Norman Thomas, Elmer Davis, Walter Lippmann, David Dubinsky, Walter Reuther, Arthur Schlesinger Jr., Hubert H. Humphrey, to name only a few—are practically ignored. The result is that Caute fails to make certain elementary distinctions which must be recognized by anyone familiar with the theory and practice of Communism, and endowed with a modicum of common sense. He does not distinguish between the necessity of a security program and the mistakes or excesses of its application, seemingly convinced that the occasional existence of the latter totally invalidates the former. In keeping with this view, to Caute it makes no difference whether a person is truly or falsely accused of being a member of the Communist Party. In either case he or she is the innocent victim of a witch hunt. And despite the record, he seems convinced that Communists are not more harmful than witches. Indeed just as the fear of witches constitutes a greater danger than witches, so to him the fear of Communism is a greater danger to democracy than the Communist movement.

At first blush, the most charitable interpretation of Caute's approach to the period he is discussing and the issues at stake is that it is a compound of political ignorance and naïveté. Even so, it is an approach worth examining because it explains in large part the state of mind, sincerely held in the case of some British officials, that made it possible for Fuchs, Allan Nunn May, Burgess, Maclean, Philby, Pontecorvo among others, to escape detection in the performance of services for the Kremlin, and whose mischievous effects for the free world to this day have not been properly assessed. This laxity and indifference toward ideological allegiance and commitment was also characteristic of the American administration before the Igor Gouzenko case broke in Canada and the publication of the explosive Royal Commission Report.[2] If anything, American officialdom at the outset was more at fault because since August 1939 it had in its possession a list of highly placed Communists in U.S. government service who were feeding information to the Soviet Union.

American liberalism before the Roosevelt New Deal era was unconcerned with the problem of security except in the guise of social security. In the main it was an opposition movement to entrenched political privilege, allied at times with populism in the interest of the social and economic "underdog." Only gradually, painfully and confusedly did it become aware of the emergence of Fascist and Communist movements working in concert with foreign powers whose threat created a problem of political security without which the desirable social securities of a democratic welfare state might be lost. It was none other than Roger Baldwin who, together with Norman Thomas had organized the American Civil Liberties Union, which once was the conscience of genuine American liberalism, who declared that "a superior loyalty to a foreign government disqualifies a citizen from service to his own." In the case of the German-American Bund, Caute has no difficulty in recognizing the common-sense justification of the safeguard. But

---

[2]*The Report of the Royal Commission to Investigate the Facts Relating to and Circumstances Surrounding the Communication by Public Officials and Other Persons in Positions of Trust of Secret and Confidential Information to Agents of a Foreign Power* (Ottawa, 1946).

with respect to the American Communist Party, he exhibits the typical ritualistic liberal syndrome, viz.—democracy has no real enemies on its Left, for Communists are extreme liberals, misguided, but well-intentioned, at most heretics not conspirators. Except for Communist Party leaders, he is often loath to identify those whose views are indistinguishable from the official party line as "Communists." They are referred to as "Leftists."

Amazing but true. Caute refuses to recognize that in the days of monolithic Stalinism, long before the emergence of polycentrism and Euro-Communism, the American Communist Party was a Leninist party, controlled in its program and leadership by the Kremlin, organized with an underground apparatus, its membership largely secret, identified by party names, and subject to the discipline of expulsion by a Control Commission in the event that a party order was disobeyed. There is a whole library of literature on this subject as well as on the canonic doctrines of belief concerning the use of force and violence, more specifically the ultimate necessity of armed uprisings, in the conquest of political power. Caute would have us believe that the American Communist Party was forced underground by the Smith Act indictments in 1948. This is false. Whatever one believes about the wisdom of the Smith Act, whose necessity was questioned by many of the Cold War liberals whose integrity Caute impugns—the Smith Act was applauded by the Communist Party when it was invoked against the Trotskyists!—the Communist Party, in accordance with Lenin's directives, and indeed as a condition of its affiliation with the Communist International, had a parallel underground organization from the very beginning.

One may attribute to credulity Caute's acceptance of the Communist Party claim that it was just an ordinary American political party, like any other, and therefore membership in or association with it, should be treated in the same way as membership in, or association with, other political parties. But unless there are no limits to Caute's credulity, it is hard to escape the impression of disingenuousness on his part, when he buys the apologetic explanation of leaders of the Communist Party when confronted with their own party texts, that they really did not believe in force and violence except in resisting a counter-revolutionary rebellion against a democratic majority that has come peacefully to power. But this is what any party that accepts democracy believes! How then explain the absolute control of the American Communist Party by the Kremlin down to the ditching of Earl Browder? Caute is aware that at a time when war with the Soviet Union over the blockade of Berlin was a real possibility the leaders of the Communist Party openly pledged that in such an eventuality their party would support the Soviet Union with every means at their disposal. To Caute this stand was still a harmless heresy, a mere matter of words, for "no plausible evidence ever emerged to prove that the CP drew contingency plans to sabotage vital industries and lines of communication in the event of war." A Fifth Column in place does not need to draw up plans in advance. In any case it is absurd to demand proof of detailed sabotage or espionage plans as a precondition for barring declared enemies from any official position of influence. As a matter of fact, a strike engineered by a Communist Party leadership in a key industry under the pretext of fighting some "job issue" could have an even more disastrous effect than a few monkey wrenches in the machinery of a factory.

The incontrovertible point here is not that Communist Party membership or leadership is or should be a criminal offense—so far as I know only Walter Lippmann and Hubert Humphrey favored outlawing the Communist Party—but that membership in the Communist Party as it was organized and oriented *at that time* was certainly *relevant*, among other considerations, in determining who was a security risk in government services or in industries related to defense. Nor in the light of all the available evidence does it follow that *every* member of the Communist Party is *ipso facto* a Fifth Columnist or espionage agent. Surely, it may be objected, and this is implicit in Caute's criticism of the American security program, a person may be a member of the Communist Party and pledged to defend the Soviet Union at all costs, and yet when actually called upon to redeem his pledge be unwilling to betray his country. Is it not possible for some members of the Communist Party to be loyal to their own country, despite their ideology, rather than to the Soviet Union, "the worker's fatherland"?

The best answer to this question was made by Clement Attlee after Dr. Pontecorvo had fled from England and the empty stables were firmly locked. The Prime Minister told the House of Commons,

There is no way of distinguishing such [hypothetically loyal Communists] from those who, if opportunity offered, would be prepared to endanger the security of the state in the interests of another power. The Government has, therefore, reached the conclusion that the only prudent course to adopt is to ensure that no one who is known to be a member of the Communist Party, *or to be associated with it in such a way as to raise legitimate doubts about his or her reliability*, is employed in connection with work, the nature of which is vital to the security of the State. (My italics.)

The connection may extend to apparently humble positions. Caute keeps on insisting that the Communist Party was no more than a gnat; but even by his own account, it was more like a swarm of gnats. And although one could dispute the methods used to get rid of gnats—some gnats carry deadly disease germs—apparently Caute would simply ignore them until they did their work of contamination.

In any case, comparison of the Communist Party to a gnat seems somewhat bizarre. Its influence especially through its transmission-belt organizations on the cultural-political life of the US during the 1930s was enormous. It has been amply documented by Eugene Lyons' *The Red Decade* (1942) among other publications. Its domination of the national student and youth movements and the mass anti-Fascist organizations was typical. During the 1940s, it recovered from the temporary set-back of the Nazi-Soviet Pact and acquired considerable strength in the trade union movement. Its potential as a disorganizing factor in production and shipping seems to have been recognized by Roosevelt himself. As late as 1948, after the "great fear" and "terror" had begun, the Communist Party was able to launch the Progressive Party which at the beginning seemed designed to be helpful to Thomas Dewey, the Republican Candidate, whose victory was preferable at the time to the Kremlin. Although the Progressive Party vote fell far short of expectations, as a result largely of the brazenness of Communist Party control of Henry Wallace's campaign, the very fact that the Communist Party could put on a national third party ticket in the field (a notoriously difficult operation in those days because of restrictive state registration laws) testifies to the extent and efficiency of the organization.

Some gnat!

As for Caute's discussion of Communist espionage trials, it is very curious indeed. He keeps on referring to American "hysteria" about the trials, overlooking both the characteristic openness with which the American press discusses any kind of criminal proceedings and the number and variety of appeals the American legal system provides to those convicted. His summaries of the trials of Alger Hiss and of Ethel and Julius Rosenberg are very sympathetic to the defendants. He does not accept the evidence of Hiss's guilt. Nothing reveals his bias so blatantly as his final comment on the Rosenberg case in which he treats Kim Philby's acknowledgment of the Rosenbergs' guilt as equally evidential with a fictional scene from E. L. Doctorow's novel. Philby wrote:

Fuchs not only confessed his own part in the business, he also identified from photographs his contact in the US, Harry Gold. From Gold, who was in a talkative mood, the chain led inexorably to the Rosenbergs, who were duly electrocuted.

Caute remarks: "Such evidence, of course, is merely suggestive." "Merely suggestive"? Why should Britain's master spy who enjoyed the Kremlin's confidence refer this way to the Rosenbergs? Why should he believe that the chain of evidence "led inexorably" to the Rosenbergs? "Equally suggestive", according to Caute, is a purely fictional account by Doctorow of the Rosenberg case in which some character remarks out of the blue that the evidence against them, which withstood repeated appeals, was "phony." Only Caute's deepseated bias can blind him to the likelihood that Philby knows more about the Rosenberg case than Doctorow.

Because security procedures had been absent or slack, when they were first introduced, there were, not unexpectedly, many mistakes and excesses in the American security program. It was the liberals whom Caute attacks who did the most to help the innocent victims of these excesses. It was not the procedures of the American Review Boards that were so much at fault—actually in crucial respects they were fairer than the UK Review Boards.[3] The situation was exacerbated by two factors: (1) the failure to understand on the part of many boards as well as of their vehement critics like Caute that the problem of security is primarily not one of detection and punishment, but of prevention and avoidance; and (2) because they were staffed not by knowledgeable men and women, who in addition to common sense possessed political sophistication and experience, but by typical investment bankers, corporation lawyers, Republic and Democratic Party regulars, who could hardly distinguish among New Deal liberals, Socialists and Communists, and were altogether mystified by the varieties and kinds of ideological allegiances and organizational affiliations of those investigated.

The troubled times, the conjunction of espionage cases at home and abroad, the objective danger of a Third World War, all created an atmosphere which made it easy for cultural vigilantes who had their own special axes to grind to press for loyalty oaths. These were not only irrelevant to national security—no oaths ever stopped

---

[3]British civil servants under investigation were rarely told of the evidence against them. They had no right to legal counsel or even to representation. Judging by the absence of appeals to them, English courts seem to have little jurisdiction over dismissals from government service.

a traitor—but insulting to honest dissenters. Irresponsible charges of communism were hurled against individuals who took unorthodox stands in the field of morals and religion. These outrages, which culminated even though they did not cease with McCarthy's charges against individuals within government and out, were documented and publicly opposed by those whom Caute holds, because of their opposition to both Communists and the cultural vigilantes, chiefly responsible for the excesses.

Once it was established that the American Communist Party, whatever its other activities were, functioned as a foreign arm of the Soviet Union, public concern was aroused about the behavior of its members in other areas of life unrelated to government service and defense industry. The source of the greatest confusion was to assimilate the problems created by Communist Party cell activities in different areas and professions to problems of security when in many cases there was not the remotest connection with national security. To make matters worse some of the political Neanderthals of the time, failing to recognize that vigorous criticism and dissent are the very life blood of a free society, became suspicious of their expression in social, political and religious affairs because Communist propaganda exploited such criticisms and dissent for its own purposes.

To be sure, there were problems of unprofessional conduct posed in some of the fields in which Communist Party cells operated. When such offenses came to light it was not the business of government to intervene; it was the responsibility of the professionals in their own field to formulate and to enforce the appropriate standards of conduct. Their failure to do this, even when there was ample evidence of violation of principles of professional conduct, played into the hands of unscrupulous politicians. Where there was evidence, e.g., of membership in an organization that issued instructions to its members to engage in unprofessional behavior, the essential issues had little relevance to the Cold War or to national security.

Liberals were divided among themselves as to the significance of membership in the Communist Party. Long before the onset of the Cold War, the question had arisen in the area of education. The New School of Social Research was founded in 1919 by John Dewey, James Harvey Robinson, Thorstein Veblen, Charles Beard, and Alvin Johnson, the leading liberal thinkers of the nation. In 1934 it organized a Graduate School staffed mainly by exiles from Nazi Germany. The faculty of the Graduate School adopted the following principles which subsequently became the position of the New School:

The New School knows that no man can teach well, nor should be permitted to teach at all, unless he is prepared "to follow the truth of scholarship wherever it may lead." No inquiry is ever made as to whether a lecturer's private views are conservative, liberal or radical; orthodox or agnostic; views of the aristocrat or commoner. Jealously safeguarding this precious principle, the New School stoutly affirms that a member of any political party or group which asserts the right to dictate in matters of science or scientific opinions is not free to teach the truth and thereby is disqualified as a teacher.

Equally, the New School holds that discrimination on grounds of race, religion or country of origin either among teachers or students runs counter to every profession of freedom and has no place in American education.

On the other hand, the attitude of the Communist Party of the United States mirrored at the time the position of the Communist Party of the USSR. Among the instructions to those of its members who were teachers, published in the official organ of the Communist Party (*The Communist*, May 1937), we find the following:

Party and YCL [Young Communist League] fractions set up within classes and departments must supplement and combat by means of discussion, brochures, etc. bourgeois omissions and distortions in the regular curriculum. . . . *Marxist Leninist analysis must be injected into every class.*

Communist teachers must take advantage of their position without exposing themselves to give their students to the best of their ability working-class education.

To enable the teachers in the party to do the latter, the party must take careful steps to see that all teacher comrades are given thorough education in the teachings of Marxism-Leninism. Only when teachers have really mastered Marxism-Leninism *will they be able skilfully to inject it into their teaching with the least risk of exposure* and at the same time conduct struggles around the schools in a truly Bolshevik manner.

The sentences I have italicized leave no doubt that there was an awareness that the actions recommended violated the norms of academic freedom and integrity. Nor can there be any question that members were expected to follow the Party line on all issues, for as one of the Resolutions of the Ninth Convention of the Communist Party put it: "In order to carry through their work effectively . . . all Communists must at all times take a position on every question that is in line with the policies of the party. . . ."

Caute is aware of the existence of these directives but ignores the issues and problems they raise. Without quoting them, he dismisses these directives as "dated" implying that they no longer hold for the period he is treating. He fails to indicate when they were officially, or even unofficially, withdrawn or modified or repudiated. This is typical of his approach in every area. There are no problems for him set by the existence of members of a Communist Leninist Party intent upon penetrating the educational and cultural institution of a democracy for purposes hostile to their proper functioning. Such an attitude is bound to provoke sooner or later a public reaction that threatens others besides Communists. More seriously, it creates an atmosphere in which the proper professional measures, under safeguards of due process, fail to be taken by the profession itself to remedy abuses.

Not surprisingly Caute is just as cavalier with the problem created by secret Communist cells in newspapers, especially when members of the Communist Party, queried about their party-angling of the news, invoked the Fifth Amendment on the ground that a truthful answer would tend to incriminate them. Some invoked the Fifth Amendment not in order to avoid incriminating *themselves*, but in order to avoid incriminating *others* which legally was an inadmissible ground. But how was one to know their real motivation? Caute denounces the *New York Times* and the local New York union of the American Newspaper Guild as well as the Guild membership of the *Times* for holding that in such circumstances the reliance on the Fifth Amendment created a doubt about the professional integrity of the newspaper reporter on whom the public relied for an honest news story.

The record of the *New York Times* throughout these years can be summarised in a sentence: sensitive to the rights and liberties of certifiable anti-Communist liberals, insensitive to the rights and liberties of the Left, of those who questioned the rectitude of the Truman Doctrine.

Caute is characteristically mistaken. The *New York Times* was sensitive to the rights and liberties of anti-Communist liberals who were being smeared or falsely accused of being Communists or subject to the discipline of the Communist Party. But, together with these liberals, it was also sensitive to the rights and liberties of those who questioned the rectitude of the Truman Doctrine as many pacifists and isolationists did. Once more Caute slyly uses that rubber-band term "Left" to conceal the fact that he means members of the Communist Party. (If by "Left" one includes belief in civil and human rights, the anti-Communist liberals whom he denigrates were more genuinely Left than those to whom Caute is referring.) It is beyond even Mr. Caute's considerable powers of invention to cite a single case when anyone, as he claims, Communist Party member or not, was denied by the government or courts any legitimate right or liberty merely for "questioning the rectitude of the Truman Doctrine."

Caute's *parti-pris* and anti-American animus comes clearly into play even when he deals with some of the truly shameful excesses of the investigatory power in the entertainment industry. Given the nature of the Communist Party, there was a legitimate Congressional interest in discussing the sources of its funding. Hollywood during the 1930s and '40s provided huge sums of money for the coffers of the Communist Party and its front organizations. V. J. Jerome, a member of the Political Bureau of the Communist Party, was the Party representative who oversaw the raising of funds and the recruitment of members. The relevant facts could have been ascertained by an investigation of the financial resources of the Communist Party, not of the entertainment industry. The result of Congressional investigation was unfortunate. Many Hollywood and Broadway performers were victimized, some of whom had very little actual relationship with the Communist Party. Racketeers appeared on the scene who offered to "clear" those identified (or suspected) as members of the Communist Party for a fee. The heads of the California movie studios and Manhattan radio and television networks abdicated their own responsibilities and judgments and supinely accepted "black-lists" drawn up by pressure groups.

There were certain problems connected with the ethics of employment involved here which Caute refuses to recognize—some flowing from the record of activity and harassment by Communists against critics of Communism (touched on by John Cogley in his two-volume *Report on Blacklisting*), and some flowing from the fact that the entertainment industry was profit-oriented. There was nothing corresponding to the BBC or the Public Broadcasting System in the United States at the time. The first set of problems could have been met by drawing up a code of professional behavior to be administered by representatives of the producers and artists as well as the industry and public. Even a good unpolitical trade union could protect members from political victimization. But such unions were lacking. The second was more difficult. There had always been a "morals clause" in the contracts signed with studios that released them from underwriting performers whose behavior might give rise to a public boycott that would lead to economic loss to the studio. The "ratings" of audience reach have always been king in this industry. The courts in the main have upheld the validity of the "morals clause" and the justification for invoking it when individuals by their defiance of the Congressional Committees or their invocation of the Fifth Amendment became objects of popular scorn or hatred, and possible boycott. Even if the "right to a job" (or to unemployment insurance) is regarded as a human right, as it should be, it cannot be a right to a specific job. In a highly competitive market, the manufacturer who sponsors a show that features a talented performer who has endorsed, say, the Ku Klux Klan and the "Protocols of Zion" or any other unpopular cause, and consequently fears a boycott of his product that could bankrupt him, cannot be expected to continue subsidizing the performer or show, particularly if he himself abominates the "cause" that has been espoused. This would by no means justify him in setting up a black-list. One might even respect the sponsor for refusing to yield to outside pressures regardless of its effect on his financial position. But one could not reasonably condemn him for insisting that the performer be dropped. Neither he nor his shareholders are in business for their health. Suppose the performer were not someone of Fascist sympathies but someone who had endorsed the Communist propaganda line that the United States had engaged in germ warfare in Korea, and a patriotic boycott by Americans had begun. Would refusal of sponsors to continue his employment be morally illegitimate? Even if one deplores the demonstrations of protest against performers on political grounds as unwise or unjustifiable, the legal right to peaceful protest must be protected just as much as the right to hold unpopular political opinions by the performers. Does this mean that performers must be protected from the economic consequences of their unpopularity?

In an essay reviewing Cogley's study in which I criticize the black-list, I consider these and other problems in the ethics of employment. Mr. Caute cites one sentence—and this only in part— from the essay to indicate the extremes to which "Cold War liberals" went in pressing for a domestic purge. He carefully refrains from citing the succeeding sentences that give my actual position. This is the sentence Caute quotes:

So long as the radio and television industries operate under commercial sponsorship, it is both unrealistic and unfair to compel sponsors whose income position is being undermined by popular boycott of Communist or Fascist performers on their programs to continue their sponsorship. . . .

Standing by itself no reader could infer from this truncated sentence what my true position was. He would be inclined to believe that I endorsed the Hollywood purges and black-lists. That is why Caute cuts the quotation short. I must beg the indulgence of the reader for the lengthy passage I now cite as evidence of Caute's suppressions of what he finds inconvenient to his obsessive anti-Communism. His procedure here is typical of his criticisms of some other leading "Cold-War liberals."

So long as the radio and television industries operate under commercial sponsorship, it is both unrealistic and unfair to compel sponsors whose income position is being undermined by a popular boycott of Communist or Fascist performers on their programs to continue their sponsorship, or to drop the show and thus harm other performers. Paradoxically, only a publicly-owned radio or television system, as in Great Britain, could withstand a popular boycott of entertainers who have outraged the conscience of the country. The Minister in charge, however, would have to answer for it in Parliament.

Under existing conditions of sponsorship no general theoretical solution is possible. It may be that with time and increasing sophistication, no matter what the politics of an entertainer, the audience will react to his talent and not to his prejudices. After all we laugh with Chaplin despite his politics, enjoy Picasso even though he is committed to communism, and listen with pleasure to Wagner without being upset by his virulent anti-Semitism. There is a kind of *Narrenfreiheit* customarily extended to artists which does not license them to violate the moral decencies but which makes for greater charity in judgment on the part of audiences. This in no way jeopardizes our right to criticize artists and our right not to listen. Where no position of executive trust is involved, it would be wiser as well as more generous, especially since no question of national security enters, to leave all careers open to talents subject to the criticism of audience response. In the entertainment industry no one can survive the audience's refusal to listen. Only the great are likely to escape the consequences of violations of basic community values. And when they do, we should forgive them their bizarre morals and politics, within the law, because of the joy they give us in enriching the human legacy.

At the moment the popular arts suffer more from low standards of taste and achievement than from threat of communist penetration. Problems flowing from the latter can best be solved by working out a code of ethical procedures *within* and for the industry. They are not a legitimate concern of any Congressional committee unless it can be shown that a definite issue of national security is involved. If it is true, as it once was true, that a large portion of the financial backing for the Communist Party comes from its Hollywood contingent and sympathizers, this is certainly a relevant question for investigation. But this could be more effectively accomplished not by an investigation of the entertainment industry but by an investigation of the financial resources of the Communist Party.

It is by selective quotations from passages like these that Caute forges his amalgam of anti-Communist liberals and Senator Joseph McCarthy as both guilty of "willingness to defend democracy by means of anti-democratic methods." Caute is not a Communist but his selective quotations are typical of Communist polemics. They bring to mind the attempt of an English Stalinist philosopher to prove that John Dewey, until his death the leading American anti-Communist liberal, was a racist.

Caute is unreliable not only in his exposition of the views of those whom he condemns, but of the position of those whom he defends—especially those who have been active on the Communist firing line. One can pick at random almost any of the figures he selects as a victim of American persecution and find evidence of violent distortion in his account. The case of Cedric Belfrage can serve as well as any other. Belfrage is depicted by Caute as merely a Communist sympathizer harassed and persecuted by the government who sought to deport him—merely for his opinions. Belfrage (of British nationality) was a resident alien who served as an editor of the Communist *National Guardian*. He is cited as a case "which most forcefully demonstrated the government's refusal to tolerate criticism from the far Left" (*sic*). But in Belfrage's case it was not merely his criticism, which was standard Communist patter, that the government was concerned with; nor even the charge of Party membership. (His Party name was Oakden.) He had been publicly identified as a member of the British Intelligence Service who had been recuited by the Soviet Secret Police operating in the U.S., i.e., as actually a double-agent with basic loyalty to the Kremlin. When asked (on 5 May 1953), "Did you ever turn over extremely valuable information from the files of the British Intelligence Service while you were here in the United States of America to Russian agents?", he invoked the Fifth Amendment. At another crucial hearing (on 10 August 1954), he was asked; "Have you ever been engaged in espionage activities against the United States or Great Britain?" He again invoked the Fifth Amendment. A deportation warrant was then issued against him. As an alien, Belfrage enjoyed rights and privileges altogether unknown not only in democratic countries on the continent, but also in his native Britain. All one need ask is: what would be the fate of an alien in Britain who in similar circumstances refused to answer a question about his espionage activities? No one in the United States, whether in Belfrage's time or today, has the power of the UK Home Secretary to send an alien packing whose presence is regarded as harmful to the national interest. In the United States the government must present reasons at public hearings, and frequent and lengthy judicial appeals can be taken from the decision of the Commission of Immigration. (The activity of American Courts on the whole gives the lie to Caute's account of "great

American fear.") Caute does not give the pertinent details about the Belfrage case.[4]

It was actually a few such cases of this kind that McCarthy demagogically exploited to gain the limited support of the American public for a brief period. The essence of McCarthyism was irresponsible exaggeration. Not everything he said was false. But he manipulated what was true to convey untruth. "Irresponsible exaggeration" is a precise characterization of Caute's assertion that the United States was in the grip of terror during the so-called McCarthy years. Even at the height of Senator McCarthy's power the leading newspapers of the country were criticizing, indeed denouncing, him. His methods, tactics and words were under impassioned attack in almost every large educational center of the nation. There is little likelihood that there will be a recurrence of McCarthyism except in the improbable event that the Caute syndrome which mistakes dangerous conspirators for harmless heretics reappears in the thought and behavior of the American administrative bureaucracy.

The gravest domestic damage of McCarthy and McCarthyism was its effect on government employees, especially Foreign Service officers who for a few years were intimidated into playing it safe in their analyses and recommendations out of fear of public inquisitorial grilling. McCarthy lost whatever public support he had when he overreached himself in his attack on the Army. His demagogy became apparent even to the relatively unsophisticated

---

[4]Nor of the Gerhardt Eisler case or of the Joint Anti-Fascist Refugee Committee. According to Caute the demand for the records of this organization by the House Committee was motiviated primarily by hostility to opponents of Franco. He omits mention of the fact that what preceded the investigation was the publication of the photostatic copies of the checks issued by the Anti-Fascist Committee to Gerhardt Eisler, at that time serving as the chief Cominform agent in the U.S. according to former leading Communists. Money raised for "the orphans and widows of anti-Fascist refugees" was being diverted, at least in part, to the support of the Communist Party functionaries. Caute applauds the refusal to submit the Communist records on the ground that the anonymity of the donor and recipients were at stake although the evidence could have been presented in executive session.

In this connection it is interesting to observe that when the director of Ku Klux Klan was sent to jail for contempt for refusing to produce Klan records of membership before a grand jury, he pleaded not only that he was bound by an oath of secrecy but that the revelation of the names of the Klansmen would be an act of betrayal and prejudicial to the interests of his fellow-members. None of those who protested the conviction of Communist front organizations for refusal to submit their records of how they spent monies raised for nonpolitical purposes protested the conviction of the Klansman.

citizenry. As subsequent events have shown—despite a chorus of anguished predictions to the contrary—he has had absolutely no effect on the vigorous expression of political dissent.

In perspective, perhaps the greatest harm from McCarthyism to the United States and to the struggle for freedom was the distorted impression it produced on European public opinion concerning the nature and consequences of Congressional investigations. They were compared with the aid of a largely hostile European press to the terroristic practices of the *Gestapo* and the NKVD. Incredible as it may seem, during and long after McCarthy's years, I found many influential European intellectuals more concerned, certainly more vocal, about McCarthyism than about the Gulag Archipelago. Some of them actually compared the political situation in the United States in 1953 to that of the Weimar Republic in late 1932 when Hitler was in the wings ready to take over. Caute's book, despite his occasional disavowals of intent, tends to perpetuate these delirious political judgments.

Finally, it remains to ask: Why was it that there was so much more concern about the problem of Communist infiltration from 1950 on in the United States than in countries like Austria (which were partly occupied by Soviet troops) or in France and Italy (with their mass Communist Parties) or in Great Britain? This is a large question, and I have attempted to analyze it in detail elsewhere.[5] Briefly, the answer is this: in countries as vulnerable as Austria, there was hardly any need to worry about the problem because it would have made little difference if anyone did. In France and Italy to this day any attempt to break up the Communist underground organizations, which function like a state within a state, or effectively curb infiltration into strategic government services, would result in crippling strikes, if not civil war.

It should also be recalled that the Korean War, although fought under the aegis of the United Nations, was experienced (because of the losses incurred) primarily as an American engagement. At about this time the United States lost its monopoly of nuclear weapons. Rightly or wrongly, this was widely attributed to Communist espionage. Most important of all, in contradistinction to the situation in Great Britain publicly sworn testimony—some of it legally substantiated when the charges were contested and most of it met with Fifth Amendment evasions—had identified highly placed government officials as members of the Communist un-

---

[5]See my *Political Power and Personal Freedom*, (1959), pp. 235–51, and my reply to Mr. James Cameron in *Encounter* (February 1977), pp. 90 ff.

derground. Communist penetration in Britain seems to have been limited to security and defense agencies. Had a comparable number of high-ranking persons in the exalted precincts of British officialdom been identified in the same way as their American counterparts, many of them in advisory and policy-making posts, popular concern would probably have mounted to the same degree. The structure of Westminster's party organization and the Official Secrets Act would have prevented a demagogue from exploiting the situation. But there would surely have been a tighter security system, a deeper understanding of ideologically motivated subversion and espionage. I am sure too there would have been a greater skepticism of David Caute's belated reverse McCarthyism.

CHAPTER FOURTEEN

The Worldly Views of John Kenneth Galbraith

Some explanation is owed the reader why a chapter should be devoted in a volume on Marxist studies to John Kenneth Galbraith. Galbraith, of course, is not a Communist, nor an avowed Marxist. He is seemingly reluctant to call himself a Socialist, although this has not deterred others from doing so. He thinks of himself as an abiding liberal, but his liberalism is not an economic category. It expresses a constellation of values that define the free and open society to which many who differ with him on specific issues subscribe with no less loyalty. Indeed, whatever its limitations, one of the virtues of this society is its toleration of dissent, its good-humored acceptance of variety and difference in the pursuit of happiness provided it does not violate the basic norms of decency in personal life and civility in public life.

I discuss Galbraith's views primarily because they exemplify a very influential, if not dominant, conception of the nature of Communism prevalent in the American academy and increasingly evident in major segments of the public media. At times in the past they have reflected the perception of political realities among certain circles of the political Establishment. It is not precluded that in the future they may be persuasive to individuals and groups once more at the helm in international affairs. I regard these views as gravely flawed. Were they to become guides to American foreign policy in the future, the prospects of survival of free Western society would be seriously affected. That is why I have included my analysis of Galbraith's recent autobiography that expresses, among other things, his views on Communism and allied themes.

Like other autobiographies of contemporary figures, John Ken-

159

neth Galbraith's *A Life in Our Times*[1] may be approached on various levels and from various points of view. As a story it is a fascinating account of the ascent of a Canadian farm boy to dizzying political heights in the United States where he became a spokesman and at times a critic of the Establishment. To be sure, those he supported, with the exception of JFK's fluke victory, lost, despite not because of his counsel. But it is hardly disputable that if Stevenson, McGovern, or Edward Kennedy had ascended to the presidency, Galbraith would have been an important power in the nation. His views on foreign policy, had they prevailed in the past, would have had momentous consequences. He is still wedded to those views and the chief moral of his tale is an apologia and defense of them. They are of primary concern to me and should be to all Americans regardless of their differences on domestic economic issues.

On these economic issues I am closer to Galbraith than most of his critics. I am still an unreconstructed advocate of the welfare state who believes its waywardness and abuses can be corrected. Nonetheless, to me the basic issue of our time is not capitalism *or* socialism in any of their variants and combinations but the defense of the open society against totalitarianism.

As a commentary on our political history since the thirties, Galbraith's book is absorbing, in places highly amusing, and fiercely partisan. Galbraith never forgets a slight nor a compliment. In many ways he confirms Auden's rueful comment on my "Ethics of Controversy": To abide by them ruins the aesthetics of controversy. But some of his malicious comments are sparked not by memory of conflict but only of friendly disagreement. Thus his characterization of Bernard Baruch as a "name dropper" seems unfair. Baruch personally knew the persons in high places whose names he mentions at least as well as Galbraith knew those whose names in far greater number stud his pages. And to imply that Baruch's friendly telephone calls before the appearance of his *Autobiography* was to insure a favorable review is hardly justified. It makes one wonder why Galbraith goes out of his way to praise, and sometimes to withhold expected criticism of, some of his colleagues. Those who stood in the way of his promotion or hold economic views at variance with his get it in the neck without a convincing exposure or refutation of their positions. This is no great fault in a work of journalism—and Galbraith is indisputably a brilliant journalist—but rather a drawback in the serious analysis

---

[1]John Kenneth Galbraith, *A Life in Our Times* (Boston: Houghton Mifflin, 1981)

of ideas and policies. And Galbraith's great public conceit is that he is a profound and original thinker.

As a journalist one of Galbraith's important contributions to the gaiety of the nation is the exhumation of optimistic predictions and assurances of bigwigs on the eve of disaster. This is a valuable and much neglected public service particularly with reference to the records of economists and military men who have profited from what Galbraith calls "our system of upward failure"—reward and promotion despite their miserable batting averages. He takes pains, in order to claim an intellectual humility he does not feel, to document some minor errors of economic and electoral prediction of his own. But on some matters of momentous significance like his celebration of the economic success of the Chinese Communist economy, then in the throes of the Cultural Revolution, he suffers a lapse of memory. Like so many other memoirists whom he reproves, Galbraith has his own historical dustbin.

There is an interesting passage in the volume that possibly accounts for this. "After a lifetime in public service[2] self-censorship becomes not only automatic but a permanent part of one's personality. Only in the most infrequent cases can there be escape for autobiography or memoir. And what passes thus for candor is only a minor loosening of the chains. . . ."

One senses this absence of candor in the account of his switch in 1960 from Stevenson to Kennedy at a time when Stevenson's prospects of winning the presidency were excellent without the necessity of Cook County electoral larceny. I still remember Agnes Meyer's blazing fury at Galbraith's "opportunism" and "betrayal" in attaching himself to the Kennedy clan whose reputation for liberalism at the time was not high, and what she said about the hardly more contained indignation of Eleanor Roosevelt, and the deep hurt rather than anger of Stevenson himself. Although Galbraith was aware of this feeling among Stevenson supporters, he shrugs it off without really explaining why as a *liberal* he switched. His appetite for power whetted by his experience during the war years had grown in the period he was out of government service to a point where it overcame his fidelity to liberal principle. He rationalized this to himself and others by saying that Stevenson was a "born loser."

Even more mysterious in such a highly principled man and one

---

[2] I have substituted the word "service" for "office" because Galbraith tells us that he had come to think of himself as part of the permanent government of the United States.

who rather smugly proclaims his inveterate tendency to be "compulsively against any self-satisfied elite," and "to oppose and infuriate" the well-heeled, is his undeviating loyalty to the Kennedys. John F. Kennedy in his campaign speeches irresponsibly attacked the Eisenhower administration for not actively supporting the Cuban freedom fighters—which was tantamount to a call for invasion. After his election he approved the ill-advised and ineptly planned Bay of Pigs imbroglio—mistakes that could only have been retrieved by American air support, cancelled after Kennedy's failure of nerve. Galbraith tells us now that he vehemently opposed all these moves except the last. But he did not go public with his opposition or resign in protest as he should have done.

His memory fails him when he writes about Robert Kennedy to whom he would have undoubtedly transferred his allegiance from Eugene McCarthy at the 1968 convention had Kennedy not been assassinated. He is silent about Robert Kennedy's role in Joseph McCarthy's rampage, and his wire-taps when Attorney General on Martin Luther King and others.

Most puzzling of all is Galbraith's undeviating support of the hero of Chappaquiddick whom he regards after George McGovern as possibly "my closest friend in politics." This is indeed passing strange for such a stern moralist for whom Nixon's character, despite Galbraith's enthusiasm for his policy of detente and the opening toward China, unfit him for any public office, even that of lowly dogcatcher. Nixon was certainly foolish beyond words and his political villainies, albeit flowing from an excess of personal loyalty to subordinates and political partisanship, are reprehensible. But if character is relevant to politics what act of Nixon's begins to compare in infamy, moral cowardice, and deception with that of Edward Kennedy's? And as for cover-ups, what act of Nixon's was as degrading as the bribe to the parents of the victim of Chappaquiddick to forbid an autopsy whose findings might have raised the question of whether what occurred, that is, the delay in getting help and reporting what happened, was purely an accident? Conscious decision by Galbraith not unconscious censorship operates here, not only in the failure to make even passing mention of the incident but in not informing the reader what advice, if any, Galbraith gave at the time.

All this is relatively minor save as an illustration of how the double standard in morals and politics pervades Galbraith's memoir. Much more significant to the serious reader is the theme song that runs through the book with respect to the mischievous role American concern with Communism has had on our foreign policy. It is this topical theme which deserves closer attention.

Galbraith is convinced that the bane of American foreign policy since the end of World War II has been its obsessive anti-Communism. It threatens to end the world in a nuclear holocaust. American statesmen have been rendered both foolish and bellicose out of fear of being considered "soft" on Communism by those who are rhetorically "hard." Communism constitutes no danger *in* the United States nor *to* the United States. All the Communist powers want are safe borders. Integral to the debilitating syndrome of the anti-Communist complex that has gripped American statesmen from the onset of the cold war is that the Communist movement is a monolithic world organization driven by an unchanging ideology which has inspired its zealots everywhere to engage in conspiratorial practices. The result is that we have done more harm to ourselves than to our reputed enemies. Although the original architects of this disastrous policy are long dead, Galbraith is convinced that their spirits have poisoned the minds of the current inhabitant of the White House and his advisors. (Party loyalty prevents him from seeing that a better case can be made for finding the roots of the current attitude in Truman's belated policy of containment than in the actions of Eisenhower and Dulles.)

It is this bitter attack on current and past American foreign policy with respect to the Soviet Union and Communism that is likely to have the greatest influence on uninformed readers. It varies little from the position of those like former Secretary of State Vance and his advisors, Marshall Shulman et al., who believe that the Soviet Union, far from being a threat to the United States, feels threatened and insecure by its "failures" in Europe, Asia, and Africa, and that the invasion of Afghanistan is a sign of Soviet "weakness." Galbraith does not yet go as far as George Kennan who has abandoned advocacy of the policy of containment for Bertrand Russell's position—"Rather Red, than Dead"—if an arms agreement cannot be negotiated. There are suggestions, however, toward the close of the book, that this may soon be Galbraith's view, too. Were he consistent, it would be because on his theory of convergence, as we shall see, technology not ideology determines our future under any system, and the technological imperatives of Communism and capitalism as industrial systems are the same.

Before addressing myself to this criticism of American foreign policy, I should like to challenge two assumptions that invariably attend Galbraith's exposition of it. The first, relatively minor, is his attempt to preempt the designation of "liberal" for his position in which he is abetted by some stupid conservatives. The only sense of the term "liberal" that would justify such presumption is one that defines liberalism as the belief that there are no enemies to human freedom on "the Left"—often a euphemistic expression for Communism. This kind of liberalism is always anti-Fascist but more often *anti* anti-Communist than anti-Communist.

The foreign policy Galbraith and his confreres are attacking is the foreign policy more strongly advocated by the liberal, organized labor movement in the United States (the AFL-CIO) than by any group of plutocratic monopolists and/or free marketeers on the scene. Yet Galbraith mistakenly attributes the chief opposition to the Communist movement to big business which notoriously has been more interested in trade with Communist countries than have the trade unions. It is the same foreign policy defended by men like Adolf Berle, Paul Douglas, Reinhold Niebuhr, and scores of others whose liberal credentials are as long standing and every whit as authentic as Galbraith's. To be sure, this has no bearing on the validity of the policy, but it is sufficient to expose—nothing can apparently limit—the patronizing arrogance of the assumption that where Galbraith stands, even in his call for quota systems and reverse discrimination, the liberal flag waves.

More serious is the factual error that United States foreign policy, of which I have often been a critic for reasons quite different from those of Galbraith, has taken as axiomatic the monolithic character of the international Communist movement. Even under Truman, despite the fact that Tito's Yugoslavia was ideologically the most intransigent and aggressive of the Communist states, the United States was quick to offer economic and military assistance to Belgrade after the Tito-Stalin rift. The development of polycentrism was a slow process in the Communist world, and the United States was not unduly tardy in recognizing it. It may be true that Kim Il Sung decided on his own to invade South Korea after Acheson had gratuitously declared it outside the confines of the American national interest. But once the invasion was launched, North Korea could not have continued to wage the war against the U.S. and UN resistance without the active collaboration of the Soviet Union and Communist China. The worldwide campaign against the United States that circulated the monstrous lie that the U.S. was waging germ warfare in Korea was initiated and orchestrated by the Kremlin.

And now that the United States has decided to play the China card in a very modest opening in order to restrain the current expansionist tendency of the Soviet Union, Galbraith and other appeasers deplore the move as a dangerous provocation even as they continue to indict American policy for its "mindless" assumption that the world Communist movement is monolithic. Actually, there is a good precedent in United States policy for helping, in the national interest and the ultimate cause of freedom, one form of totalitarianism resist another, about which we hear little from human rights absolutists, namely, United States military and economic aid to the Kremlin after Hitler double-crossed his erstwhile ally and invaded the Soviet Union on June 22, 1941. Such aid, under existing law, would not have been possible then.

Of course it is fatuous to contrast "hard" and "soft" attitudes toward Communism. Nor do I recall any policy being accepted or rejected by leading American statesmen in these terms despite Galbraith's assertion that their use was systematic. All American political figures, including Henry Wallace and George McGovern, have been *against* Communism. But that is not enough to develop "intelligent" and avoid "unintelligent" policies resisting it. "Intelligent" and "unintelligent" are the only appropriate epithets to apply in considering alternatives of policy, not "hard" or "soft." Although knowledge of Communist theory and practice is certainly no guarantee of wisdom here, that is, of developing an intelligent policy, ignorance of Communist theory and practice almost invariably results in unintelligent policies, policies, for example, that assume that since Communists are just as human as we are, their foreign policy is therefore motivated by the same considerations as those of other non-Communist states, or that since they are Russians, their foreign policy must therefore be a continuation of czarist foreign policy. Granting that Communists behave like human beings, and that they behave like Russians, too (or Chinese, as the case may be), the question is: Do they behave like Communists? Those who are ignorant of the theory and practice of Communism cannot answer this question. Note that even if one believes that the rulers of the Soviet Union behave like Communists, this does not mean that they behave *only* as Communists or *always* as Communists. Ideology is not everything. But it certainly is not nothing as the history of our century shows.

Although I found it difficult to believe, I have reluctantly concluded, on the strength of this book and some others of his writings, that Galbraith really is innocent of knowledge of the theory and practice of Communism. For him Communism is purely an economic system in which private property in the instruments of social production has been abolished. On this view, the only individuals who are obsessively hostile to it are those who mainly live on profit, rent, and interest, and who sense in the intrusion of government into economic life the ultimate takeover of the system of collectivism. Galbraith has no notion of what the dictatorship of the proletariat means in Communist theory and practice, of the dictatorship of the Party as the necessary and only means of carrying it out, and of the theory and practice of democratic centralism which insures the dictatorship of the Political Committee of the Communist Party to oversee and enforce the political, cultural, social, and intellectual orthodoxy of the members of the Communist Party and of the entire population over whom they rule. In short, Communism as a system of totalitarianism is beyond his ken. One may doubt whether totalitarianism as an "ideal type" in Weber's sense exists anywhere in the world. Neither does democracy. But the existing differences in one type or another, and the possibility that under certain historical conditions one may be transformed into the other, do not preclude the proper use of the designation.

My reasons for concluding that Galbraith lacks understanding of the nature of Communism are varied. Before detailing them I must confess that the conclusion is a blow to my vanity. In 1952 as one of the organizers of Stevenson's campaign, Galbraith asked me through Arthur Schlesinger, Jr. (the suggestion, I was told, originated with John McDonald, a former colleague of Galbraith's at *Fortune*) to write two speeches on Communism for Stevenson. Not only were they not used, they were apparently unread (perhaps they were lost in the mail).

The most striking of Galbraith's assessments of a Communist society is to be found in his book *China Passage* published after his visit to mainland China in 1972. It is odd that although large chunks of his other volumes are reproduced or summarized in this memoir there is no reference to the book in its pages or a revaluation of its judgments in the perspective of later years. Galbraith was in China while "the cultural revolution" was still raging, when its economy was crippled, its universities paralyzed, and the manifold terrors of the Chinese Gulag Archipelago pervasive in most areas. Nonetheless he reported to the world that China's economic system is "highly effective," that it "functions easily and well," with a performance rivaling Japan's. (The true state of affairs, economic as well as political in China at that time, or at any time, could have easily been learned by talking to recent refugees in Hong Kong—especially those who fled to avoid religious persecution and who had no political axe to grind.) Feasting on the elaborate, exotic *haute cuisine* in a succession of banquets the Chinese lay on for distinguished visitors—just like those the Kremlin provided for visiting Western dignitaries during the famine of the early thirties—Galbraith does not in so many words say that the general population ate as well, but implies that it was well fed, despite the suspicious absence, noted by one of his companions, of any cats or dogs.

To Galbraith's credit he forbears mentioning the absence of flies in China. But neither does he note anywhere the absence of freedom except in a Pickwickian sense. He has a peripheral consciousness of some oppression, but it is the easy and satisfactory functioning of the economy that impresses him most. "Dissidents are brought firmly into line in China but one suspects with great politeness." And why does he suspect this? Because his Chinese hosts invariably smiled at him. He actually writes that the Chinese "command with a smile," No one was ever a more willing and self-deluded victim of skillful Chinese Potemkins. He has an appreciative eye for the aesthetic delights of the countryside but seems blind in both eyes to the totalitarian character of every social landscape. He prefers not to stress the drab unisex uniforms of Chinese adults in order to point up the brightly attired five-year-olds. He remains silent about the educational and cultural significance of these children pirouetting and celebrating with Mao's little Red Book in their tiny hands.

His final pronouncement: "For the Chinese, the system works. . . . It is the Chinese future." We may not like it nor the French. The Chinese do. It is a pity Galbraith does not tell us how he knows that the Chinese like it. When did they choose it? The only choice the Chinese have had since the Communists took over was when the Chinese prisoners of war, after the Korean conflict, were given an opportunity to return home or go elsewhere. Despite the bullying of their Indian interviewers, the great majority chose the bitter bread of exile. When the Communist Chinese officials lifted the bamboo curtain for a few days, they hurriedly dropped it lest southern China be depopulated.

Galbraith's insensitiveness to the totalitarian character of Communism is a corollary of his theory of convergence according to which the society and culture of the future are determined by the technological imperatives of large-scale industrial organization. He denies therefore that there is much sense in defining the world conflict as one between capitalism and Communism as economic systems or especially between democracy and totalitarianism. All the palaver about free enterprise is so much hokum or what Thurman Arnold, who long ago recognized Galbraith's economic genius loyally reciprocated by Galbraith, called "folk lore." And as for Marxism-Leninism, and all its variants, that is so much theology whose chilling language imperialists and militarists, and their academic hirelings, often cite out of context to increase appropriations. Denounce totalitarianism as one pleases. It cannot survive, according to Galbraith, where we have large industrial organization "that sustains technology, and the nature of the planning that technology requires." Celebrate democracy as one pleases, the same technological imperatives "impose a measure of discipline . . . of subordination of the individual to the organization which is very much less than the individualism that has been properly identified with the Western economy." We can now understand how anachronistic free trade unionism is in the new industrial state!

Galbraith sees no threat to his abiding liberalism in the convergent tendencies of industrial societies which result in oligarchies both in Communist and capitalist societies. "Ideology is not the relevant force." In 1966 to make this simplistic technological determinism more palatable he predicted that the Soviet Union "will necessarily [sic!] introduce greater political and cultural freedom" (New York Times, December 18, 1966). Why this did not occur in the new industrial states of pre-war Germany and Japan he does not explain. Actually, political and cultural conditions in the Soviet Union since Galbraith made this prediction have worsened but he still clings to his simplistic technological determinism that would have shamed Howard Scott, the father of the technology movement. On his theory, why should the Soviet Union become like the West rather than the West become like the Soviet Union since ideology is irrelevant and technology is decisive?

Anyone who believes, as Galbraith does, the proposition that "technical specialization cannot be reconciled with intellectual regimentation," to use one of his favorite expressions, is capable of believing anything. The proposition is demonstrably false—historically, psychologically, and politically. Technology makes certain ideal uses possible; it does not determine them. He obviously has not pondered the moral of the Nobel Peace Foundation, which grew out of the desire to compensate for the potential destructiveness of dynamite and other explosives. Some thought that the invention of dynamite made war itself obsolescent rather than certain modes of war obsolescent. Galbraith falls below the level of a sophisticated Marxism in failing to realize that human ideals, which are always at the heart of an ideology broadly conceived, cannot be reduced to economic or technological equations of the first or any degree.

A cognate failure to grasp the animating ideals of Communism as a movement grasping for power by any means is evidenced in his discussion of the Vietnam war. Here, too, there is a hard and fast treatment of the facts. The theme is too complex for exhaustive or even adequate analysis here. Suffice it to say that the initial error of the United States was not to bring pressure on France, as it did on the Netherlands with respect to Indonesia, to live up to de Gaulle's war-time pledge to give Vietnam independence. It was imprudent to get involved in an area so distant, but it is false that the United States was seeking to impose its own way of life on a foreign nation. It was Adlai Stevenson who stated the true issue on the day of his death. "My hope in Vietnam is that resistance there may establish the fact that changes in Asia are not to be precipitated by outside force. That was the point of the Korean War. This is the point of the conflict in Vietnam." It was the same point that led the United States government to condemn and therefore reverse the war of England, France, and Israel against Egypt a decade earlier. This was during the very week in which the Soviet Union invaded Hungary to suppress with ruthless bloodshed the indigenous political development of a government formed, according to the words of George Lukács at the time, "to represent every shade and stratum of the Hungarian people that wants peace and socialism."

Once the United States became involved, given the ineptness of the military, the hostility of the media which turned the defeat of the Viet Cong Tet offensive into a psychological and political victory, and the political constraints on military operations, the real question was how to get out of Vietnam without inviting horrible excesses on a population unwilling to accept Communist despotism, and whom we encouraged to resist. Another major mistake to which Galbraith contributed was to conspire against Diem who might have come to terms with the North before our massive involvement. Galbraith himself defended not complete withdrawal but a system of enclaves in South Vietnam, which would have resulted in a series of Dien Bien Phus but which might have provided for a short time a sanctuary "for those who have joined our enterprise in Vietnam." But there is something macabre in his self-vindicating remark: "My warning of the boat people was better than I guessed." Were his concern with the myriad of victims of a Communist takeover more than a face-saving piety, he would have at least supported the Accords Kissinger worked out with the North Vietnamese, protested the congressional cutoff of arms to the South Vietnamese to defend themselves, and urged some counteraction when with blatant cynicism the North

Vietnamese violated the Accords we had pressured Thieu into accepting.

Galbraith never asks himself why the Communists feel free to violate their agreements whether at Yalta, Potsdam, or Helsinki. Distrust of agreements with Communist powers and insistence upon safeguards that are verifiable (which require mutual site inspections) he tends to regard as a kind of paranoia. Of course, Galbraith would be the first to oppose Soviet aggression if there were any evidence of it that trenches on our vital interests. The changes in global power reflected in the changes in the map of the world since the end of World War II do not constitute persuasive evidence to him. They show Communist influence in areas far removed from where our national interests lie.

I am put in mind of a conversation I had with Charles Beard whose attitude toward Japanese and Nazi aggression was somewhat similar to that of Galbraith's toward Soviet Communism. Beard's eminence as a historian and his reputation as a master craftsman among his colleagues far exceeds Galbraith's standing among professional economists. When I visited Beard late in 1940 in the company of Herbert Solow he scoffed at the idea that Hitler was out to conquer Europe, no less the world. As for the defense of freedom, Beard told me: "I am prepared to fight Hitler in defense of freedom in the streets of New Canaan." I am convinced that if George Kennan does not win him over and he continues to resist what his friend, George Ball calls, "the lunacy of unilateral disarmament," Galbraith, too, would fight for human freedom in Cambridge, Massachusetts, or Townsend, Vermont, and once he grasps the true nature of Communism, anywhere its aggressions entrench on the vital interests of the free society in which he has been nurtured.

It is both in large matters and small that Galbraith reveals his innocence of Communism as an ideology and as a movement. He is scornful of the necessity of a security program in the apparent belief that membership in the Communist Party is hardly different from membership in any other political party. When he mentions Communists who have served in government, or those suspected of Communist connections, here as in his other writings, they are portrayed as victims persecuted because of their views, victims of a witchhunt. The one exception is Lauchlin Currie, of whom Galbraith strangely says nothing at all. He is tolerant of what he calls "enlightened malfeasance" in destroying official files on possible security risks. One does not have to endorse every silly decision of uninformed security boards, who disregarded or could not distinguish the difference between Norman Thomas Socialists and Communists, or countenance McCarthy's demagogic antics to accept as a premise, to which even Roger Baldwin subscribed, that anyone who owes a superior allegiance to a foreign government is unqualified to serve his own in any sensitive post. Some might say any post. To be sure, because the American Communist Party pledged allegiance to the Stalinist regime to a point where its leaders publicly acknowledged that in the case of conflict between the United States and the USSR they would side with the latter, it did not follow that every individual member would carry out instructions to betray his country. But there is no way of telling in advance who will and who will not. It is notoriously true that the most dedicated Soviet agents are drawn from the nationals of satellite Communist Parties, a proposition that only a fool would simply convert into the statement that all members of the Communist Party are Soviet agents. But the fact that some may be cannot be dismissed.

Like so many others, Galbraith seems unaware that a security program is designed not to detect or apprehend those guilty of malfeasance, a task beyond its powers and irrelevant to its task, but to prevent the likelihood of such malfeasance by identifying and excluding security risks. It goes without saying that he ignores— elsewhere he scoffs at—the possible usefulness and effectiveness of intelligence agencies and espionage in our modern world. He probably has not heard of Richard Sorge whose report to Stalin that the Japanese warlords had decided to strike at the United States and not at Russia—something Stalin carefully concealed from the United States while accepting its aid—enabled Stalin to transfer the Siberian regiments in time to save Moscow from the Nazi assault. There is a monument to Sorge in Moscow and he has been immortalized like Lenin and Stalin on postage stamps. The Kremlin knows better than Galbraith how useful its agents can be.

Galbraith's *A Life in Our Times* concludes with a plea for nuclear arms control about which no person of intelligence need be persuaded. The fear-and-tear-jerk rhetoric in its behalf is unnecessary. To this cause Galbraith pledges the rest of his life. It is to be hoped that he will devote his thought to its many intricate problems, especially to the difficulties of reliable inspection without which arms control may prove a sham. In an open society there is sure to be a public-spirited citizen who will blow the whistle in the ever vigilant press at our slightest transgression. In closed societies any attempt to do so would invite summary execution.

It is also to be hoped that in his discussion of the subject Galbraith will avoid the elementary confusion between *cause* and *ground* that mars almost every mention he makes of defense and defense appropriations as well as taxes. He has a lamentable tendency to impute motives of self-interest to those with whom he disagrees about defense appropriations and taxes without adequate assessment of their argument. There are many *causes* for a person's beliefs but in considering their validity only the *grounds* are relevant. A person's belief in vegetarianism may be caused by his aversion to killing, a weak stomach at the sight or thought of blood, or an allergy to meat. But if he argues that the imposition of unnecessary suffering on sentient creatures is morally wrong and that mankind can survive without the necessity of consuming the flesh of slaughtered creatures, the causes of his beliefs are irrelevant to the logical force of his position. Galbraith tends to believe that those who argue for greater military appropriations or tax policies of which he disapproves do so out of self-interest. That may or may not be so, and in many cases it certainly is not so, but that has no bearing on the truth or falsity of their position. I have no doubt that some who urge higher defense appropriations have stock in defense industries, but if there has been an absolute and relative decline of American defense power with respect to the Soviet Union, they may be right. I know very well why some physicians are opposed to socialized medicine, but anyone who favors it must be prepared to meet their arguments against it. Naturally, knowledge of the causes of their belief will impel one to look hard and carefully at their arguments and evidence.

I had looked forward to reading Galbraith's memoir of his busy political life for revelations that are not on the public record. They are not to be found. His pages tell more about himself than about others but still not enough. His style is lively and entertaining. One can forgive his apparent arrogance since it is an obvious protective device against the suspected judgment of economists of the first rank. My disappointment may be due to the fact that my expectations were so high. I cannot believe that his much vaunted arrogance which impresses so many of his friends and enemies is more than a semi-humorous ploy. If I am mistaken and he is indeed serious, then one must observe that however boastful he may be of his size and achievements, at second glance there is not as much to him as meets the eye.

PART TWO

Beyond Marxism

CHAPTER FIFTEEN

What Means This Freedom?

Just as man does not live by bread alone, so a nation cannot survive merely by material wealth and physical arms in a dangerous world where the sudden death of cultures is not a remote possibility, but a contingency inherent in the development of nuclear technology.

Despite the existence of all our sophisticated weaponry, what was true of the past, when human beings faced one another with not more than their muscles and sticks and stones, is still true today—the arm is no more powerful than the will and resolution behind it, and no wiser than the ideas that guide it. Ideas by themselves, of course, like the will in the absence of healthy muscles, are powerless, never sufficient to achieve their goals in a world of physical forces, but in the affairs of men ideas are always necessary and sometimes decisive. William James claimed that it is more important for a landlady to know the philosophy of her boarder than the contents of his trunk—for if she wants to predict his behavior, the more reliable index is not how much money he has, but his conception of right and wrong, obligation and honor. One however, might object: "Aren't those ideas related to and ultimately caused by material self-interest?" To which I reply—not altogether, and in any event it is the ideas that may play the decisive role. Karl Marx once maintained: "It is not consciousness of men that determines their being but, on the contrary, their social being that determines their consciousness." This is a half-truth. I defy anyone to explain Marx's own consciousness and behavior, or Friedrich Engels's, for that matter— the two men whose shadows still loom large in the contemporary world—in terms of their social existence. Karl Marx, who never saw the inside of a factory, was offered a post in the Prussian government by an emissary of Bismarck. Engels could have spent his life as a playboy luxuriating on the surplus values his father's factories sweated out of the workers of Manchester. *Their* ideas cannot be explained by their social existence as well as many other intellectuals who threw their lot in with the oppressed and exploited.

No, it is not economic conditions alone, it is not wealth or weapons alone, that determine the patterns of history. We need not buttress this conclusion with recondite illustrations. The North Vietnamese prevailed not because they were better fed or better armed, but in large measure because they were more resolute. They knew what they were fighting for, whereas their battlefield opponents and, in the last analysis, the American public and Congress did not.

This brings me to my theme—the meaning of freedom. The task is difficult because of the fundamental ambiguities of the term "freedom." There are many varieties of freedom, and whole libraries of literature are devoted to each. No one has even been able to establish that all of these meanings are logically related. For example, the much-debated question of freedom of the will has no bearing on whether the existence of a free society is more desirable than other alternatives. Individuals who agree that man's will is completely determined by antecedent causes may still differ about the desirability of a free society, and, conversely, they may agree about the latter and disagree about the former. Then too, regardless of the meaning we give freedom today, we will discover that before long the word will be appropriated by those who do not really subscribe to our meaning. Because of its positive emotive associations, it will be kidnapped by those who are its enemies. This has occurred with respect to other terms like "democracy" and "peace." We live in an age where we daily witness a phenomenon I once called "the degradation of the word." Every Communist nation in the world calls itself "democratic," for example, East Germany. Along the western border of the so-called German Democratic Republic, there exists a lethally charged electric wall built not so much to keep others out, but to pen its own denizens in, a wall on which hundreds of people have been martyred in their desperate efforts to escape to the free society of the West. However, if we are clear in our minds as to what *we* mean by "freedom," we will not be confused by the calculated policies of semantic corruption of those who do not believe in it.

The first step toward clarity is to understand that in most of our current usages of the term "freedom" we mean "political freedom." When we say we should put "freedom first"—in essence we are referring to the right and power of a people to determine the nature of the government under which it lives, and who its

rulers should be. It is one specific form—a *desirable* specific form—
of a larger conception of freedom whose root notion is the absence
of coercion or restraint by others on the effective expression of
our desires. A free government is not always or necessarily a good
government, although those who support it, recognizing that it is
fallible and can make mistakes, still believe that it is better than
any unfree government feasible at the time. Some honest totalitarian
thinkers from Plato to Santayana have opposed free democratic
government because they believed that a majority of mankind is
either too stupid or too vicious to be entrusted with self-government.

Political freedom is obviously a matter of degree, but in the
most consistent use of the term "free," a government is called
"free" when a legally recognized opposition exists and is permitted
to function, thus making it possible for a minority peacefully to
become a majority. Therefore, it is integral to the very conception
of political freedom—if we hold it to be desirable—that the
processes by which political consent is won must be free, that
there cannot be any honest or informed assent unless there exists
the legally protected right to dissent. More specifically, unless the
freedoms of speech, press, assembly, and association, and the
cluster of freedoms allied to them in a Bill of Rights, written or
unwritten, have legally protected sanctions, there is no genuine
political freedom. And by "legal sanction," I mean that it is not
enough for these rights to exist on paper, they must be enforced.
After Sidney and Beatrice Webb visited the Soviet Union, they
came back and wrote a huge two-volume work in which they
hailed that country as a new and free civilization. When asked
how they knew it was "free," they pointed to the Stalin constitution
of 1936, which contained a long list of "freedoms"—at the very
time when the most monstrous purges and frame-up trials were
the order of the day, and when Stalin was carrying out his genocidal
practices against the Russian peasantry. Since Khrushchev's revelations before the Twentieth Congress of the Soviet Communist
Party in 1956 about the Stalin regime, this kind of naively adulatory
literature about the Soviet Union has become scarce. But as if to
prove Hegel's dictum that the only thing we can learn about
history is that people do not learn from history, not so long ago
we read scores of travelers' reports about Red China in the vein
of the Webbs' book—in which we never heard of any dissidents.
Today we are learning of the existence of a Chinese Gulag
Archipeligo as vast as the Soviet Union's.

There are a great many problems connected with the freedoms
that are central to a free society. I can touch on them only briefly.

For example, one may ask: Are there any limits to the freedoms of speech, press, and assembly, or are they absolute, never under any circumstances to be abridged? And are they to be enjoyed even by those who use them to destroy the political system that makes them possible? My answer to such questions briefly is that these rights are strategic. They are not absolute. There are certain circumstances in which in order to preserve the entire structure of our freedoms, it may be necessary for a limited time to abridge one or another freedom.

I want to make three points to which I direct your critical attention because they are crucial to my argument. The first one I have already made in passing, but I want to make it explicit: When any sane person says he believes in freedom he always has a specific, desirable freedom in mind. He does not really believe in the root conception of freedom as the power to do as one pleases without let or hindrance by others. I have never found anyone who knowingly affirms his belief in freedom as the power to do anything one pleases without let or hindrance by others, for if he did so, he would be justifying the most horrible crimes not only against others but against himself. It is *psychologically* impossible, therefore, to advocate unqualified, unrestricted, generalized freedom in that sense.

Second, it is *logically* impossible to approve all freedoms of action. For whenever we advocate a specific freedom, we are also advocating that the *freedom of others* to interfere with or frustrate that freedom be restrained or abridged. If I believe in your right to freedom of speech, then I must believe that the freedom of others to curb you from speaking should be restrained. If you believe in my right to property, you must believe that others have no right to act in such a way as to deprive me of what I own. There are some persons who say that because we believe in tolerance we must also be tolerant of the actively intolerant. They speak this way because they are confused as to what they really believe. To believe in religious tolerance—or any other kind of tolerance—entails the belief that it is wrong to tolerate the intolerant actions of religious fanatics who would prevent the exercise of religious freedom.

Third, and most important, no specific right or freedom is absolute because the specific freedoms of which we approve often conflict. On many occasions we are committed to incompatible freedoms. We want speech and the press to be free; we also want a man to have the right to a fair trial. But what if, as is sometimes the case, we cannot have both? The situation here is comparable to a moral situation in which we ask: What should I do? Such situations arise not when good conflicts with bad—we really have no problems then because we know what to do at that point!—but when good conflicts with good, when right conflicts with right, and when good conflicts with right. I want to be just and I want to be kind or merciful, but can't be both; I want to support my parents and want to go to school to further my career for the sake of my own family, but can't do both. These are paradigmatic moral situations. Every enumeration of desirable freedoms or rights contains a potential conflict among them; for instance, you cannot always square the right of the public to know with the individual's right to privacy. Ask some arrogant newspaper man who screams that the right of the public to know is absolute when he is forbidden by a court to publish details of some court proceeding—ask him what of the public's right to know his private sources, or the public's right to know who leaked classified information to him, and he will suddenly change his tune.

No, we cannot substitute a table of rights for the hard thought necessary to resolve the conflicts of rights in specific situations. There is no recipe book which if mechanically followed will give us satisfactory solutions. The balancing of rights and freedoms against each other in the light of the public interest or of the preservation of the entire structure of our *prima facie* rights, is the heart of the democratic political process.

But, one may object, do not dictators in totalitarian or politically enslaved countries say the same thing—that they too believe in all these freedoms but not in absolute freedoms, that they too have to suspend them sometimes for the good of society or the good of the revolution or what not? Yes, they say it—but they do not say the truth. The truth is that they do not suspend these freedoms for the *public* good, as ascertained by permitting citizens freely to determine for themselves by open discussion what this good is, nor do they permit a free electoral process to choose who is to administer that good. Rather, they suspend the freedoms for the good of the minority party or its leadership, as they conceive it, without any popular check or control. They do not suspend these freedoms subject to the sanctions of an independent judiciary. They do not suspend these freedoms sometimes but *always*. They do not suspend them temporarily—for history shows they are never voluntarily restored. For example, the ironclad dictatorship of the Communist Party of the Soviet Union was originally justified as a transitional device until a classless society could be established. Well, they now claim to be classless, on the basis of their own

definitions, but their dictatorship and other features of their totalitarian state, instead of withering away, are stronger than ever
before. Nor is it true, as some of their apologists assert, that this
dictatorship exists only because of the necessities of national
defense, since the dictatorship was internally less repressive when
its national strength was weaker and became internally more
repressive as its defensive and offensive military capacities grew.

Well, then, we may ask: What *is* the basic difference between
the free and open societies of the West and their totalitarian
enemies? It is of the very first importance that we grasp this
difference, that we understand the conflicting social and political
values that underlie the diplomatic, military, and economic conflicts
that daily arise. Let us begin by considering some of the ways in
which the difference has been formulated.

One school of thought, which claims to be evenhanded in its
approach, contends that we are confronted with different conceptions of freedom or democracy, all equally legitimate. It is a position
sometimes expressed by revisionist historians of the Cold War
about whom I shall have more to say later. According to them
the West is characterized by a formal political democracy which
they admit is absent in the minority party dictatorships of the
Communist world. But, they assert, there exist in that world other
kinds of democracy which they sometimes refer to as economic
democracy, ethnic democracy, and even educational democracy.
They profess to believe that both cultures are converging and that
someday the formal political democracy we find in our world will
be extended to the economic, ethnic, and educational spheres,
while the Communist world mellows or matures to the point at
which political democracy, now lacking, will be added to the
allegedly "new" forms of freedom and democracy which the
Communist world has pioneered.

Let us analyze this contention. Whatever "economic democracy"
means, it must include the right of those who work to freely
determine the rewards and conditions of work; whatever "ethnic
democracy" means, it must include the right of ethnic groups to
freely determine the values, traditions, and customs of their ethnic
legacy; whatever "educational democracy" means, it must include
the right to freely experiment and select the curricular patterns
and models of excellence in courses of instruction. But how is it
possible, I ask, to exercise the right to determine the rewards and
conditions of work; how is it possible to interpret and develop
the traditions of one's ethnic heritage; how is it possible to exercise
the right to determine the curricular subject matter, techniques,

and values of education—without freedom of inquiry, freedom of speech, freedom of press, and freedom of association, which constitute the very essence of *political* freedom and democracy? The whole notion of different *kinds* of freedom and democracy in this context is absurd, a violation of the ethics and logic of discourse. While we may admit that political freedom or democracy by itself is incomplete, we must insist that economic freedom or ethnic freedom or educational freedom *without* political freedom is impossible, an abuse of terms. When we say we put freedom first we mean that political freedom is the *sine qua non* of every other form of desirable social freedom.

We sometimes hear it said—most often by the Communists themselves—that the fundamental difference between their society and ours is the opposition between capitalism and socialism as economic systems, and that all other differences are derivative from it. I submit that on both analytic and historical grounds this is a profound error. In the first place, it is questionable whether capitalism—in the sense of the free enterprise system of Adam Smith and the unrestricted rule of the market—can be said to exist in the economies of the welfare states in the West in which the public sector constitutes from 25 percent to 40 percent, directly or indirectly by subsidies and regulatory controls, of the productive output. The recent domestic outcry against governmental intrusion into economic affairs—whether one believes such intrusion to be justified or not—is a measure of how far we have come from a state of affairs in which the mechanisms of the market are accepted as the determinants of economic policy or even of prices. It is just as questionable whether socialism—in the sense intended by Karl Marx and other classical advocates of a cooperative society—exists in the Soviet Union or any other Communist society today. No, with respect to the economy, the basic issue is *not* capitalism or socialism, but whether a people is to have the right to choose for itself the economic arrangements under which it is to live, or whether these arrangements are to be decided for it by a handful of persons responsible to no one but themselves.

If the fateful issue is conceived in terms of a conflict of economic systems, why should we expect anyone to risk life, honor, and fortune in defense of a scheme of economic arrangements? Can we conceive of it as a rallying cry? Why die for capitalism? Even the capitalists would be loathe to do so. Indeed, in purely economic terms, it makes no sense to die for anything. When we reflect on the massive trade with Soviet Russia in which capitalists from the very outset of its existence have engaged, thus helping to build up a powerful economy and war machine whose ideology keeps up an intense drumfire of propaganda and hatred against the free world, all the while proclaiming the inevitability of the world triumph of Communism—one wonders whether the capitalists realize what they are really doing. A very formidable case can be made for the thesis that the tremendous industrial expansion of the Soviet Union and its potential for destabilizing the free world has been in great part the result of the cooperation of Western capitalists. It is noteworthy that the AFL-CIO opposed the policy of bailing out the Polish regime after the suppression of Solidarnosc, whereas the American banking community insisted on doing business as usual despite the imposition of martial law, the imprisonment of Lech Walesa, and the violent dispersion of unarmed protesters.

Nor does the difference between the Communist and the free worlds consist in the fundamental difference between irreligion and religion. In a famous speech a president of the United States declared that "atheistic communism" was the real enemy of our free society, leaving open the implication that if communism were not atheistic, it would constitute no greater threat to us than other ways of organizing society. This is a serious misconception. The issue here is not the Judaic-Christian-Moslem faith or its absence; it is not between supernaturalism or naturalism. The issue is the right of a people freely to worship or not to worship God according to its conscience; the right to believe in one, many, or no god or gods; the right to decide what to believe about first and last things, without interference from the state.

Similarly, whether with respect to any doctrine in science or philosophy or any form or style in art, the issue is not the truth or falsity of belief, or the validity or invalidity of any specific practice, but the freedom of the mind—which includes the right to be wrong—in the perennial quest of the human spirit to discover new modes of expression. The issue is the right to think differently, to say "no!" to the established order and its conventions, and, within the limits of mutual respect for the rights of others, to lead one's own life.

There are some who see the difference between the open and totalitarian societies primarily in *material* terms. They point to the immense superiority of the open society with respect to the production of goods and services compared to the scarcities of the Communist world, where the frenzied attempt to catch up with and surpass America has until now failed. Some may recall the famous kitchen debate between Khrushchev and the then Vice-President Nixon, when the latter visited the Soviet Union. It was a spontaneous, informal debate in which each vied with the other in reciting the record of his nation's achievements. Despite the propaganda of Communist countries about a poverty-afflicted America, the population of those countries is not taken in by it. Even with all the material and technological help the Soviet economy has received from the shortsighted businessmen and governments of the West, it lags far behind. Nonetheless, that is not the basic issue. In a command economy where all resources of materiel and men can be mobilized, where no strikes are permitted and forced labor is the rule, it is not impossible that in some area of production a Communist society may succeed in outproducing the free societies. After all, the Soviet Union put a Sputnik in the sky before we decided to launch our own satellites. It is not inconceivable, although highly unlikely, that in the future the Soviets may become number one in almost every field. Suppose a day comes when Communist countries are richer than those of the West. Will the issues that divide us be any less? I do not think so. They will appear more starkly than ever.

Those issues are many, but in the end they all relate to the legacy of the founding philosopher-statesmen of the American republic—the right to live under just laws whose authority rests upon the consent of the governed, with individuals free, beyond the necessary confines of public order, to lead their own lives, think their own thoughts, and pursue patterns of happiness for which they themselves take responsibility.

Leaving aside the conceptual formulations of the meaning of freedom today, and what the issues are that divide the free world from the closed societies of our time, we may take a denotative approach and point to the actual ways in which the different societies are organized, justice is administered, and public policies are developed in relation to public opinion. The contrasting qualities of the lived experience illustrate the difference.

We may grant that these differences are not always, and never completely, ideological. Some of them are national, ethnic, and traditional. We should also grant that there are problems and evils in the world over and above those that flow from ideological conflicts, no matter how acute. Even if there were no Communist regimes in the USSR and China the world would be plagued with a great many problems—poverty, overpopulation, ecological dangers, rampant and aggressive nationalisms. We must grant that in our own country there are abuses of freedom and threats to the birthright of moral equality proclaimed in the Declaration of Independence. There is an uncompleted agenda of social and economic action which must be carried out in order to fulfill the promise of American life. We are a nation of many faiths and religions, of different races, ethnic groups, and historical traditions, all bound together by belief in our moral equality. Many of our problems today flow from the fact that we have taken our philosophy of political freedom for granted, that we do not really understand it or cultivate in our social and political life the virtues and habits that are required to keep it healthy, and that are necessary to defend it in a dangerous world. In this world, the largest nation on earth, the Soviet Union, and the most populous nation on earth, Red China, are at one with each other—despite the current differences of their dictatorial regimes—in their common hostility to the free world.

The source of their hostility to the free world does not lie in the aggressive actions of the United States against them. It is false to assert, as have the so-called revisionist historians, that the United States is solely or mainly responsible for the Cold War. This contention rests upon the cool disregard of the ideology of communism and its conspiratorial practices, directed from the Kremlin, and the scandalous distortion of events at the close of World War II, when the Kremlin violated the agreements of Teheran, Yalta, and Potsdam which provided for free elections in Eastern and Central Europe. I shall mention only briefly some of the incontestable facts that expose the absurdity of the revisionist view, a view which, unfortunately, because of the absence of historical memory, is rapidly becoming canonical doctrine in many of our academic centers.

First, at the close of World War II the United States withdrew its troops from Europe while the Soviet Union kept its armies in all the countries it had occupied, including areas of Germany from which the United States had needlessly withdrawn. Second, to rebuild their war-shattered economies, the United States offered the Marshall Plan without strings to all the European nations, including Czechoslovakia and Poland, which at first accepted but under Stalin's pressure declined. Third, when the United States had a monopoly of atomic weapons—at a time when that erstwhile pacifist and future savage critic of American defense efforts, Bertrand Russell, was urging the United States to use the atomic bomb against the Soviet Union—the United States offered to surrender its monopoly to an international atomic authority, a proposal accepted by all the nations of the United Nations except the Soviet Union and its satellites. Hard on this rejection came the Communist coup in Czechoslovakia, the Berlin blockade, the Soviet and Chinese support of the North Korean invasion of South Korea, and the unleashing of ferocious campaigns of political propaganda and subversion, supplemented by intense espionage operations, against the United States. The rearming of the United States and the establishment of NATO were defensive measures designed not to roll back the Soviet armies, but to prevent the overrunning of Western Europe. No effort was made to come to the aid of the East German workers in 1953, the freedom fighters of Hungary in 1956, or the embattled Czechs in 1968 when Soviet tanks rolled over them.

I leave to those who are better informed an evaluation of the comparative military strengths in Europe of the forces of the East and West. I am no expert on military technology. But I do know something about the morale of Western Europe and its psychological readiness to resist aggression. They are at a very low ebb. I vividly recall the spirit of the population of West Berlin in 1948 when, together with Mayor Ernst Reuter and other popular leaders, we stood on the ramparts dividing the city and shouted "Es lebe die Freiheit," when the half-starved population of that war-battered metropolis refused to be bought off by Communist offers of coal, food, and clothing from its militant opposition to the efforts to cut Western access to it. There is little of that spirit left. In the eyes of Western Europe, the adoption of a one-sided Ostpolitik and the Helsinki Declaration grant official American recognition of Soviet hegemony in Middle and Eastern Europe and of the permanent separation of the two Germanys. Neither France nor Italy has the will or capacity to resist a Soviet incursion into West Europe. The only thing that stands in the way of such possible action is the presence of the American military in Western Europe, though not until the Kremlin is surer of Peking's intentions is the Soviet Union likely to move. The removal of American troops would be construed by the Kremlin as an invitation to Finlandize Europe. The mood which led to the widespread acceptance of the slogan "Why Die for Danzig?" in France on the eve of World War II pervades much of Europe today, strengthened by endemic anti-Americanism among intellectuals and neutralism among other classes.

Yet, so long as the American will to resist aggression remains firm, so long as the reaffirmation of the legacy of freedom is not undermined by skepticism, pacifism, and the erosion of patriotism, the Western Europeans will enjoy peace and be able to enjoy the luxury of their neutralism and anti-Americanism. For so long as the Communists are uncertain that they can win an armed conflict, we shall have peace. The statesmanship of the West, among other commitments to preserve security and prosperity, must see to it that the Communists remain uncertain.

The future becomes problematic, however, when we soberly assess the *American* mood. How strong is the American will and dedication to freedom in face of the growth of neo-isolationism, the persistent refusal to challenge Communist advances where there is little risk in doing so, and an ambiguous policy of detente that in an earlier period was called appeasement. The danger of appeasement—as the historical record shows—is that it has two possible upshots, both equally unpalatable. It emboldens an aggressor to take actions in the expectation of continued appeasement until a point is reached at which the alternatives seem to be either capitulation or a resistance that will end in defeat or a pyrrhic victory.

The situation becomes graver still because of the nature of modern weapons, and the awesome and incalculable consequences of the resort to them. Peace until now has rested on the precarious balance of terror which is threatened by the tendency to nuclear proliferation, and by the development of elaborate systems of civil defense by totalitarian powers, defense designed to make most of their industry and populations invulnerable to retaliatory response from the West. Prospects for the preservation of peace now mainly depend upon multilateral disarmament under strict international controls.

We must not deceive ourselves with excessive hopes or fears. With respect to those who make a fetish of survival at any cost, even the cost of freedom, we must recognize that the difficulty, the uncertainly, and the dread of the unknown gradually have a corrosive effect upon their will to resist any kind of aggression. But we know that whoever makes mere life, rather than a good life, the directing goal of existence; whoever makes survival at any price the be-all and end-all of existence, has already written for himself an epitaph of infamy. For there is no cause or value or person he will not betray. Not only is it an ignoble position, it is an unwise and impractical one. It is unwise because to proclaim—and there are many different ways of doing it—that one will not resist aggression, because allegedly, "There are no alternatives to peace," is to invite further aggression. It is to overlook the moderating effect of the passion for survival among the enemies of freedom themselves. It is to overlook the historical evidence that those in the past who have sought to save their property and life by sacrificing their freedom have often lost not only their freedom, but their property and life as well.

CHAPTER SIXTEEN

In Defense of the Cold War
Neither Red nor Dead

The strongest justification of the Cold War between the U.S. or the West and the Soviet Union is that it prevented a hot war and the triumph of Communism in Western Europe. It did not prevent a hot war in other areas of the world, but these did not directly involve the Soviet Union or threaten Western Europe. The tendency has been therefore in Western Europe to assess the Cold War narrowly without regard to the potential effects of the conflicts in other areas of the world on the prospects of its survival as a relatively free society. Indeed this tendency has developed to a point where it would hardly be an exaggeration to say that influential sectors of public opinion in Western Europe regard what they call "the cold war mentality" as a greater threat to their security than the intense, unabated campaigns of subversion, propaganda, and political pressure which the Soviet Union has been waging against the free world for decades. It is as if the Cold War were a set of activities initiated by the West or practiced only by the West while the actual expansion of the Soviet Union, directly or through its proxies, although deplored, is explained as a response to Western Cold War activities.

This is very strange because the ostensible and declared purpose of the Western proponents of the Cold War was one of containment of Communism, an essentially defensive strategy. The strategy of containment was itself adopted after the U.S. policy of accommodation proved unable to halt Soviet expansion. This policy was slow in emerging. In the interest of historic justice, because of present day revisionist interpretations, one should point out that at the close of World War II the U.S. demobilized its troops in Europe and dismantled its defense establishment, cutting its outlays from $81 billion in 1945 to $13 billion by 1948, while the USSR retained the bulk of its forces in place; that the U.S. offered Marshall Plan aid to all European nations, including those under Russian occupation, which was brusquely rejected by the Soviet Union, and that, when it had a monopoly of atomic weapons, the U.S. offered to surrender it to an international authority, the Baruch-Lilienthal plan, an offer spurned by the Soviet Union. So generous were the provisions of the Baruch-Lilienthal plan that Bertrand Russell at the time unwisely urged that the United States atom bomb the Soviet Union if it refused to accept the proposal. For Russell was convinced that the Soviet refusal presaged a renewed attempt to impose its way of life on the world as soon as it acquired atomic weapons. Fortunately the United States turned a deaf ear to Russell's pleas, and Russell himself as if to prove that the opposite of an absurdity could be just as absurd, became an ardent advocate of unilateral disarmament by the West.

Whatever the justifications of the policy of containment, a sober assessment of the situation today reveals that the containment policy has not been successful. The Soviet Union directly and through its proxies expanded into areas beyond its theater of national interest and indeed into regions that exceeded the reach or even concern of the czarist empire. Accompanying this expansion has been an absolute and relative decline in American defensive power. As the proportions of the G.N.P. not only in the U.S., but in Europe devoted to defense declined (from the early sixties to the late seventies) the proportions of the Soviet defense expenditures to its G.N.P. increased. One of the ominous consequences of this reversal of military power between the U.S. and the USSR is that the latter is now within easy striking distance of the oil fields and sea lanes on whose flow Western Europe and Japan are presently heavily dependent. Accompanying this has been the manifest decline and failure of American intelligence capacities, conspicuously illustrated in recent events in the Near East and Middle East but by no means restricted to these areas.

The upshot of all this, and of cognate developments on the diplomatic and economic front, has been a widespread perception among American allies, especially in Europe, of an erosion in the American will and capacity to defend the free world against aggression by an increasingly powerful Soviet Union both in conventional military weapons as well as nuclear ones. This in turn has naturally intensified the fears of many Europeans of needlessly exposing themselves by measures of concerted self-defense that might provoke Soviet punitive measures against them, especially as the deterrent power of the Western nuclear umbrella loses credibility.

We must also recognize that despite the fact that the balance

of terror—which is not the same thing as the balance of power—
has kept the peace in Europe, in recent years there has emerged
in Western Europe powerful movements favoring unilateral disarmament, political neutralism, and even outright pacifism. The
relative prosperity of Western Europe, compared to the immediate
post-World War II years, has dulled the sense of history and blotted
our consciousness of the basic values at stake in the struggle
against Communism leaving only the obsessive fear of war in
which even military victory may be catastrophic. The ancient
illusion that passive disobedience may be more effective than
armed resistance to aggression is being revived as well as the
misleading citation of the Gandhian example which overlooks the
crucial facts that Gandhi appealed to values that were integral to
the ethos of the British, whereas passive or nonresistance on a
small scale to totalitarian dictators has led to mass butchery. Another
comfortable illusion that has nurtured pacifist fantasies is that, in
the event of a Communist takover, the worst eventuality would
be a decline in both the standard of living and the loss of political
and cultural freedoms to the level of the Soviet satellites today.
This is extremely questionable. Once the countervailing presence
and power of the contrasting example of functioning open societies
is removed, there is nothing to prevent the culture of the Gulag
Archipelago or, more accurately, the standard of life and repression
within the Soviet Union from becoming general. Where all resistance
and threats of resistance to its global power are removed, the
Soviet Union is not likely to countenance a higher level of existence
or greater freedom of expression in its satropies than within its
own borders.

There is an alternative to capitulation and all-out war. Properly
waged this is the Cold War, which in effect was abandoned when
the policy of detente was introduced. Basic to the strategy of the
Cold War is the development and deployment of the means of
military defense which would make extremely problematic all-out
aggression against the free world. This strategy rests on the
reasonable assumption—reasonable because based on historical
evidence and the geography, so to speak, of the Communist mind—
that, unless their domestic spaces are invaded, the leaders of the
Soviet Union will not undertake a war they are uncertain to win,
or one whose costs are so heavy as to make even a technically
favorable outcome a pyrrhic victory. The cold war of containment
is designed to deny them any such assurance and therefore is a
policy of peace. And why indeed should the leaders of the Soviet
Union think otherwise? Unless the disproportion of strategic forces
in their favor is so overwhelming that resistance on the part of

the West would be minimal or hopeless, why should the Communist high command incur unnecessary risks?

Even without all-out general war, the power and influence of the Soviet Union on a global scale, despite occasional setbacks in some areas and despite domestic difficulties, are growing. Extrapolation in human affairs is dangerous because it assumes the constancy of key variables, but some of the key variables have changed. Whenever there was a risk of war in the past, notably at the time of the Berlin air-lift in 1948 and the Cuban missile crisis in 1962, the Kremlin has exercised what used to be called Bolshevik realism, and climbed down. Unfortunately for us today the present danger has developed because of the reversal in the positions of overall military strength between the two super powers. Unless that disproportion is reversed and the balance of strategic weapons is restored, the danger will grow that the leaders of the Soviet Union may abandon the cautious strategy of the past. In 1973, at the time of the Yom Kippur War, the 1962 positions of the U.S. and the USSR were reversed. One year after the ten point "Declaration of Basic Principles of Relations Between the U.S. and U.S.S.R." were signed in Moscow, in which both nations pledged themselves not to stir up conflicts in troubled areas of the world and obtain unilateral advantages at the expense of the other, the USSR encouraged Egypt and its allies whom it had rearmed, to attack Israel. After the initial defeats, Israel reversed the tide and by a pincers movement of its invading armies was about to destroy the Egyptian Eighth Army. At that point the Soviet Union threatened to intervene with its own armed forces. The U.S. protested. Soviet forces then went on a nuclear alert to which the U.S. responded with its own nuclear alert. The situation was every whit as serious as the confrontation in 1962. But a special meeting of the National Security Council informed President Nixon that the U.S. was no match at the time for the USSR. The result was that the American government brought pressure on the Israelis who reluctantly and under protest released the Egyptian Eighth Army from the grasp of the Israeli military forces. (Admiral Zumwalt is the source of this story, which has been confirmed by leading dignitaries at the time in the American defense establishment.)

This defeat, instead of being a signal to restore the equilibrium of strategic nuclear power, was a preface to detente. The domestic paralysis produced by Watergate had more to do with the failure to arrest the decline of American military power in the mid-seventies than the consequences of Viet Nam.

Redressing the balance in military power on all levels—conventional as well as nuclear—will be a long, arduous, costly process in which the Welfare States of the West may have to sacrifice some hard-won social gains. I do not agree with some pessimistic voices who lament that it is already too late. But it is obvious that it will be extremely difficult to achieve, in the face of Soviet diplomacy that seeks to create rifts in the Western alliance and strong domestic currents of opposition, the necessary increased defense expenditures as well as the punitive commercial actions that break the economic ties with the Soviet Union established during the period of detente. These ties were supposed to bind the Kremlin with cords of self-interest and prevent it from pursuing adventurist policies that would upset the *status quo*, but in effect they seem to have bound certain Western economic interests to acquiescence in Soviet actions in other areas of the world that weaken the West. One thing should be clear although it may be impolitic to make much of it. The U.S. cannot undertake to redress the balance of strategic power without the whole-hearted coop-eration of its European allies. This cooperation will be difficult not only because of increasingly onerous costs but because it requires a psychological reorientation in order to make nuclear deterrence effective.

The major psychological reorientation requires an understanding of the nature of the deterrent effect of nuclear weapons. The mere presence of these weapons is not sufficient to deter a potential aggressor. He must be convinced of the will and readiness to make *defensive* use of them, otherwise they lose their deterrence and end up contributing to a deceptive sense of security. There are several ways of communicating the presence and strength of this will and readiness—by frequent drills accompanied by preparedness for civilian air defense. The paradox which seems hard to accept in some quarters is that the more effectively is this will and readiness communicated, the more likely is it that these weapons will never be fired.

Further, the Cold War until quite recently, and this is still true among America's European allies, has been conceived as having its locus primarily in Europe—the region of the greatest threat. Defense planning both for strategic forces and theater nuclear forces has been geared to this eventuality. But in recent years the growth of Soviet military power together with the extension and intensification of its political power have made other areas peripheral to Western Europe highly vulnerable. But some of these other areas are vital to the security and industrial vitality of the West, particularly the Persian gulf. The resources of the U.S. are not sufficient to counter the Soviet threats, their power and maneuverability have increased in virtue of the fact that geo-political changes have strengthened Soviet interior lines of communication. In their own interest America's European allies must broaden their conception of the Cold War and actively participate in the devising of common measures to deal with threats outside Western Europe.

I want to stress that in my view the primary responsibility for the failure to keep abreast with Soviet military power in Europe and to block its political incursion in other areas, rests with the United States. Its policy of detente signaled a change, welcomed by its European allies, that in effect represented an abandonment of the Cold War of containment for one of accommodation and appeasement. The very expressions "Cold War" and "Cold Warrior" became epithets of disparagement in the West. The situation was symbolized by the refusal of President Ford, on the advice of Kissinger, to receive officially Aleksandr Solzhenitsyn during the week in which Brezhnev was receiving Gus Hall, head of the American Communist Party. From the point of view of the West, it is certainly not true that the policy of detente was the continuation of the Cold War waged by other means. Such a characterization applies more accurately to the Soviet conception of detente. In November 1980 in an address in Madrid, Ambassador Max Kampelman quoted from a speech by a leader of the Soviet Union in Prague in 1973 in which the latter made clear that the policy of detente was a strategy to effect a decisive shift in the international balance of power. Said the spokesman for the Soviet Union: "We have been able to achieve more in a short time with detente than was done for years pursuing a confrontation policy with NATO . . . Trust us, Comrades, for by 1985, as a consequence of what we are now achieving with detente . . . we will be able to extend our will wherever we need to." Even discounting for exaggeration, there is a grain of truth in the observation.

The adoption of the policy of detente by the U.S. was bipartisan. Its abandonment today should be equally bipartisan. But it seems to me still an open question whether our European allies have abandoned the policy of detente. There are disquieting signs that as the burden of the mounting costs of upgrading military defense becomes more onerous, especially in a period of economic retrenchment, the illusions that the status quo in Western Europe can be preserved without increasing sacrifice, born out of fear of a nuclear holocaust, will revive. The program adopted by the British Labour Party as well as the current orientation in international affairs of the Socialist International, may be harbinger of the drift of dominant European opinion. This could spell the end of NATO and I fear the reversion of American public opinion toward an isolationist foreign policy and the illusion of a Fortress America psychology rationalized by the consideration that one cannot defend the freedom of people who are unwilling to risk anything in their own defense. The withdrawal of American troops from Europe whose presence is now a guarantee that the fate of Western Europe and the United States is intertwined, would follow. The ghost of Senator Mansfield's proposal to call U.S. troops home who are now stationed in Europe still stalks the halls of Congress.

There is a misconception that the prosecution of the Cold War and negotiations on arms reduction and other issues are incompatible. This is a profound error. It has often been pointed out that the limited nuclear test-ban treaty was signed in 1963 at the height of the Cold War. This indicates that specific peace initiatives can be proposed and negotiated in an illusionless Cold War atmosphere. But there are negotiations and negotiations. Agreements must be strictly reciprocal and *verifiable*. It is not true that compliance can be monitored by satellite, sometimes called "natural means of verification." There must also be mutual *on site* inspections. As Eugene Rostow has observed: "No·camera can tell how many separate war heads are carried by a single missile, or measure its thrust, its accuracy, or the explosive power of the weapons it carries . . . Nor can it identify missiles in warehouses and underground." It is a commonplace but it has ever relevant practical implications—the broadcast of knowledge of violations of agreements entered into in an open society, where the press and public opinion are independent, is almost a matter of course. In a closed society, however, violations of agreements by contracting governments can be carried out with impunity. The West should make it clear that when the Soviet Union fails blatantly to live up to its obligations under existing treaties as is the case in the current flagrant violations of the provisions of Basket Three of the Helsinki Final Act, the other signatory powers should declare that they are relieved of their obligations under the Final Act—including the *de jure* recognition of the Soviet boundaries so coveted by the Soviet Union that it professes to accept Basket Three, which it has systematically violated.

So long as the ramparts of freedom are abundantly defended the Cold War will not become transformed into a hot war between the U.S. and the USSR. The conflict for the minds of men and women will go on. There will not be a final conflict but one long drawn out in the hope—so far nugatory—that changes within the

Communist world will lead to a degree of liberalization that will significantly modify its totalitarian character. The Cold War, as I conceive it, should be designed to achieve this result—to accept the fact that both systems are in a state of competitive peaceful coexistence struggling to win the allegiance of mankind.

It is sometimes said that facts, especially the facts of power, are ultimately more decisive than ideals and ideologies. But it is just as true that the weight and effects of power often depend upon our perception of them, and our conceptions of legitimacy and justified authority. The propaganda of all totalitarian countries recognizes this. Communist societies are particulary vulnerable to their own rhetoric and propaganda, especially in their proud claim of being a worker's state, committed to disarmament and peace, and human welfare. From this point of view (until very recently) the behavior of the West is a history of lost opportunities in exposing the weaknesses and hypocrisies in the roots of the totalitarian Communist structure itself. Next in importance to containing and frustrating Soviet expansion, is this effort at ideological destabilization of the potentially restive populations of Communist regimes not by inflammatory rhetoric but by the sober propaganda of truth—even truth about some of our own shortcomings. Its success may inhibit the appetite for foreign adventure among the Communist leadership.

The exodus of hundreds of thousands of Cubans at the risk of life and limb from Castro's island paradise was mishandled from the point of view of its educational potential, as well as other mass flights of refugees from Communist countries. Not enough has been done to expose the absurdity of equating the political and civil rights of the U.N. Declaration of Human Rights with the social and economic rights of the workers, for in the absence of the first, the second are uncertain and in times of crisis, nonexistent. In the absence of political freedoms, not even a slave system can provide security.

The Polish situation is a paradigm case of the bankruptcy of Communist professions of being a worker's state. No matter what the specific outcome of that situation will be in Poland, from now on it will be a perpetual reminder to all Communist satellite nations and to the workers of the Soviet Union itself that free and independent trade unions are incompatible with the monopoly of political power by a dictatorial Communist minority, and that a nation physically unarmed but spiritually mobilized—symbolized by slogans like "while there is death, there is hope"—may moderate the severity of totalitarian rule in the direction of a more humane

order. Beyond that we cannot see at the present moment. Of one thing we can be confident. No words of support to Solidarity or contributions of food or clinical supplies, despite *Pravda*, will be a pretext for the Kremlin to do what it would not have done otherwise.

The Polish situation was a pitiful revelation of the unreadiness of the Western world, particularly the U.S., to wage an effective Cold War which the Communist authorities and their spokesmen in the West ungratefully charge the U.S. of engaging in. The decision of the AFL-CIO to contribute to the Polish Workers Aid Fund threw Washington, not the Kremlin, into panic and led the State Department to supererogative assurances to the Kremlin that the American government was not involved in the charitable efforts. Perhaps it was a hangover from previous administrations, but it seemed as if the Sonnenfeld doctrine was still active, although its own author had repudiated it, and that the West, as Tom Kahn caustically observed, "had developed a vested interest in the stability of the Eastern bloc." I am not well informed about the reaction to the Polish events in Western Europe, but my impression is that they were met with more alarm than elation. I have been informed that some Social Democratic figures showed a fine sense of international solidarity by proclaiming, "the U.S. out of El Salvador and the USSR out of Poland." There is something preposterous in this equation between several divisions of Soviet soliders in full armor with a handful of American technicians aiding the government to carry out its plans for land reform against reactionary right-wing terrorists and left-wing terrorists of a Communist-dominated coalition fueled and armed by clients and proxies of the Soviet Union.

It is not inconceivable that if the situation in Poland develops along pluralistic lines that reveal the lineaments of the human face some heretical Communists talk about but so far have nowhere produced that the West should actually help to ease Poland's economic burdens. It would be well worth the cost of an example that might inspire instability in other satellites and similar liberal developments. Hopefully the appetite for freedom will grow upon what it feeds and even infect the rank and file of the captive trade unions of the USSR. The exact form of that cooperation cannot be forseen now, but it is not beyond imaginability that the kind of support extended to hard-line Yugoslavia under Tito at the first manifestations of Communist polycentrism be directed toward Poland if its free trade union movement is permitted to flourish.

In contradistinction to hot war, Cold War is not a monopoly

of government. Private groups can wage it, sometimes, as in the case of organized protest against the systematic harassment of Sakharov, even more effectively. The refusal of American scientists and mathematicians to meet with their Soviet counterparts until the persecution of Sakharov ceases, by itself may seem a slight form of pressure that the Soviet Union can shrug off. Multiplied and extended to other areas of science and scholarship this intellectual and cultural boycott may prove costly enough to occasion second thoughts in the Politburo.

I want to conclude by stressing a proposition that I believe can and should be a focal point in current Cold War agitation on which Western public opinion and Western governments can unite, to wit, that the Brezhnev doctrine is incompatible with the spirit, text, and principles of the Helsinki Final Act Accords just as much as the censorship, imprisonment, exile and confinement in psychiatric institutions of dissidents. The Brezhnev doctrine that no satellite of the Soviet Union has the right to modify its current political and social structure in the direction of greater democracy and pluralism was never freely voted on by any people to whom it has been applied. It is a naked assertion of *Faustrecht*. Let us challenge it before the conscience of the world not only at Madrid but wherever East and West meet.

CHAPTER SEVENTEEN

On Western Freedom

Rarely in modern times—especially in times of relative peace—has one man's voice provoked the Western world to an experience of profound soul-searching. What Aleksandr Solzhenitsyn said not only at Harvard in June 1978 but also earlier before the AFL-CIO (which provided him a platform when the President of the United States, at the urging of his Metternichian Secretary of State Henry Kissinger, refused to receive him) has stirred the reflective conscience of the Western world more profoundly than even the eloquent discourses of Franklin Roosevelt and Winston Churchill. This is all the more unprecedented because Solzhenitsyn speaks in a foreign tongue and uses expressions that remain opaque in translation. Nonetheless, the continuing comments on the Harvard speech testify to the power of his words and to the fundamental character of his challenge to our mode of life, to its basic values, fears, and illusions, and to a philosophy of civilization concealed by the apparent absence of any philosophy.

My response to Solzhenitsyn's Commencement address falls into four sections, followed by a restatement of what I regard as Solzhenitsyn's morally valid challenge to the West despite the multitude of defects and inaccuracies in his analysis of the nature of freedom and democracy and the causes of the weakness of the West.

First I shall deal with his general indictment of the West. Second, I shall consider some of his specifications of its decline and dangers. Third, I shall discuss his peculiar conception of democracy, his failure to appreciate the distinction between legality and morality, even granting the large measure of truth in his observation about the excesses of a freedom conceived only as the absence of restraint or the rejection of rational regulation. Fourth, I shall consider his causal analysis of our predicament, his central contention that all our evils can be attributed to the rise of secular, rational humanism and its belief that an acceptable human morality is intrinsically related to the consequences of our actions on human weal and woe. According to Solzhenitsyn, such a belief generates the heresy that morality is logically independent of religion and theology, especially of the existence of God as "the Supreme Complete Entity." Here Solzhenitsyn reveals not only his literary but also his spiritual kinship to his great countrymen, Dostoyevsky and Tolstoy.

Finally, after giving full measure to all of Solzhenitsyn's misunderstandings of Western culture, I should like to restate what I take to be his crucial, abiding, and valid messages to the partisans of human freedom in our time. On the basis of his central insight, I am confident that those who are opposed to *all* varieties of totalitarianism can work out a unifying moral program that is independent of all our theological and religious differences. Such an approach can serve as a common rallying point for those who still believe that in the current conflict between free and unfree societies, there are alternatives other than war and surrender. It makes possible a strategy for freedom that still holds out the promise not merely of survival but of a society worthy of human beings.

HIS INDICTMENT OF THE WEST

The central point in Solzhenitsyn's indictment of the West is that it has suffered a colossal failure of nerve concerning its own animating philosophy of freedom, as expressed in its basic documentary ideals. According to him, the map of political freedom in the world is shrinking, and Western ideals are in eclipse even in those areas of the world that they helped to liberate. The vast gains in all forms of human freedom that have been made in social and political life are either denied or downgraded, in his eyes, by the continuing shortcomings that are apparent when we measure (as we should) the status quo against our highest standards.

In the Communist world, Solzhenitsyn charges, there is no genuine reciprocity either in cultural exchanges or in the honoring of pledges and agreements. The Helsinki Accords, in which the West formally acknowledged the de facto suzerainty of the Soviet empire in Eastern Europe, have been violated by the failure of the Soviet Union and most of its satellites to live up to the elementary provisions of human rights to which they have pledged lip allegiance. The degrading treatment of the Scharanskys, the Ginsburgs, and the Grigorenkos, the enforced incarceration of dissidents in psychiatric torture chambers, continues. The Soviet Union's failure to uphold the Belgrade agreement to investigate the compliance with human rights brought no remonstrance from the United States.

In the so-called Third World, according to Solzhenitsyn, we have witnessed a strange transformation: colonially liberated countries whose ideals were related to, if not rooted in, the American Declaration of Independence are now ruled by one-party dictatorships whose treatment of the people equals or even surpasses in cruelty the oppression from which they were liberated. The United Nations has in effect become an association of anti-American nations more intent on transforming Israel, the victim of a systematic terror campaign, into a pariah state than on coping with the genocidal practices of Amin's Uganda or Kampuchea.

But the main point in Solzhenitsyn's indictment of the Western world concerns its very conception of freedom. He believes the West is so obsessed with its notion of freedom that in exercising that freedom it cannot distinguish between what is desirable and what is undesirable to pursue. It defends individual *rights* to the point of making them almost absolute, refusing to understand that our essential freedoms cannot function properly unless we recognize that certain human *obligations* are just as binding upon us. "Legal limits (especially in the United States) are broad enough," he says, "to encourage not only individual freedom but also certain individual crimes. Supported by thousands of public defenders, criminals can remain unpunished or receive undeserved leniency. When a government seriously undertakes to fight terrorism, public opinion immediately accuses it of violating the terrorists' civil rights."

Many of Solzhenitsyn's formulations are inexact or exaggerated, but I think it is fair to restate his main philosophical points in the following assertions.

First, freedom is misconceived if it is defined as the right to do anything one pleases. Every specific freedom we can reasonably defend must be one that is desirable or normative.

Second, no desirable freedom can be unqualified; every right, whether moral or legal, carries with it a restriction or prohibition of the correlative right to interfere with it. If you sincerely believe that a person has a right to speak, write, assemble, and worship according to his conscience, then you must believe that no one has the right or freedom to prevent him from exercising this right, that the freedom to interfere with this right must be restrained. If you believe in tolerance, then you cannot believe in tolerating those who are *actively intolerant* of others. Otherwise you do not understand the meaning of tolerance or are insincere in professing belief in it.

Third, no matter what schedule of desirable rights or freedoms you draw up, none is absolute, because in every moral situation, rights conflict. In his own way Solzhenitsyn realizes what philosophers like John Dewey and others have expressed more precisely, that the moral situation confronts one with a conflict not between good and bad, right and wrong, but between the good and the good, and the right and the right and the bad and the worse. For instance, you cannot always give a man a right to a fair trial and permit complete freedom of the press. Kindness and truth are not always compatible. Lying is wrong, but so is murder— and sometimes you may have to choose between telling the truth and saving a life. Divorce American style where children are involved is deplorable but if the only alternative were "Divorce Italian Style," according to the famous film of that name, even a religious fundamentalist would have to give preference to the American style as the lesser evil.

LEGALISM VS. MORALITY

The biting impact of Solzhenitsyn's speeches lies not in his recognition of these truths but rather in his dramatic illustrations of what he regards as improper choices when values conflict. Two illustrations must suffice.

Of course Solzhenitsyn believes in freedom of the press—since he has been imprisoned and exiled because of its absence. But in the West he sees a press "more powerful than the legislature, the executive, and the judiciary," and a claim for its freedom regardless of the consequences for the nation's well-being and security. He asks: If everyone is to be held morally responsible and legally accountable in a just and democratic society, who holds the press responsible and accountable, especially if it enjoys a practical monopoly? He speaks of cases in which reporters steal government secrets and the press publishes them under the claim "the public has a right to know": when legal inquiries are made into the secret sources of a reporter's news, he says, even if a man's life or freedom is at stake, the press unanimously denies that the public has a right to know—on the grounds of freedom of the press. But if that is true, then may it not also be true that in the interests of preserving a free society—without which there could be no freedom of the press—the government may also claim that there are some secrets that the public does not, at least for a limited period, have a right to know?

A second illustration. Coming from a country in which people are often severely punished for living up to the laws of their own land, as the Soviet dissidents claim, Solzhenitsyn is taken aback by what he sees in this country as an excess of legalism over morality in the judicial system. This is related to what others have recently referred to as our imperial judiciary. At a time when there is a sharp incidence in major crimes of violence, he finds increasing concern with protecting the rights, not of the victims and potential victims of crime, but of those guilty or accused of crimes. He claims to find a jurisprudential theory according to which criminals are the victims of society and therefore not really responsible for their evil deeds; this results in the legally countenanced resort to technical procedures and prolonged delays that defeats the ends of justice. (If he had mentioned the absurdity of the exclusionary rule as currently applied in the area of evidence, he would have been much more eloquent and morally indignant.) Rightly or wrongly he associates these judicial conditions with the decline in private and public morality, with an increase in selfishness, with the philosophy of grab-and-run-if-you-can. There is something wrong with a society when "the center of your democracy and culture is left for a few hours without electricity, just that, and instantly crowds of American citizens rush to loot and rape."

THE PRESS AND AMERICAN DEMOCRACY

Let us now turn to a more central point. Even if we grant the validity of many of the *specific* criticisms in Solzhenitsyn's indictment (and in these matters of the law and abuses by the press the picture seems to me to be very grim indeed), what does Solzhenitsyn suggest as a political cure or alternative? Here a fatal ambiguity in his conception of democracy manifests itself, and I shall relate this to his fundamental theology.

First of all, Solzhenitsyn fails to realize that many of the defects in the current American legal process are not rooted in the democratic system. In democratic countries like England and Canada, and even in some less democratic jursidictions, without the slightest abridgment of justice, the courts work much more effectively and the law is by far less egregiously an ass than in so many of our state and federal jurisdictions.

This is even more obvious with respect to the press. Given the present state of investigative reporting, the growth in some quarters of advocacy reporting, and the view that because complete objectivity is impossible, therefore the whole concept of objectivity is a myth, no man's or woman's reputation is safe from careless and irresponsible misrepresentation. In this respect, professional standards of media reporting in England are superior to those in the United States, though even there they leave something to be desired. Even without taking recourse to the English laws of libel and the Official Secrets Act, one can repair to a Press Council if one has been victimized by a false or malicious press story. But in the United States—

When the Twentieth Century Fund, on the advice of some leading figures in American journalism and based on the success of the British example, established a Press Council, such leading papers as *The New York Times* and *The Washington Post* refused to cooperate with that council. Indeed, the American Society of Newspaper Editors a few years ago voted three to one against the establishment of even its own internal grievance committee [Max Kampelman, "The Power of the Press," *Policy Review*, Fall 1978].

Lester Markel, a former editor of the *New York Sunday Times*, a few years ago wrote:

The press, pretending to believe that there is no credibility gap and asserting its near-infallibility, countenances no effective supervision of its operation; it has adopted a holier-than-thou attitude, citing the First Amendment and in addition the Ten Commandments and other less holy scripture [*New York Times*, February 2, 1973].

John B. Oakes, emeritus editorial-page editor of the *New York Times*, added his voice to the criticism of journalistic irresponsibility. In discussing the "Dwindling Faith in the Press" he pointed to the necessity of making the press "voluntarily more accountable as well as more accessible to the public" (*New York Times*, May 24, 1978). The more powerful it is, the more accountable it should be. Sometimes it abuses its power, as when by false reporting it transformed the military *disaster* suffered by the Viet Cong in its Tet Offensive into a military *victory*. The effect was to give a political victory to the Viet Cong in this country, force a President out of office, and profoundly affect the ultimate outcome of the war.

These are some of the evils of a democracy. But the cure, surely, is not *no* democracy but a *better* democracy. And there are ways and means of bettering a democracy without relying on the famous trinity of the Dostoyevskian tradition: mystery, authority, and miracles. What Solzhenitsyn fails to appreciate about Western democracy is the nature of its political faith. There is nothing sanctified about the will of a majority even when it recognizes the civil and human rights of its minorities. It is not infallible. The majority may be unenlightened, but as Felix Frankfurter put it, "the appeal from an unenlightened majority in a democracy is to an enlightened majority," and so long as the political process of registering freely given consent exists, the evils are remediable.

The real question we must ask Solzhenitsyn is whether he is prepared to accept the *risks* of a democracy and its right to be wrong, provided it has a chance to correct that wrong. Or does he believe, as do all totalitarians from Plato to those of the present, that most members of the community are either too stupid or too vicious to be entrusted with self-government? I, for one, believe that despite some ambiguous expressions, Solzhenitsyn, like his great compatriot Andrei Sakharov, can be counted on the side of democracy.

The fundamental argument for democracy against those who are convinced that they know the true interests of the people better than the people itself is: those who wear shoes know best where they pinch and therefore have the right to change their political shoes in the light of their experience. Of course, children and mentally retarded persons do not always know when and where their shoes pinch. The totalitarians and their apologists justify their "paternalism"—which rests more on force and self-interest than on genuine concern for the people's welfare—by the arrogant assumption that the people are in a permanent state of childhood.

THE WEST'S FAILURE OF NERVE

I come now to Solzhenitsyn's analysis of the causes of the failure of Western courage, the inadequacies of its democracy, and the weakness of its morality. And here I find him, together with a long line of distinguished predecessors and successors, profoundly, demonstrably, and tragically wrong. To Solzhenitsyn the cause of Western democratic decline and the collapse of its morality is the rise of secular humanism and rationalism, which began with the breakdown of the medieval synthesis and the emergence of the scientific world outlook. Put in its simplest terms, what Solzhenitsyn is saying is that the basic cause of our world crisis is the erosion of religion, the decline in the belief in the existence of a Supreme Power or Entity, and our reliance not on transcendental faith but on human intelligence as a guide to man's nature and conduct.

I cannot accept Solzhenitsyn's causal analysis for many reasons. Historically, neither Judaism, Christianity, nor Islam is responsible for the emergence of democracy as a system of community self-government resting upon the freely given consent of the governed. None of these religions ever condemned slavery or feudalism in principle, and often they offered apologetic justifications for them. Logically, from the proposition that all men are equal in the sight of the Lord, it does not follow in the least that they are or should be equal in the sight of the Law. The belief in the divine right of kings is older than the equally foolish view *vox populi vox Dei*. The existence or nonexistence of God is equally compatible with the existence of any social system whatsoever, except when God is so defined that His moral attributes require that the system be democratic.

My criticism goes even further. Theology is irrelevant not only to democracy and capitalism and socialism as social systems but to the validity of morality itself. Solzhenitsyn echoes Smerdyakov's dictum in Dostoyevsky's *Brothers Karamazov* that "if God does not exist, everything is [morally] permissible." But this is a non-sequitur. Men build their gods in their own moral image. When we profess to derive a moral command from a religious revelation, it is only because we have smuggled into our conception of Divinity our own moral judgments. By definition God cannot do evil, but we ourselves are responsible for the distinction between good and evil. What makes an action morally valid is not a command from on high or from anywhere else but the intrinsic character of the action and its consequences for human weal and woe.

Some of the profoundest theologians of the West, from the author of the original version of the Book of Job to Augustine to Kierkegaard, have maintained that the religious dimension of human experience transcends the moral experience. The bone in the throat of Western theology is the problem of evil—the ever-recurrent question why an allegedly all-powerful and all-benevolent Supreme Being permits in every age the torture of innocent multitudes. Kierkegaard in his *Fear and Trembling* portrays Abraham, because of his willingness to sacrifice his son, Isaac, on divine command, not as a great *moral* figure, comparable to Agamemnon or Brutus the Younger, who also were willing to sacrifice their offspring, but as a divinely inspired *religious* figure. It would not be difficult to show that Kierkegaard's reading is quite arbitrary and that in the end Abraham's action in sacrificing an animal instead of a human being testifies to the supremacy of morality, to the birth of a new moral insight or judgment for which he and we as individual human beings must take responsibility, and not to a pious, unreasoning acceptance of a command from an allegedly divine power.

But the argument is unnecessary. For it should be clear that if like Solzhenitsyn we wish to unite mankind in the defense of rational freedom, in the preservation of a free society, it is not necessary to agree on first and last things about God, immortality, or any other transcendental dogma. Actually the great majority of mankind do not subscribe to the Judeo-Christian faith—they are Hindus, Buddhists, Confucians, Shintoists, naturalists, and animists. Religion is a private matter, and religious freedom means the right to believe or disbelieve in one, many, or no gods. If we wish to unify or even universalize the struggle for freedom, I propose that we find a set of ethical principles on which human beings can agree regardless of their differing presuppositions, a set of common human needs and human rights that will permit human beings of different cultures, if not to live and *help* each other to live, at least to live and *let* each other live. What unites Solzhenitsyn and Sakharov and us with them—our love of human freedom and our desire to preserve a free society—is more important than any of our differences. Solzhenitsyn's strategy divides us in the common struggle by his criticism of secular rational humanism.

A GREAT MORAL PROPHET

Despite my differences with Solzhenitsyn on the matters I have mentioned and on others also, I regard him as one of the great moral prophets of our time. After all, what is it that has moved him to his thunderous evocations of despair with the values and absence of values in the West? It is his observation, repeated in various ways, that the relatively free areas of the world are becoming progressively weaker *vis-à-vis* the totalitarian powers and their assorted varieties of Gulag Archipelagos. And he has been struck to the very heart of his being by the growing feeling among some leading intellectual figures of the West, like George Kennan, that "we cannot apply moral criteria to politics," and that since resistance may lead to a universal conflict in which the survivors will envy the dead, the West starting with the United States must "begin unilateral disarmament."

And what if the enemies of a free society are not inspired by this spirit of Christian submission? What if, interpreting pacifism and appeasement in good Leninist fashion as an expression of cultural decadence, they move to take over the remaining centers of freedom? Better that, says George Kennan, than the consequences of resistance. Echoing Bertrand Russell in his last years, Kennan proclaimed, in his famous interview in the *New York Times*, "Rather

Red, than Dead." Solzhenitsyn finds that this is a mood not far below the surface in Western Europe and other areas. In moments of crisis we find it expressed in many ways. How often have I heard variations on the themes "It is better to live on your knees than die on your feet" and "It is better to be a live jackal than a dead lion."

Now, for one thing—although Solzhenitsyn does not say this— Kennan's and Russell's strategy of ultimate surrender may not work in a world where two super-Communist powers possess nuclear weapons with which they threaten each other. We may first become Red and still end up dead![1]

As I read him, Solzhenitsyn is saying something different. He claims that our greatest danger is the loss of moral nerve, the loss of will power, the loss of belief that some things are morally more important than mere life itself, and that without such belief, weapons, "no matter how great the accumulation, cannot help the West overcome its loss of will" to defend free institutions. In one of the memorable sentences in his Harvard address, he quietly says, "To defend oneself, one must also be ready to die"—and the context shows that by this he means the defense of our free institutions as our ultimate concern. There is a profound historical and psychological truth here. The lean and hungry hordes ready to die have always triumphed over those who have sought primarily to save their goods or to save their necks. (Not infrequently they lost both, and their honor as well.) Deny Solzhenitsyn's proposition and what conclusion must one draw? That survival is the be-all and end-all of life, the ultimate value. But if we are prepared to sacrifice all our basic values for mere survival, there is no infamy we will not commit. The result would be a life morally unworthy of man's survival.

Solzhenitsyn's abiding message is that if we renew our moral courage, our dedication to freedom, we can avoid both war and capitulation in the grim days ahead. Our choice is not between being "Red or dead"—provided we are prepared to stake our lives, if necessary, on freedom. For we are dealing not with totalitarian madmen but with Leninists who worship at the altar of history,

---

[1] It is noteworthy that Bertrand Russell, when he had reached the age of Socrates, still gave precedence to freedom over mere survival—even after the hydrogen bomb had been invented. "Terrible as a new world war would be, I still for my part should prefer it to a universal Communist empire" (*New York Sunday Times Magazine*, September 27, 1953). Subsequently he was to defame those who defended this position.

who believe their triumph is inevitable without war, and who, by virtue of every principle of their ideology, will never initiate a world war unless they are certain they will win it. Our task is to be strong enough to prevent their belief in such a certainty. Why should they risk a war when they are gaining power and growing stronger without war, using other nations as mercenaries in local military engagements?

One need not endorse Solzhenitsyn's specific political judgments to agree with him that so long as the West remains strong enough to preclude any guarantee of totalitarian victory, and so long as it recognizes that the essential moral element in that strength is the willingness to risk one's life in the defense of freedom, there will be no world war. World peace, which has existed under the balance of terror, will be preserved as we rely on multilateral disarmament and the hope of evolutionary peaceful changes in totalitarian societies. We have seen fascist countries become transformed into imperfect democracies without war. So long as we keep our guard up and do not capitulate *à la* Kennan or Russell, *perhaps* someday totalitarian Communist countries may through internal development democratize themselves without war.

Differing as profoundly as I do with Solzhenitsyn about so much, I am nonetheless confident that he would agree with a short answer I have made to the Kennans and Russells of this world in the form of a thumbnail credo:

It is better to be a live jackal than a dead lion—for jackals, not men. Men who have the moral courage to fight intelligently for freedom and are prepared to die for it have the best prospects of avoiding the fate both of live jackals and of dead lions. Survival is not the be-all and end-all of a life worthy of man. Sometimes the worst thing we can know about a man is that he has survived. Those who say life is worth living at any cost have already written for themselves an epitaph of infamy, for there is no cause and no person they will not betray to stay alive. Man's vocation should be the use of the arts of intelligence in behalf of human freedom.

I am also confident that if Hitler and the Nazis had developed atomic weapons and threatened the West with their use, many of those who currently find plausible the Kennan-Russell line—which in effect is one of capitulation—would have rejected the variant "Better Nazi, than Dead" and accepted the spirit of the passage above.

CHAPTER EIGHTEEN

A Critique of Conservatism

One of the recurrent phenomena of social life is a periodic swing in thought and attitudes between polar positions. In the arts the movement is from order to revolt, from tradition to experiment, and back again. In education the movement is from a curriculum of the tried and true fundamentals to varied and individually oriented offerings, from the discipline of method to the permissiveness of self-expression. In politics and economics today we are experiencing, at least in ideologicial emphasis, a reversion from the so-called welfare state to the liberal state of a century ago, from government conceived as an instrument of social progress and justice to government conceived merely as a watchman upholding public order.

The significance and infectious influence of Proposition 13 is currently being widely interpreted as a repudiation of the philosophy of the welfare state, of the role and rule of Big Government, bureaucratic intervention into the economy, over-regulation, and over-centralization. And oddly enough, almost everyone, including former opponents, seems to have become a partisan of Proposition 13, fiercely embattled against government intervention in the economy except, of course, where one's special economic interests are involved. *Herbert Spencer Redivavus* could well be the rallying cry of the ideological spokesmen of the flight from the welfare state.

The most paradoxical feature of the current attack on the welfare state is that it is being conducted under the rallying cry of "freedom." Freedom has become the shibboleth of the libertarian movement and all the prophets of the market-enterprise system. To the extent that this commitment to freedom is sincere, then even Social Democrats, who put freedom first, must meet the challenge posed by this attempt to undermine the precarious achievements of the welfare state, which from our point of view has still far to go to meet the legitimate expectations of free men and women. To us the opposite of the welfare state today is the ill-fare state, indifferent to the remediable ills of its citizens.

To begin with, I for one wish to stress that I hold no brief for the present plethora of controls and regulations on current production and consumption. Many of them are unnecessary. Everyone can furnish his own illustration of bureaucractic ineptitude. As one who believes in the moral right to commit suicide, I myself see no need for a host of regulations and controls, provided things are properly labelled and identified, that would protect mature persons from the consequences of their own reflective decisions. Nor am I prepared to defend the whole complex of government supports and subsidies, many of which have been adopted at the bidding of special-interest groups who profit most from them. Here, an intelligent approach requires a case-by-case analysis and decision.

But the real target of the conservative and libertarian revival is not this or that particular government program or regulation. It is rather the whole policy of government intervention itself they wish to reverse.

It is one thing to introduce regulation of social and economic behavior in the interest of safety and informed risk. It is quite another thing to presume to dictate to citizens what their lifestyle should be on the basis of an arrogant and bureaucratic decision as to what is good for them. This is typified in the failure to distinguish between the regulations that prevent the distribution of drugs like thalidomide and those that would prevent the customary use of cyclamates and saccharin when these are properly labelled. Unfortunately socialism and even social democracy have been identified too much with wholesale regulation and control of human conduct and not enough with the expansion, the enrichment, and the varieties of personal freedom. Yet historically the socialist movement developed out of a protest against the indignities of an industrial system that tied workers to fixed schedules and modes of conduct whose deadening monotony was felt to be incompatible with natural growth and the spontaneity of freely selected vocation.

Common sense would indicate that in part a cost-benefit analysis be undertaken here as in all other situations in which we have to balance good against good when we cannot have both, or bad against worse when we must choose one or the other. But the so-called libertarian ideology rejects this approach because it assumes that the only alternative to existing bad regulation is necessarily no regulation rather than a better or worse regulation.

One would have thought that the regulations that were introduced after the thalidomide disaster to insure greater safety in drug use would meet with no principled opposition. But even with respect to these regulations, it has been argued that they are unacceptable because their restrictions resulted in a severe reduction in the development and marketing of new drugs that allegedly could have saved more lives than were blasted by the monstrous deformities of thalidomide-affected births. When those who hold this view are questioned, they point to the fact that in certain other countries new life-saving drugs were used before they were adopted in this country. But they play down the fact that in every one of these countries, regulatory controls on the marketing of dangerous drugs exist, so that even if one accepted all the factual allegations made, this would be no argument for the abandonment of regulations on drugs but only for more intelligent regulations. To the opponents of regulation, the measure and content of freedom are determined not by specific consequences but by the degree to which the economy is free from any kind of direction or control. This in effect is to make a fetish of the free market, whereas for Social Democrats the economy is the means by which a whole cluster of other human freedoms are furthered.

Let us grant that one of the major functions of government, even the major function, is to protect freedom. Let us also grant on the basis of logic and historical experience that unlimited government is evil because it countenances no checks on its power to restrict freedom. This is an undeniable truth. But no less undeniable is the truth that the unlimited absence of government would be even more oppressive than unlimited government because that would spell anarchy—the rule of a thousand despots.

Those who speak of government, the agency of organized society, as if it were an inherent foe of human freedom seem to me guilty of a fundamental error. They assume that freedom exists in a state of nature, that it is a natural good that comes with the environment, and that it is surrendered when human beings are organized under laws which necessarily limit some freedom of action. Unless one defines freedom as the right and power to do anything one pleases— which no one can consistently do who becomes a victim of the cruel or malicious action of others—this view of freedom is a myth. There is no human freedom in *rerum natura:* it is an outcome of society, of a free society. Government and the state are not artificial accretions to the human estate. Long ago Aristotle recognized that the individual as a human being, as distinct from a biological organism, could not exist outside of society, that in such a situation he would have to be something more than man (divine) or less than man (animal).

To be sure governments can be restrictive and oppressive, and of such governments we can say that they are best when they govern least. But it is just as true to say that sometimes government can protect freedoms and not merely threaten them, that sometimes government can expand freedoms rather than restrict them. Whatever freedoms or rights we deem desirable, including the right to privacy, the right "to be left alone," governments and laws are necessary to secure them in a world where others are intent upon violating them. Our own historical experience is evidence of that. It was not the operation of the market that extended and protected the civil rights of the negroes in the South but the government, and the central government at that. It was not the operation of the market but of the government that guaranteed the rights of the American working class to collective bargaining. Since there can be no government without law, what is true for government is analytically true for law. In a sense *every* law, no matter how wise and enlightened, restricts someone's freedom. As Bentham put it, "every law is contrary to [someone's] liberty," i.e., it is contrary to the liberty or freedom of those who would do what the law forbids them to do and who would interfere with us in the exercise and enjoyment of our rights. The government or the law can only protect our liberty by depriving others of their freedom to act as they please. That is why it is simply false to argue that there is always an inherent opposition between law and freedom, and that the more we have one, the less we have of the other. Would any sensible person argue that the fewer the traffic laws, the greater the freedom motorists would enjoy in our crowded cities and highways to get to their destinations quickly and safely? And even if it were true for motorists, it would certainly not be true for pedestrians.

So long as human beings have conflicting desires, laws are inescapable, regulations are inescapable. Legislation is or should be the process by which we determine what kind of trade-offs we wish to make in the conflict of freedoms, and which are to be given priority.

But the real gravamen of the criticisms of the conservatives against the program of the welfare state is that by its interference with a free-market economy it necessarily limits, coerces, and ultimately destroys human freedom which can flourish only on the basis of a market economy. This is the burden of William Simon's bestselling *A Time for Truth*, enthusiastically endorsed in special introductions to the volume by the high priests of the free-market economy.

I propose that we take as our postulate the desirability of human freedom—which the free-market defenders also stress—and examine the bearings of the market economy on the freedom not only of those well-endowed with the goods of the world but of those who are not, on the freedom not only of the haves but of the have-nots. Is it true that all, or most, human beings are really free even in an ideally perfect market economy? No action is free unless it is uncoerced, unless it is based upon freely given consent. If I have no food or water or the wherewithal to live for myself and my family, how free am I to exchange my services in bargaining with someone else who has more than enough to live on? What alternatives have I to match his? In such bargaining situations, the individual who has more than he needs can command anything from me, including my freedom, for what sustains life. In an ideal free market, on paper everyone starts from scratch—everyone has equal means, equal needs, equal power. But in the real world, we do not start from scratch, there are great and growing disparities of power between those who have and those who have not that often make the notion of a fair and equal exchange a myth.

Suppose a man says to me: "Your money or your life"—and I give him my money. He is caught and pleads that I gave the money to him freely, that I *had* a choice. According to him, I could have saved my money at the cost of my life. Would anyone else say that I was a free agent? To say so would sound like a macabre joke. Now suppose I am without any means in the free market, and someone offers me work for a bare pittance under humiliating conditions—and there is no other work available or work I can do—am I really a free agent in that case? The situation is such that I am essentially faced with the objective ultimatum: "Your labor or your life," actually "Your labor or your life and the lives of your dependents." The coercion of hunger or the fear of hunger can be just as persuasive, although different, as the coercion of physical violence or its threat. The chief difference is that one is long drawn out, the other sudden and more immediately painful.

The basic point is incontrovertible. In any society, whether it possesses a market economy or a socialized economy, property is power. Whoever owns poperty has the power to exclude others from the use or possession of what is owned. Whoever owns property in the means of life which I must operate to earn a living—whether the property is owned by the state or an individual—has the legal right to exclude me from its use. Therefore property in things, especially in the social instruments of production, means power, power over human beings. In the very interest of the human freedom that upholders of the free market advocate, we Social Democrats contend that such power must be made socially and morally responsible to those who are affected by its exercise.

This is not the place to demonstrate in detail the multiple ways in which a market economy functions to affect the lives and freedom of those who contract to work within it. Take as a paradigm case the shut-down of a large plant in a community or town in which the plant or factory is the sole or chief supplier of employment. The individual worker in such situations is almost as helpless and unfree as he is in a natural castastrophe, with the normal expectations and life-style of himself and his family destroyed. The decision as to where to work, the conditions under which to work, and the rewards of work seem to be made by forces beyond his control. In the long run, the apologists of the free market argue, the individual will somewhere and somehow be able to find work again. But even if true, what happens until then? Even if true, who pays for the agony and costs of waiting for the market to stabilize itself? If we are to strengthen genuine freedom of choice and even approximate the quality of opportunity which the ideal market economy presupposes, we must do something to provide those who are thrown on the slag heap of the unemployed through no fault of their own, who are willing and able to work, with some alternative possibilities of existence.

After all, as a rule those who close down their enterprises because they are unprofitable, or not as profitable as other kinds of investment, have other means of existence at their disposal. In the very interest of freedom of choice, unemployment insurance and some kind of welfare payments to the victims of hazards beyond their control seem required to redress the bargaining balance. But this and similar government interventions into the economy are precisely what the high priests of the market economy deplore.

Let us openly admit that we share with the conservatives a fear of concentrated government power, but on the same grounds we are fearful of large concentrations of private property that can also have oppressive effects. Like them we seek the dispersion of power, but unlike them we seek to avert those gross inequalities of power that unduly influence the political process in these days of multiple mass communication. Even Thomas Jefferson, in the days in which the economy was mainly agricultural and rural, deplored extremes of wealth as subversive of the democratic spirit of a self-governing nation. The only way in which these extremes can be prevented today is through intelligent and equitable tax policy, through wiser and better government, not absence of government.

There are some concentrations of economic power that can be countered only by the power of government. It was none other than John Stuart Mill who proclaimed that "Society is fully entitled to abrogate or alter any particular right of property which on sufficient consideration it judges stands in the way of the public good." This recognizes that property is a human right but not all forms of it have the same weight and justification in the light of the public good.

The concept of the public good is a complex and difficult one, hard to define, except in terms of the reflective process in which we balance good against good and right against right. But without the existence and power of government, we could not peacefully determine or enforce the public good. Even those who would limit the power of government to that of watchman of the rules of the road, or to the exercise of police power, are committed to the notion of the public good.

Although it has been denied, I am prepared to show that even on the premises of the watchman theory of government, the public good requires some concern for public welfare, the extent of which depends on public resources. One form of this theory of the state and government professes a belief not only in equality before the law but in equality of opportunity, not equality of outcome. If we take equality of opportunity as an ideal, we must grant that so long as differences in family and home environment exist, as they always will, as well as extreme genetic variations in capacity, absolute or literal equality of opportunity is unattainable. But this is true of all ideals! That absolute health and wisdom are unattainable is no reason for not attempting to become healthier and wiser. The inability to establish absolute equality of opportunity is no justification for ceasing to move toward greater equality of opportunity. If democracy as a way of life implies an equality of concern for all members of the community to develop themselves to their full capacities as human beings, then it is obligatory on the democratic community to move toward greater equality of opportunity in all areas, especially education, housing, health, and employment, required for the development of the individual's best potential. That is why the American slogan of equality of opportunity is one of the most far-reaching principles ever enunicated and expressive of the ethics of Social Democracy. It is a premise for continuous social reform. And that is why the most influential school of thought in the conservative revival is abandoning the principle of equality of opportunity, and insisting that the only kind of equality which is compatible with a truly liberal society is one in which there is simply and only equality before the law.

In this view there is no such thing as "social justice" but only conflicting claims equally justified. Equality of opportunity is "a wholly illusory ideal." Justice is procedural, the impartial application of a rule or principle to all who fall under it regardless of the consequences of the rule.

There is one obvious and fatal flaw in any conception of justice that makes it merely procedural—the impartial application of a rule. It cannot distinguish between the just and unjust rules and cannot grasp the difference in significance between the statement that "justice consists in treating all persons in the same or relevantly similar circumstances equally" and the statement "justice consists in mistreating all persons in the same or relevantly similar circumstances equally." Equality is a necessary, but not a sufficient, condition of any intelligible theory of justice. Over and above formal legal equality, the just law must concern itself with the effects of law on human weal and woe. What modern-day conservatism fails to realize is that the pursuit of justice can be distinguished from, but ultimately not separated from, the pursuit of happiness or human welfare. No one in the world is really a self-made man or woman. When we consider what we owe to the community—our language without which there could be no thought, our skills that are dependent upon the cumulative traditions forged by generations of early pioneers, our knowledge most of which we have inherited, our safety, health, and even our goods possessed not only in virtue of our own efforts but because of the activities and forbearances of others—we become conscious of a debt that cannot be discharged if we are indifferent to the fate of our fellows. Concern for the public welfare does not require self-sacrifice but the wisdom of common sense that recognizes the obligation of unpaid debts and the dictates of enlightened self-interest.

As if this were not confusion enough, there has developed, out of inability to see how differences among men can be resolved by rational moral principles, a call for a return to transcendental religion. It is alleged that all our social problems and evils are a consequence of failure to grasp the supernatural truths concerning

God's existence and his supreme goodness as well as power. The failure of moral nerve in the West and the cult of irresponsibility and hedonistic abandon, with all their degrading side effects, are attributed to the loss of religious faith. We are told that a politics oriented toward man and the fulfillment of his needs on this earth can end only in the worship of Caesar.

With the profoundest respect for the great moral figure of our time who has recently articulated this point of view, Aleksandr Solzhenitsyn, we must repudiate it on many grounds. First of all, it is irrelevant to the basic issues that divide the free world from its chief totalitarian enemy. Those issues are rooted in freedom of choice. In a free and open society, freedom of religion is central to be sure, but freedom of religion means not only the right to worship God according to one's conscience, but the right not to worship, the right to believe in one, many, or no Gods.

Second, it is historically false to assert that religious faith is necessarily on the side of a free human society. The totalitarianism of the Soviet Union and of the fascist states both in the past and present has had its religious defenders.

Third, it is logically false to make any kind of religious belief the basis of human morality because men build their gods in their own moral image. What makes an action good or bad is not any divine command but the intrinsic nature of the act and its consequences for human weal and woe. It is not true that morality logically depends on religion. It is the other way around. We must first know what the good is before we seek its alleged source.

Finally, to introduce religious faith as a necessary condition of a humane society is divisive. We can rally mankind around a program of autonomous human rights, In a world of conflicting religions in which Christians are a minority, in a world of conflicting faiths even among Christians, it is wishful thinking to expect agreement on any transcendental dogmas. If we can agree and unite on the basis of acceptance of universal human rights, we do not have to agree on their religious or philosophical justifications.

As Social Democrats we yield to none in the cause of freedom— whether moral or political. And we repudiate as unfounded, indeed untrue, the conservative view that we need the unconscious help either of a pure market economy or a Supreme Being to realize that freedom in our institutions. It is true that we cannot properly plan for an entire society. Nor can we rebuild any aspects of it without regard for human history and the limitations of human nature and power. It is true that human reason is neither all powerful nor infallible. But these truths are no grounds to forego the use of intelligence and the self-corrective methods of experience in trying to cope with the problems of our economy—the chief of which are to provide full employment at an adequate wage level, economic growth, and minimal inflation.

There are redefinitions of conservatism that go beyond the libertarian ideology of the free market and seek to enstate the varied traditions of Savigny, Hegel, Burke, and even the Church fathers and philosophers. We are confronted by a curious melange of insight, ambiguity, and prophetic utterance which despite its emphasis on history neglects the liberating effect in its time of the ideals of free enterprise on the encrusted privilege, cruel prejudice, hereditary squalor, and periodic purges of the underdogs of the past. They mock with justification the invisible hand of the market but substitute for it the Cunning of Reason, the compensatory rhythm of history, or the Hand of Providence and other obscurantist notions.

Burke's maxim, "Change is the means of our preservation," can be accepted even by antagonists in a death struggle—it all depends upon the nature, direction, and degree of change. The traditions of the past are multiple not unitary, authorities are usually conflicting, interests are not always common or shared. All too often conservatism is a way of doing nothing disguised by the consoling rationalization that whatever predicaments society faces are integral to the human condition. The paradox of some conservative traditions that fear reforms as a prelude, rather than as an alternative, to revolution is that the historical figures they venerate, whether it be the Richelieus and Talleyrands, the Disraelis and Metternichs, the Frederick the Seconds or Bismarcks, were movers and shakers of events—many of them of unhappy consequence—rather than servitors of the *status quo*.

The contrast between "conservatism" and "liberalism" today is not very instructive because these terms have been labels for varied and ambiguous positions. It is more illuminating to discuss *issues*, particularly when according to some conservatives ideas of any generality are considered abstractions applied mechanically to any situation regardless of its specificity and history. When a problem arises our quest should be not for *the* liberal or *the* conservative solution, but for one we consider the most intelligent under the circumstances evaluated in the light of the consequences of alternative courses of action on the preservation of a free society.

In furthering the ideals and institutions of a free society, choices must sometimes be made that require genuine sacrifices by the citizens of the community. For example, sufficient means may not be available to provide adequately both for the necessary defense and the public welfare. In such cases measures of economy may have to be adopted that result in genuine hardship. The regulating principle in such situations should be an approximate equality of sacrifice for all groups. No formula can be worked out in advance, and there will always be dissatisfaction with the results. But so long as these differences are submitted to the arbitrament of the democratic process there is hope that the considered judgment of the community will be accepted, that the unifying allegiance to the process will override other residual differences. These in turn become the subject for further discussion and possible remedial action.

The differences between conservatives and liberals, when the terms are reasonably construed, are family differences among adherents of a free society, defined as one whose institutions ultimately rest on the consent of those affected by their operations. When the security of a free society is threatened by aggressive totalitarianism, these differences must be temporarily subordinated to the common interest in its survival. There is always the danger that in the ever-present and sometimes heated struggles between conservatives and liberals, each group may come to fear the other more than their common enemy. If and when that happens, the darkness of what Marx called "Asiatic despotism," in modern dress to be sure, will descend upon our world.

Index

Acheson, Dean, 164
Afghanistan, 94, 163
AFL-CIO, 164, 182, 195, 197
Africa, 3, 38, 52, 94, 163, 199
Alienation, 46–53, 63, 64, 69
American Artists Congress, 85
American Civil Liberties Union, 144
American Jitters (Wilson), 108
American Newspaper Guild, 151
American Review Boards, 148
American Society of Newspaper Editors, 202
Anarchism, 7–8, 19, 89
Ancient Society (Morgan), 37
Anderson, Sherwood, 84
Anti-Dühring (Engels), 28, 37
Anti-Semitism, 116–17, 154
Antonov-Ovseyenko, Anton, 136–40
Antonov-Ovseyenko, Vladimir, 136
Aristotle, 123, 210
Arnold, Thurman, 167
Attlee, Clement, 146
Augustine, St., 60, 204
Austria, 91, 111, 157
Aveling, Edward, 114–15, 118

Bakunin, Mikhail, 13, 35
Baldwin, Roger, 144, 171
Ball, George, 170
Baruch, Bernard, 160
Baruch-Lilienthal proposals, 142, 188
Bauer, Bruno, 6
Beard, Charles, 30, 58, 149, 170
Beer, Max, 116
Belfrage, Cedric, 155–56
Bentham, Jeremy, 30, 58, 63, 211
Beria, Lavrenti, 45, 138
Berle, Adolf, 164
Bernstein, Eduard, 26, 28, 36, 60, 67, 114, 116, 120

Bismarck, 175
Blacklisting, 152–57
Blacks, 90
Blanqui, Louis, 13, 14, 35
Bliven, Bruce, 112
Boas, Franz, 37
Böhm-Bawerk, Eugen, 31
Bolshevik Party. *See* Communist Party, Soviet Union; October Revolution
Bolshevik Revolution. *See* October Revolution
Brest-Litovsk Treaty, 74
Brezhnev, Leonid, 140, 192, 196
Browder, Earl, 44, 85, 145
Brozozowski, Stanislaw, 59
Bryant, Louise, 130–31
Buber, Martin, 47
Bukharin, Nikolai, 111, 112, 136
Bulganin, Nikolai, 45
Bulgaria, 45
Bullitt, William, 131
Burke, Edmund, 217
Burnham, James, 67–68
Butler, Nicholas Murray, 57

Cambodia, 93, 199
Camus, Albert, 93
Canada, 201
Capital (Marx and Engels), 5, 23, 27, 28, 41–49, 51, 55, 57, 60, 64, 99, 100, 102, 104, 121, 124
Capitalism, 99; American Communist Party and, 86, 88; dictatorship of the bourgeoisie under, 12, 14; freedom in, 4–7; inequalities of distribution under, 9; Marxism and, 31, 39, 54–55, 104; mixed economy in, 34; mode of production in, 26–27; socialism compared to, 181; specialization of labor in, 5–7, 65; as term, 57; welfare state and, 100–102

219

Carlyle, Thomas, 48
Castro, Fidel, 93, 194
Caute, David, 141–58
China, 3, 19, 22, 25, 31, 38, 40, 45, 57, 93, 110, 117, 143, 161, 162, 164, 166–67, 177, 183, 184
China Passage (Galbraith), 166
Chomsky, Noam, 93
Christ and Christianity, 3, 23, 25, 35, 52, 80, 99, 135, 216
Churchill, Winston, 137, 197
Civilization and Its Discontents (Freud), 124
Civil Rights Act, 101, 128
Class, 85–89; classless society, 3–4, 12, 27, 31–33, 39–40, 51, 65, 88–89, 125–26, 140, 179–80; class struggle, 32–33, 55, 68, 100, 106, 125–26
Cogley, John, 152, 153
Cohen, M.R., 57
Cohen, Stephen, 136
Cold War, 85, 94, 142, 145, 149, 153, 180, 184, 187–96
Comintern. See Communist International
Commission of Inquiry into the Truth of the Moscow Trials, 38, 91, 112
Communism, Marxism and, 3–22, 34–46, 50, 87–88
Communist International (Comintern), 17, 20, 21, 37, 43, 72–83, 111, 133; Second Congress, 83; Seventh Congress, 74, 85
Communist Manifesto, The (Marx and Engels), 5, 13, 27, 48, 69, 85, 97, 127
Communist Party: Bulgarian, 45; Central Committee, 15, 18, 43–44, 142–43; dictatorship of, 14–19, 42–43; French, 44, 76, 80; German, 82; Party Congress, 43–44; Polish, 58; Soviet Union, 16, 34–46, 57–58, 72–83, 85–95, 108–13, 135–40, 142–43, 150–51, 179–80; United States, 17, 44, 45, 84–95, 108–13, 141–58, 171
Comte, Auguste, 123, 125
Constituent Assembly, 15–16, 21, 36, 80–81, 133
Corey, Lewis, 110, 111
Cowley, Malcolm, 108–13
Critique de la raison dialectique (Sartre), 47
Critique of Political Economy (Marx),

96–97, 121
Critique of the Gotha Program (Marx), 7
Cuba, 3, 93, 106, 162, 190, 194
Culture and Crisis, 84
Currie, Lauchlin, 170
Czechoslovakia, 19, 93, 142, 184, 185

Dante, 3, 65
Darwin, Charles, 20, 23, 52, 122
Davis, Elmer, 143
Debs, Eugene V., 76
de Gaulle, Charles, 169
De Leon, Daniel, 26
Democracy, 11, 43, 61, 166; Communist Party and, 18; equality in, 214–15; freedom and, 180–84, 201–3; religion and, 203–5; socialism and, 27; Solzhenitsyn on, 197, 201–3; totalitarianism and, 25, 203
Demuth, Fred, 119
Demuth, Helene, 118–19
Determinism, Marxist, 28–31, 65–66
Dewey, John, 38, 62, 64, 91, 109, 112, 123, 125, 149, 155, 200
Dewey, Thomas, 147
Dialectics of Nature (Engels), 37
Dictatorship: of the bourgeoisie, 12, 14; of the Communist Party, 14–19, 42–43; of the proletariat, 12–19, 42–43, 68, 75, 80, 166
Dietzgen, Joseph, 58
Division of labor, 5–7, 65
Djilas, Milovan, 39
Doctorow, E. L., 147–48
Dos Passos, John, 84, 111
Dostoyevsky, Fyodor, 198, 204
Douglas, Paul, 164
Drachkovitch, Milorad M., 72–83
Dubinsky, David, 143
Duclos, Jacques, 44
Dulles, John Foster, 163

Eclipse of Reason, The (Horkheimer), 122
Economic and Philosophic Manuscripts (Marx), 46, 50, 69
Egalitarianism, 7–9, 61, 214–16
Egypt, 169, 190
Eisenhower, Dwight D., 162, 163
Eisler, Gerhart, 156n
El Salvador, 195
Emerson, Ralph Waldo, 48

Engels, Friedrich, 12–14, 18, 22, 25–28, 30, 35, 37, 38, 42, 43, 50, 56, 60–62, 66, 68–69, 71, 80, 83, 85, 98, 115, 119, 121, 122, 127, 139, 175–76. See also *Capital; Communist Manifesto*
England, 12, 13, 17, 32, 38, 45, 92, 100, 105, 106, 114, 146, 148, 154–55, 157–58, 169, 192, 201, 202
Erfurt Program (1871), 27
Ethical principles, 11, 22, 60, 125–26
Existentialism, 46–53
Exploitation, 61

Fabian Society, 115
Fascism, 21, 24, 82, 85, 87, 90–92, 94–95, 99, 105, 126, 142, 144, 147, 153
Fear and Trembling (Kierkegaard), 204
February Revolution (1917), 136
Feuer, Lewis, 59
Feuerbach, Ludwig, 51, 64, 69, 117, 124
Fifth Amendment, U.S. Constitution, 151, 152, 155, 157
Ford, Gerald, 192
Ford, James W., 84, 109
Foster, William Z., 17, 44, 84, 89, 109, 110
Foundations of Leninism (Stalin), 15
Fourier, François M. C., 7
France, 32, 78, 92, 157, 169, 185; Communist Party, 44, 76, 80; Paris Commune of 1871, 10, 14, 42, 68, 117, 118
Franco, Francisco, 156n
Frankel, Leo, 14
Frankfurter, Felix, 203
Frankfurt School, 59, 120–29
Freedom, 3–5, 11, 21–22, 27–28, 106, 127; in capitalism, 4–7; democracy and, 180–84, 201–3; in existentialist view of Marxism, 46–53; market economy and, 212–14; problems of, 178–79; Solzhenitsyn on, 197, 198–200, 205–7; as term, 176–77; in totalitarianism, 179, 182–83; welfare state and, 208–12
Freeman, Joseph, 110
Freud, Sigmund, 124
Fromm, Erich, 47, 120
Frossard, Louis-Oscar, 76
Fuchs, 144, 148

Galbraith, John Kenneth, 86n, 159–72

Gandhi, Mahatma, 189
Gelb, Barbara, 130, 131, 134
Germany, 21, 29, 38, 74, 82, 91, 92, 105, 111, 116, 132, 168, 176, 184, 185; Social Democratic Movement, 12, 26–34, 36, 60, 67
Goebbels, Joseph, 95
Goethe, Johann Wolfgang von, 6, 65
Gold, Harry, 148
Goldenweiser, Alexander, 37
Gorky, Maxim, 78, 111
Gouzenko, Igor, 137–38, 144
Gramsci, Antonio, 59
Great Fear, The (Caute), 141–58
Grün, Karl, 48
Gulag Archipelago, 205; Chinese, 22, 166–67, 177; Soviet, 22, 56, 67, 93, 136, 137, 157, 189

Hacker, Louis, 57
Hall, Gus, 192
Harrington, Michael, 96–102, 121
Hegel, G. W. H., 9–10, 22, 37, 49, 51, 62, 65, 69, 96–99, 102, 117, 121, 122, 124–25, 177, 217
Hegel and the Revolution (Marcuse), 124
Heilbroner, Robert, 103–7
Helsinki Final Act, 193, 196, 198
Hero in History, The: A Study in Limitation and Possibility (Hook), 20
Hess, Moses, 48, 60
Hingley, Ronald, 137
Hiss, Alger, 141, 147
Hitler, Adolf, 21, 45, 54, 82, 85, 87, 91, 105, 110, 111, 137, 140, 157, 165, 170
Hobbes, Thomas, 51, 63
Ho Chi Minh, 93
Holland, 13, 169
Holmes, Oliver Wendell, 123
Horkheimer, Max, 120–24, 128
Human Nature and Conduct (Dewey), 64
Humphrey, Hubert H., 143, 146
Hungary, 43, 85, 93, 169, 185

India, 117
Individuality, 4–8, 60
Indonesia, 169
Infantile Sickness of Left-Communism (Lenin), 15
Institute of Marxism-Leninism, 18
Intercollegiate Socialist Society, 84

International, Third. *See* Communist International

International, Second, 28, 35, 36, 60, 83

I Speak for the Silent (Tchernavin), 137

Israel, 169, 190, 199

Italy, 82, 92, 105, 157, 185

James, William, 123, 175

Japan, 92, 99, 111, 166, 168, 170, 171, 188

Jaurès, Jean, 60

Jefferson, Thomas, 213–14

Jerome, V. I., 152

Jewish question, 116–17, 153, 154

Johnson, Alvin, 149

Johnson, Lyndon B., 101

Journal du Peuple, 80–81

Kadar, Jan, 43

Kahn, Tom, 195

Kamenev, Lev Borisovich, 78

Kampelman, Max, 192, 202

Kampuchea, 93, 199

Kant, Immanuel, 9, 37, 103

Kapp, Yvonne, 114–18

Kautsky, Karl, 12, 26, 30, 59, 60, 67, 96

Kelles-Krautz, Kazimierz, 59

Kennan, George, 163, 170, 205–7

Kennedy, Edward, 160, 162, 165

Kennedy, John F., 160–62

Kennedy, Robert, 162

Kerensky, Alexander, 16, 21, 74, 132, 136

Khrushchev, Nikita, 17, 38, 41, 45, 85, 92–93, 112, 136, 138–39, 177, 182

Khrushchev Remembers (Khrushchev), 138–39

Kierkegaard, Sören, 103, 204

Kim Il Sung, 164

King, Mackenzie, 137–38

King, Martin Luther, 162

Kissinger, Henry, 169, 192, 197

Kitchin, George, 112

Knowledge, 70–71, 104–5, 122–23

Kolakowski, Leszek, 58–71

Kommunist, 18

Korean War, 142, 143, 153, 157, 164, 167, 169, 185

Krivitsky, Walter, 140

Krzywicki, Ludwig, 59

Ku Klux Klan, 153, 156*n*

Lafargue, Paul, 60, 118

Lange, Oscar, 40, 59

Lazitch, Branko, 72–83

League Against War and Fascism, 85

League for Industrial Democracy, 84

League for Peace and Democracy, 85

League of American Writers, 85, 109

League of Professional Groups, 84, 109, 110

Lenin, Nikolai, 12–22, 31, 35–46, 54, 61, 67, 70, 90–92, 96, 100, 105, 111, 130, 132, 135, 137, 139, 145, 171; Communist International and, 72–83; on the Constituent Assembly, 15–16; dictatorship of the proletariat and, 14–15, 42, 68

Lenin and the Comintern (Lazitch and Drachkovitch), 72–83

Lerner, Abba, 59

Levin, Dr., 111

Levine, Isaac Don, 137

Liberalism, 63, 159, 161, 163–64, 168, 217

Liberman, E. G., 41

Liebknecht, Karl, 37

Life in Our Times, A (Galbraith), 160–72

Lippmann, Walter, 143, 146

Lissageray, 118

Locke, John, 63

Lovestone Communist Opposition, 110

Lowie, Robert, 37

Ludwig Feuerbach and the Outcome of German Philosophy (Engels), 28

Lukács, Georg, 59, 62, 66–67, 71, 169

Luxemburg, Rosa, 16, 35, 77, 133

Lyons, Eugene, 147

McCarthy, Eugene, 162

McCarthy, Joseph, 142, 149, 154, 156, 157, 162

McDonald, John, 111, 166

McGovern, Goerge, 160, 162

Machajski, Waclaw, 58

Maclean, 144

Main Currents of Marxism (Kolakowski), 58–71

Malenkov, Georgi, 45, 138

Man, Henri de, 58

Mansfield, Mike, 193

Mao Tse-tung, 54, 93

Marcuse, Herbert, 21, 120, 124, 126–29

Markel, Lester, 202
Marshall Plan, 142, 184, 187
Marx, Eleanor, 114–19
Marx-Engels Institute of Moscow, 114
Marxism: capitalism and, 31, 39, 54–55, 104; Communism and, 3–22, 34–46, 50, 87–88; contradictions in, 23–26; existentialist version of, 46–53; Harrington on, 96–102, 121; Heilbroner on, 103–7; Kolakowski study of, 58–71; revisionism of Frankfurt School, 59, 120–29; revival of interest in, 55–58; Social-Democratic version of, 26–34, 50
Marxism: For and Against (Heilbroner), 103–7
Marx's Concept of Man (Fromm), 47
Materialism, 12, 28, 30–31, 37–39, 54–55, 60, 69, 92, 117, 121; alienation and, 46–49; Heilbroner on, 105–7
Materialism and Empirio-Criticism (Lenin), 37
May, Alan Nunn, 144
Mein Kampf (Hitler), 87
Menshevik Party, 16, 78
Merleau-Ponty, Maurice, 47
Meyer, Agnes, 161
Michels, Robert, 32
Mill, John Stuart, 63, 214
Mills, C. Wright, 96
Molotov, Vyacheslav, 138
Morality, 9; freedom and, 178; of Marx, 118–19; Solzhenitsyn on, 197–98, 200–201, 203–7, 216
Morgan, Lewis, 37, 97
Moscow trials, 38, 91, 111–12
Mussolini, Benito, 21, 82, 105

National Association of Manufacturers, 32
National Guardian, 155
Nationalism, 19, 55, 68, 99
NATO, 185, 192–93
Naturalism, 122
Nazism, 21, 82, 87, 95, 105, 110, 171. *See also* Hitler, Adolf
Nazi-Soviet Pact, 85, 91, 147
Negroes, 90
Netherlands, 13, 169
New Class . . . , The (Djilas), 39
New Class Divided, The (Parry), 40

New Deal, 20, 108, 144, 148
New Left, 52, 79, 81
New Masses, The, 109, 111, 112
New Republic, 109, 111, 112
New School for Social Research, 149–50
Newton, Sir Isaac, 20, 23, 52
New York Times, 151, 202, 205
Niebuhr, Reinhold, 164
1984 (Orwell), 137
Ninth Convention, 150
Nixon, Richard M., 101, 162, 182, 190
Nobel Peace Foundation, 168
Notebooks (Lenin), 37

Oakes, John B., 202
October Revolution (1917), 12, 14, 16, 20, 21, 26, 31, 35–36, 38, 42, 61, 74–77, 91, 92, 100, 105, 130–33, 136
Official Secrets Act (U.K.), 158, 202
Old Left, 115
One Day in the Life of Ivan Denisovich (Solzhenitsyn), 138
O'Neill, Eugene, 131
"On Slogans" (Lenin), 16
Origin of Species (Darwin), 122
Orlov, Alexander, 137
Orwell, George, 68, 137

Pareto, Vilfredo, 32
Paris Commune of 1871, 10, 14, 42, 68, 117, 118
Parry, Albert, 40
Partisan Review, 67, 128
Pass, Joseph, 110
Peirce, Charles S., 6, 56, 123
Philby, Kim, 144, 147–48
Philosophy and Myth in Karl Marx (Tucker), 47
Plato, 6, 103, 123, 129, 177, 203
Plekhanov, George, 26, 30, 60, 78, 96
Plotinus, 49
Poland, 58–59, 94, 111, 117, 142, 182, 184, 194–95
Pollack, Frederick, 120
Pontecorvo, Dr., 144, 146
Popper, Karl, 51
Positivism, 62, 104, 123
Pragmatism, 123, 124
Press Council, 202
Production, modes of, 26–27, 41–42, 69–70, 92, 96–98, 105, 121–22, 182–83

Professionalization, 5–7
Proletariat: dictatorship of, 12–19, 42–43, 68, 75, 80, 166; revolutionary change in, 126
Property, power and, 212–14
Proposition 13, 208
"Protocols of Zion," 153
Proudhon, Pierre Joseph, 14
Psychoanalysis, 124
Psychology of Socialism, The (de Man), 58

Radek, Karl B., 78
Rappaport, Charles, 80
Reason, 122–26, 129
Red Decade, The (Lyons), 147
Reed, John, 130–34
Religion, 215–16; democracy and, 203–5. See also Christ and Christianity
Renan, Ernest, 135
Report on Blacklisting (Cogley), 152
Reuter, Ernst, 185
Reuther, Walter, 143
Revolution, 17, 18, 20, 21; inevitability of East-West, 44–46; Socialist, 13, 14, 19, 20, 38–39. See also October Revolution
Riazanov, David, 114
Robinson, James Harvey, 149
Roosevelt, Eleanor, 161
Roosevelt, Franklin Delano, 85, 86, 137, 144, 147, 197
Rorty, James, 111
Rosenberg, Ethel, 141, 147–48
Rosenberg, Julius, 141, 147–48
Rostow, Eugene, 193
Rousseau, Jean-Jacques, 43
Royal Commission Report, 144, 144n
Russell, Bertrand, 163, 184, 188, 205, 206, 206n, 207
Russia. See Soviet Union

Sadoul, Jacques, 79
Sakharov, Andrei, 94, 196, 203, 205
Santayana, George, 77, 177
Sartre, Jean-Paul, 47, 52–53, 93
Savigny, Friedrich Karl von, 217
Schapiro, J. Salwyn, 57
Schlesinger, Arthur, Jr., 143, 166
Schumpeter, Joseph, 31
Scott, Howard, 168

Shakespeare, William, 65, 97
Shulman, Marshall, 163
Simon, William, 211–12
Sinclair, Upton, 131
Smeral, Bohumir, 76
Smith, Adam, 101, 181
Smith Act, 142, 145
Social Democratic movement, 208, 210, 213, 215, 216; German, 12, 26–34, 36, 60, 67; Marxism of, 26–34, 50; Soviet Union, 12–22, 34–46
Social Fascism, 90, 91, 110
Socialism: capitalism compared to, 181; democracy and, 27; egalitarianism under, 8, 11; revolution and, 13, 14, 19, 20, 38–39
Socialist Party: Austrian, 91; French, 78; United States, 76, 110
Socialist Revolutionary Party, 15, 16, 78
Solow, Herbert, 170
Solzhenitsyn, Aleksandr, 67, 94, 137, 138, 192, 197–209, 216
Sorge, Richard, 171
So Short a Time (Gelb), 130, 131
Soule, George, 112
Souvarine, Boris, 80
Soviet Union, 3, 25, 31, 32, 59, 70, 105; capitalism and, 181–82; classless society in, 39–40; Communist Party, 16, 34–46, 57–58, 72–83, 85–95, 108–13, 135–40, 142–43, 150–51, 179–80; dictatorship of the proletariat in, 15–16, 68; freedom in, 177; Gulag Archipelago, 22, 56, 67, 93, 136, 137, 157, 189; production modes in, 41–42, 182–83; Social-Democratic movement in, 12–22, 34–46; state in, 40–41; treaty violations of, 184–85, 198–99; United States anti-Communism and, 141–58, 164–65, 168–70. See also Cold War
Specialization of labor, 5–7, 65
Spender, Stephen, 63
Spengler, Oswald, 121
Spinoza, Baruch, 66
Stalin, Joseph, 15, 17, 35, 37, 39, 40, 44–46, 61, 67, 68, 78, 79, 85, 90, 91, 93, 111, 112, 130, 133–40, 164, 171, 177, 184
State, Marxist view of, 33–34, 40–41
Steffens, Lincoln, 87
Stein, Ludwig, 123

Stevenson, Adlai, 160, 161, 166, 169
Stewart, Donald Ogden, 85
Surplus value doctrine, 61, 99, 105–6

Tchernavin, 137
Ten Days That Shook the World (Reed), 130–34
Theatre Arts Union, 85
Third World, 106, 199
Third World Congress, 73
Thomas, Norman, 143, 144, 171
Tillich, Paul, 47
Time for Truth, A (Simon), 211–12
Time of Stalin, The: A Portrait of a Tyranny (Antonov-Ovseyenko), 136–40
Tito, Josip, 136–37, 164, 195
Tolstoy, Leo, 198
Totalitarianism, 83, 94–95, 129, 133, 165–69; democracy and, 25, 203; freedom in, 179, 182–83; as outgrowth of Marxism, 4, 12–13, 68; religion and, 216
Towards Soviet America (Foster), 17
Towards the Understanding of Karl Marx (Hook), 54, 86
Triumph of American Capitalism (Hacker), 57
Trotsky, Leon, 38, 67, 68, 76–78, 91, 92, 105, 111, 130, 134–36, 139
Truman, Harry, 142, 163, 164
Truman Doctrine, 151
Tucker, Robert, 47, 49
Tukhachevsky, Mikhail, 111
Twentieth Congress, 38, 112, 138, 177
Twilight of Capitalism, The (Harrington), 96–102, 121

Uganda, 199
Union of Soviet Socialist Republics. See Soviet Union

United Nations, 157, 184, 194, 199
United States, 12, 13, 32, 38, 52, 56, 70, 71, 75, 100–101, 105, 116; aggression resistance by, 184–86; anti-Communism of, 141–58, 164–65, 168–70; Communist Party, 17, 44, 45, 84–95, 108–13, 141–58, 171; freedom in, 199–200, 205–7; Socialist Party, 76, 110. See also Cold War
U.S.S.R. See Soviet Union
Utopianism, 5, 65, 101, 127

Vance, Cyrus, 163
Veblen, Thorstein, 30, 149
Vietnam War, 93, 94, 101, 169–70, 176, 190, 202
Vinci, Leonardo da, 6, 7, 65
Vyshinsky, 112

Wagner Labor Relations Act, 88
Walesa, Lech, 182
Wallace, Henry, 147, 165
Washington Post, 202
Watergate, 94, 190
Webb, Beatrice, 177
Webb, Sidney, 177
Weber, Max, 30, 166
Welfare state, 20, 29, 31, 33, 39, 54, 92, 99–102, 191, 208–11
What Is To Be Done? (Lenin), 35
Whitehead, Alfred North, 30
Wiesengrund-Adorno, Theodor, 120
Wilson, Edmund, 84, 108, 109
Wolfe, Bertram, 132

Yugoslavia, 39, 45, 164, 195

Zetkin, Clara, 82
Zimmerwald Movement, 73
Zinoviev, Grigori, 78
Zumwalt, 190
Zur Judenfrage (Marx), 116